Transforming Leadership

new vision for a church in mission

Norma Cook Everist

Norma Cook Everist
Craig L. Nessan

Fortress Press
Minneapolis

Cover graphic: © iStockphoto.com/Achim Prill
Cover design: John Goodman
Interior design: Douglas Schmitz

Library of Congress Cataloging-in-Publication Data

Everist, Norma Cook, 1938–
  Transforming leadership : new vision for a church in mission / Norma Cook Everist & Craig L. Nessan.
     p. cm.
  ISBN-13: 978-0-8006-2048-6 (alk. paper)
  ISBN-10: 0-8006-2048-8 (alk. paper)
  1. Christian leadership. 2. Missions. I. Nessan, Craig L. II. Title.
  BV652.1.E94 2007
  253—dc22   2007034411

The paper used in this publication meets the minimum requirements of American National Standard for Information Sciences—Permanence of Paper for Printed Library Materials, ANSI Z329.48-1984.

Manufactured in the U.S.A.

12   11   10   09   08   2   3   4   5   6   7   8   9   10

Dedication

*We dedicate this book to the graduates
of Wartburg Theological Seminary,
who embody transforming leadership in their ministries.*

Contents

 # Introduction

ALL CONGREGATIONS ARE in the process of being transformed. They are caught up in the ongoing transforming activity of a living God. Leadership is a communal activity of people involved in God's mission asking the question about who God is and what God is intending to do in the world. This is not a book directed only at some congregations that supposedly need transformation. Every congregation is in the process of development or redevelopment. The church is always in the process of being reformed and transformed. We are moving not toward the return of an idealized past but toward the newness of God's future.

God is reforming and transforming us as we are called to transformational ministries in order to be a transformational church that works for peace and justice in the world. This book aims to instill the conviction that every congregation is being transformed by God and to help leaders to become intentional about participating in the transforming process. God's Spirit will not leave us alone. God's Spirit is intent on making what is latent manifest and making whole what is now present only in part.

Transformation has to do with God's work of creating *life-giving relationships* among us. Within the biblical tradition, the theme of *shalom* describes the inbreaking of the peace of God. This *shalom* of God is the source of a network of life-giving relationships. God's desire is that life-giving relationships exist between human beings and God, among all human beings, and between human beings and the whole created environment. Life-giving relationships are based on unconditional acceptance. Life-giving relationships make us into the persons we were intended to be—created in the image of God; re-created by Christ through his incarnation, death, and resurrection; and transformed for ministry by the power of the Holy Spirit.

We live into what God is growing us to be through the gifts God gives uniquely to each person and corporately to the church. While this transforming process can cause us to suffer pain, as God prunes what is unfit, finally it is the genesis of a real and deep joy. Within this network of life-giving relationships, we begin to change one another. However, transformation does not erase our created identity, such as our gender or ethnic origin. Mutual transformation enriches our diversity and at the same time strengthens our unity in community.

Giving attention to the quality of these relationships is not peripheral to God's transforming work. Transformation is about the gospel itself. The Transforming God cares about our interactions as leaders and desires to repair our brokenness so that we can be a new community in Christ. How we relate to one another is indicative of how we will relate to those we are seeking to reach with the gospel and invite into Christian community. *Transformation, in other words, is not only the destination toward which we are moving, but the journey itself.*

Three Dimensions of Transforming Leadership

Transforming leadership has three dimensions. First, we are talking about *leadership that transforms congregations* toward participation in God's mission of justice and justification. Second, we are referring to *leaders themselves* being formed and transformed. Third, transformational leadership entails belief that all members of the body of Christ have gifts to be shared and that these people *also will be transformed* as part of this journey.

Leadership that transforms congregations toward mission equips them for becoming welcoming, evangelizing, and serving communities of faith. Clearly, each congregation is unique and has specific needs for transformation, specific to its history, context, and calling. At the same time, each congregation can benefit from seeing itself as involved in an organic process that is common to all: God calls each congregation to repentance and new life that liberates it for transformation.

Leaders are being formed and transformed by the power of the Spirit. God takes the unique gifts of each person and forges these into the service of Christ. All leaders will at some time face discouragement, even despair, at what they experience from others and at their own failures. God's unconditional love sustains and transforms.

The transformational process needs to be broad and wide. It is collaborative, literally "laboring together" towards the transformation of the congregation. By congregation, we mean all types of faith communities, including also campus ministries, camps, social ministry organizations, etc. Leadership is a function of the entire group, not just of a single individual. Specific leaders, in partnership with others, are attentive to the transformation of the whole.

God's Ongoing Transforming Action

Does history summon forth leaders, or do leaders make history? We have said that God's transforming activity is ongoing. Certainly, there are historical moments that are ripe for transformation. Such moments can transform an ordinary person into an extraordinary leader. But this does not happen automatically. Congregations should not depend upon a particular leader to "save" them and bring them to the Promised Land. Together, a faith community needs to read its own history carefully, discern the variety of leadership tasks that are necessary at a particular moment, and support one another as it grows into the transformational process. This involves genuine partnership between the called leader and all of the people who *are* the congregation.

The God who created the world and human beings in it is a Transforming God who continues to delight in the diversity of all forms of life that continue to emerge. Although change can be frightening, and we often resist it, we can trust the fact that we have a God who loves all of the created ones. However, the pervasiveness of sin, brokenness, alienation, mistrust, and hatred—certainly evident also inside the church—can leave leaders devastated. Sometimes faith communities live in such a constant state of conflict and disappointment that the reign of God is blurred beyond recognition. But as surely as sin corrupts community, the resurrection is sure and certain. Christ transforms our despair into hope. The Spirit is ready to take the most recalcitrant community—including leaders—and transform them into a renewed people who trust God and one another to discover new directions for mission. God's grace often surprises. Such hope is not illusory. Transformation is possible!

Commitments

This book operates with some deep and abiding commitments. These assumptions under gird everything we as authors say in this book.

1. Transformed and transforming leaders are essential for transforming congregations.
2. God calls us to ministries of inclusivity.
3. Justification and justice belong together.

4. Christ's call to discipleship includes evangelical outreach.
5. Church conflict is a congregational reality.
6. Not one but many paradigms for transforming congregations are needed; context is crucial.
7. Collegiality and healthy collaboration are essential for transformation.

These commitments are interwoven throughout the chapters and pages of this book. They are foundational to transforming leadership.

Contents of the Book

Section One: Community Formed

Chapter 1 builds on the premise that trust is essential for building transforming relationships. It describes how to begin by listening and setting a trustworthy environment, how mutual respect helps communities sustain good communication and collaboration, and how, when trust breaks down, to draw on a trustworthy God.

Chapter 2 stresses the vital importance of attending to context as a foundation for transforming leadership. A variety of methodologies are introduced for interpreting context. Most of the chapter is devoted to "The Top Ten List" of congregational realities that play themselves out in most every context.

Chapter 3 lays ecclesial foundations that the Church is both local and universal, both saint and sinner, both set apart and sent forth. The Church itself is continually being transformed. It is called to be a suffering servant as it gathers strangers into community as gift to one another so that they can serve the world.

Chapter 4 refines the definition of leadership as engaging people in facing their most difficult problems. In congregational life this means leaders focus on the crucial areas of identity and mission. Ten key leadership practices are elaborated to help mobilize congregations to keep clear these focal concerns, while drawing upon the deep values of the people.

Section Two: Identity Claimed

Chapter 5 deals with authority in pastoral and diaconal ministry. After defining *power* and *authority*, this chapter analyzes the process by which one claims one's gifts in assuming a ministerial office. One is called to live into one's office as it is articulated in the ordination/consecration rites through relational ministry, moving from formal to acknowledged authority.

Chapter 6 shows how leaders face the temptations of becoming either authoritarian or abdicating their leadership role. Genuine servant leadership is rooted in the liberating Word of God and expressed through power, presence, knowledge, roles, relationships, decision making, and proclamation.

Chapter 7 investigates what it means to be a Minister of the Word by exploring this ministry in relationship to the work of a rabbi. How does ministry of the Word provide coherence to all the tasks undertaken by pastors and diaconal ministers? How can concentration on the ministry of the Word help alleviate the dangers of ministerial "maceration"? Practical implications of this focus are developed.

Chapter 8 focuses on power and leadership by looking at gender issues and also at issues of race, class, nationalism, and more. Through "The Power Cycle" the powerful either retain their privilege through trying to ignore, trivialize, ridicule, and finally eliminate people or become open to transformation for partnership.

Section Three: Integrity Tested

Chapter 9 concentrates on the indispensability of disciplined spiritual practices. Ministers are responsible to be faithful stewards of their own lives, precious and finite resources that require great care. Reference is made to the value of classic spiritual practices for the lives of ministers, the necessity of nurturing an intentional circle of support, and the importance of establishing clarity about boundaries in ministry.

Chapter 10 looks at how admiration, respect, and affection are elements of caring, transformational relationships. This chapter examines various combinations of these three terms, exploring how their absence or misuse can be dangerous and how their presence provides for healthy, life-giving relationships.

Chapter 11 deals with prominent ethical dilemmas faced by ministers. The chapter stresses the value of a professional code of ethics and encourages the clergy profession to adopt one. Particular attention is devoted to the ethical themes of confidentiality, collegiality, and finances. Transforming leadership is jeopardized where improprieties and hypocrisy are detected, and it is enhanced by lives of integrity.

Chapter 12 explores how leaders, overwhelmed with the stress of multi-tasking and unending responsibilities, need to be grounded in the God who has given the gift of both holy work and Sabbath rest. This chapter suggests specific ways leaders, who all have different images of time, can actually transform their relationships with time.

Section Four: Opportunities Unleashed

Chapter 13 concentrates on three crucial issues for unleashing transforming ministry in the church. First, the chapter introduces the method of appreciative inquiry and the process of asset mapping. Second, the chapter advocates that transforming leaders be engaged intentionally in leadership development in their faith communities. Finally, the chapter imagines what it would mean to approach money as a matter of spiritual health, rather than only a means to an end.

Chapter 14 emphasizes the value of understanding congregations through the insights of systems thinking. The implications of several basic concepts are developed. Leadership strategies are developed to counteract some of the most prevalent patterns that prevent congregations from engaging vigorously in God's mission. Constancy of leadership is crucial for changing a congregational climate.

Chapter 15 explores people on the edge of leaving and others on the edge of responding to an invitation to enter the church. The chapter also examines "church shopping," the "revolving door" of membership, and "hide-and-seek" episodes as well as the edginess of conflict, the reality of fatigue, and the need for belonging.

Chapter 16 emphasizes all members of the body of Christ being transformed daily for their various ministries where they live and work all week long. Vocation is rooted in the forgiveness of sins. Members need each other in order to discern those ministries and for appreciation, empowerment, and mutual accountability.

Readers and Use of the Book

This book is written primarily for leaders called to public ministry (those professionally educated and called to serve in public ways on behalf of the church). As authors we have deep respect for the full range of such leaders, including pastors, bishops, associates in ministry, deaconesses, youth workers, directors of Christian education, camp staff, and those called to special ministries in evangelism and social justice, to name only a few. By virtue of their call, these people are acknowledged and looked to for theological acumen, vision for transformation, and leadership skill. In this book we will refer to this full range of such public ministries in the language of two of the historic offices of leadership in the church: pastoral and diaconal ministry. We intend these terms to be inclusive of all the categories of leadership that exist in each church body across the ecumenical spectrum. We trust that *Transforming Leadership* and its various particular chapters will be equally, if differently, valuable for those entering new leadership positions and for those who desire to reflect on the leadership they have been exercising for many years. We write also for other leaders within faith communities, including lay leaders—elected or volunteer, formal or informal. We trust that all of these leaders will find themselves in this book.

We envision the use of this book by church councils, church committees of various kinds, adult study groups, first call pastors and diaconal ministers, seminary students, campus ministries, church staff, social ministry organizations, judicatory leaders, teachers of the church, and others. The book, though written by two professors from a Lutheran seminary, is very suitable for an ecumenical group of leaders. It might also be used in an inter-faith context if the group establishes an environment in which people of different faiths can fully share the beliefs that under gird their tradition's leadership. A group of community leaders from a variety of professions could also find many chapters in this book helpful. Use of the book is limited only by the readers' creativity.

Opportunities for Reader Engagement

At the end of each chapter four opportunities for reader engagement are provided: *Personal Reflection* provides questions for the individual reader to consider in relation to his or her own growth in transforming leadership. These questions could be answered as one reads the book through, or pondered in a slower way, as thought-provoking reflection over the course of time. They may prompt journal entries. They may encourage deeper reflection with a mentor or close friend.

Group Conversation provides questions for reflecting with colleagues, whether a congregation staff, a church council, or other leadership grouping. Discussion of these questions may also be appropriate for an adult forum or retreat setting. Take time to set a trustworthy environment for in-depth conversation. The goal is engaging in real conversation around issues that we face together.

Spiritual Practice affords the occasion for using the themes of this book prayerfully and devotionally. God seeks continually to transform each of us in our faith journey, as the Spirit acts to make us whole. Through these exercises we intend to connect the reader to the rich tradition of spiritual discipline that are again today renewing the church and its leaders.

Transforming Action encourages readers to implement ideas and strategies consistent with the aims of the book. Some suggestions are for the reader alone, and some are for a small group or the congregation as a whole. One learns not only by thinking oneself into action but sometimes ever more effectively by acting oneself into a new way of thinking.

The Authors

We write as colleagues who have taught together the themes in this book for more than a dozen years. We also are friends. We have been mutually enriched and deeply influenced by what we have learned from each other. God has transformed us through our relationship. Both authors have written extensively in the areas of leadership. Norma also has published work in the areas of educational ministry, church conflict, and feminist theology. Craig additionally has published in the areas of ethics, congregational mission, and liberation theology.

Norma has served as a deaconess, pastor, and, for many years, as seminary professor. She has exercised theological and strategic leadership throughout the church in the U.S. and beyond. She enjoys visiting ministerial leaders and congregations across the country, offering insight and support.

Craig has served as pastor of two congregations, seminary professor, and academic dean. He has been involved as a teaching theologian for the church on a variety of themes. He has offered particular leadership in the areas of congregational mission, contextual education, ethics, and theological education.

Our Appreciation

We give deep appreciation to all those who have contributed their gifts in the preparation of this book for publication. Our conversations with Beth Lewis and Rick Rouse served as a catalyst in transforming of our collaborative teaching into a book. Our thanks also go to our very able and thorough student assistants, Sandra Burroughs, Kathryn Neal, Ashley Nicolls, who deserve special thanks for compiling the indexes; Mary McDermott, our dedicated and skillful faculty secretary; and Scott Tunseth and Tim Larson for shepherding this manuscript though the publishing process.

We are grateful for a teaching and learning community of faculty colleagues, staff, and students who support us and one another in our collaborative ministry. As authors, our respective families continue to sustain us through their care, encouragement, and love. For all these gifts we thank God!

Community
Formed
section one

Trust is foundational in forming the community called church. How one enters a new community requires wisdom, insight, and strategic planning. Setting and collaboratively maintaining a trustworthy environment fosters healthy relationships. Transforming leaders attend to context, appreciating the community already there and understanding the realities of life together. Building on the concept that the church is both global and historic, we know we live in a rich ecclesiological heritage, with its flaws and shortcomings, but as a gift of Christ. Finally, transforming leadership is the task of every new generation, reclaiming our true identity in Christ, courageously following God's call into mission.

Living in Trust:
Setting the Environment

TRUST IS AN ESSENTIAL ELEMENT for all of ministry. Without trust, a leader cannot lead. With trust in God and with trust in one another a faith community can move mountains. Transforming leadership is at its core relational. And what is a relationship without trust? Transforming leadership generates life-giving relationships. Transformation is not only the destination toward which we move, but the very way in which we relate to one another in the process. This is what God desires for God's people: trusting, life-giving relationships with God and with one another so that together we might serve in transformative ways in a world hungering for God's unconditional love.

Beginning Each New Call

Because trust is such an indispensable feature of ministry, how one enters a new context is crucial. Whether a first call, or a new call many years into one's public ministry, this relationship formally begins with the call process and involves all of the earliest contacts with members of a congregation. When one actually arrives on the scene, trust building begins with one's commitment to take much time to listen, ask interesting questions, and then really hear what is said. Trust-building, furthermore, means intentionally fostering a climate of open communication where people take the time to listen to each other. This may seem simple, but congregations often have established unhealthy patterns of talking "at" each other or "about" each other. Likewise the leader may have had past experiences where trust was in short supply. Establishing trust involves creating times and places where interaction is relaxed enough so that time is available to really pay attention to what others are saying.[1]

Part of listening deeply and insightfully involves understanding the story of the faith journey of the congregation.[2] Equally important is visiting with the people themselves in order to know the stories of their lives. Pastoral visitation in many places seems on its way to becoming a lost art. Part of the reason for this is the concern for clear boundaries about where one visits as a result of many tragic cases of clergy sexual misconduct. Certainly, one needs to be very intentional about maintaining accountability structures when one visits privately with congregational members. But there is a serious loss in the quality of pastoral relationships where one does not continue to invest in visitation. Meeting with people in their homes is deeply significant for growing trusting relationships. Where prudent, one might take a trusted member of the congregation along in making such visits. Home visits reveal so very much about the identity and values of those we encounter. Words spoken and unspoken, body language, and symbols of meaning in the room all speak volumes. Visitation is an important part of the ministry of all called leaders.

Visitation, however, is not just about home visits. Visitation occurs at church—when one sets aside the time—before and after worship services, in the hallways, and in the parking lot, as well as through formal office hours. Visiting places where members serve through their ministries in daily life, including, where possible, places of employment, both honors the ministry of the baptized and deepens our knowing one another. In many communities, vital conversation takes place where people gather for social interaction—at school activities, the coffee shop, or the post office. Intentional visitation contributes much to building essential trust. Visitation likewise is not just about intentional conversations with members of the congregation. From the very beginning, transforming leaders also will visit with people beyond the congregation, whether that be on the street, at the hospital or funeral home, or at that very same coffee shop where members gather. To engage in such mission is not to neglect members—something we dare not do—but to say Christ is always already present beyond our definitions of "church."[3] From the very beginning we need also to listen deeply to the social justice issues of a community.

James Glasse once wrote about the importance of "paying the rent" in parish ministry: "preaching and worship," "teaching and pastoral care," and "organization and administration."[4] If one takes care in "paying the rent," a climate of trust is created in which people eventually will be ready to follow one's leadership, even in challenging or controversial matters. They might even be ready to allow for principled disagreement on issues where they cannot follow. If the congregation trusts that the called leader, whether pastor, youth minister, deaconess, or another role, is tending the basic responsibilities of that call, the leader will be more able to become involved in prophetic ministry within and beyond the congregation. This wisdom about "paying the rent" remains sage to this day. [5]

Relational transforming leadership begins and ends in the intercommunion of our Triune God, who is by nature relational.[6] This is the meaning of the Holy Trinity: the One God interrelates as Father, Son, and Spirit in life-giving mutuality. This Triune, Relational God has created us to live as the very image of God as a faith community. We were made for life in communion with God, with one another, and with all creation. We long for life-giving relationships that finally grant us the wholeness for which we search. Augustine wrote: "The heart is restless until it rests in you, O Lord."[7] A life-giving relationship with God is the source of our salvation, and life-giving relationships with others are a reflection of the nature of new life together which the Triune God intends for us as we become a transformational church.

Time for Trust to Develop

Love the people! The truth of this statement is deeply connected with the insight that ministry is relational. Only by investing heart, mind, and soul in relationships with the people one serves, and by doing so over time, can one attain the social capital needed to engage in mutual transforming ministry. One develops trust by being responsible, responsible in the sense of "responding" to people and tasks in wise, capable, and timely ways that develop and strengthen relationships. This does not make relationships into a means to an end. Relationships with others are always an end in themselves. Rather, this assertion names a reality that many pastors and diaconal ministers ignore at their own peril. It takes time for life-giving relationships to be established and for trust to emerge. In fact, this process takes far longer than most of us would like to admit.

Under the best of circumstances (this means in settings where there has been no misconduct or inordinate conflict), it likely will take three to five years for sufficient trust to emerge before a leader will sense that truly mutual ministry is beginning to develop. That's three to five years under the best of conditions! The *average tenure* of an ordained minister in a particular parish is less than four years. Developing or redeveloping a youth ministry program in a congregation likewise takes longer than the average stay of a youth minister.

Most leaders do not—or are not able to—stay in a place long enough to establish the basic conditions for transforming ministry to take root and begin to flourish. Therefore, we can see why transforming leadership appears to be so rare. Where misconduct or unresolved conflict prevails in a place, the length of time to build trust may be much longer than three to five years. Yet these are the very places where the average tenure is typically very short. Pastors do not stay long enough—or are driven away—years earlier than would be necessary to see significant transformation emerge.

Perhaps the most integral factor toward promoting the increase of transforming leadership in the church is to increase the average tenure of those who have been called and commissioned to serve as leaders. Yet there are very good reasons why ministers choose to seek another call rather than remain in a congregation that is challenging and difficult. Salaries too often are inadequate. Enmeshed, conflicted congregational systems block new leadership. One's spiritual life may languish. Isolation leaves one bereft of relationships that promote life. A leader faced with these challenges may begin to sense this is not the kind of ministry that he or she envisioned, in partnership with people in God's mission.

A number of crucial factors need to be addressed if the whole church is to begin to provide the necessary prerequisites for transforming leadership. A Mutual Ministry Committee[8] can provide a place to address and work on issues that hinder healthy relationships. A salary structure will need to be devised that is just and encourages ministers to remain in those very contexts that would be best served by long-term ministries.[9] Not only are there large discrepancies in salary based on local economic conditions, but this also has consequences for immense differences in accumulated pension monies.

Transforming leaders also will need to invest in spiritual practices that sustain ministry for the long haul. This entails training, support, and accountability for life-giving practices of prayer, meditation, Bible study, and devotion. Such practices are best nurtured early in life at home and in congregations. They need to be incorporated in the formation processes of theological education.

In addition to these factors, ministers also need to be enveloped in support systems beyond the congregation. Leaders need to have a network of supportive persons to offer emotional and spiritual sustenance in the midst of the many challenging experiences in ministry. Judicatory leaders can encourage and help provide this, but leaders themselves need to make the establishment of such a network of support a high priority for their own ministry early upon arrival in a new place (see chapter 9).

Setting a Trustworthy Environment

Transformation will remain at a surface level unless people trust each other enough to care about one another and to risk new adventures. An essential task for transformative leaders is to set the tone and engage the community in helping to sustain a trustworthy, safe, healthy, hospitable environment so that they can really hear and speak truth to one another in order to participate in transformative ministry. People will need to know that their leader keeps confidences (see Chapter 11). People believing that the environment is trustworthy will take time. Trust does not rest on a singular event, but is built through a succession of trusting experiences. God's covenant relationship with God's people is an ongoing relationship. We who enter this covenant by God's grace are empowered to build a transformational community. People need to return to the issue of trust again and again. It needs to be demonstrated and reinforced.

People will bring their own insecurities to meetings, most of which are not immediately observable. Inside, a person may be thinking, "Will I have anything useful to say?" "Will they listen to me?" "Am I dressed appropriately?" "Do I even belong here?" All of these, and more, are part of the human propensity to devalue ourselves, mistrusting that God really has created us to be a gifted people to live in community.

On the other hand, human beings also have the propensity to think more highly of themselves than they ought to think, failing to believe that other people, all kinds of people, are of great worth in God's eyes with gifts to offer. A person who lacks humility and a vision of the whole community may not say it out loud, but may be thinking, "What are *those* people doing here?" "My time is very valuable; why do we have to have such a drawn-out discussion?" "How can I persuade them to come around to my views?"

An environment that is trustworthy, safe, healthy, and hospitable is not devoid of different opinions, even disagreement. On the contrary, in an unsafe environment, a wide range of views may never even surface. When people have been abused by ecclesial authority their wounds carry over into new church relationships.[10] Therefore, it is even more important to assure people, again and again, that they will be respected as persons, their voices carefully heard, and their opinions honored. With such respect, our diversity will enhance community.

An environment that is safe will be comfortable, not comfortable in the apathetic sense of the word, but in the "able to comfort others" sense. More women than men may express the need for "safety"; however, safety is essential for both men and women if the community is ever going to have a trustworthy environment. People need to feel physically safe (yes, there are some places in the church where this is not so) in order to be present without fear, emotionally safe in order to know they are people of worth, intellectually safe in order to explore new ideas, and culturally safe in order for all to come together in honesty and integrity.[11]

Some people may think that a "safe" environment lacks risk. On the contrary, congregations where trust is solid will have the courage to care about and engage in courageous ministry in dangerous places in need of justice and love. As prophets they will attune their vision to "witness more deeply the living presence of God in all who cry out for love and justice" and "find the courage to enter into the most fractured and marginalized places in reality, and thereby become the hopeful beams of light that break into dark, empty spaces."[12]

A hospitable environment offers generous welcome, even and especially to strangers. Xenophobia is pervasive in every community. Even if all the right words are said, people can tell if the space they are entering is hostile or hospitable. Leaders need to use their appropriate authority to make sure people dwell in a hospitable space of security and freedom.[13] We will need to address conflict and to tend and mend the broken places, particularly in our relationships, so that no one can dominate and no one is left outside in the cold.[14] We need to accommodate one another in order that an environment of mutual accommodation and trust can flourish.

A healthy environment provides opportunity for all of the members of the body of Christ to grow. One can actually sense if a church environment is stifling ideas and relationships. One can also sense if there is a warm hum of joy and enthusiasm. Leaders can help foster a healthy environment that fosters calm, not chaos; respectful conversation, not disdain; openness, not closed-mindedness. Leaders, of course, cannot do this alone. It is a gift of the Spirit and therefore also the responsibility of all members to try to keep themselves spiritually healthy, through prayer and meditation on Scripture, so that they can care for the church so that it can be or return to being a healthy place.[15]

Maintaining the Environment:
Collaboration and Communication

When a trustworthy environment is established, a wide range of leadership styles will work. Without an atmosphere of trust, most likely no leadership style will save the day. Maintaining a trustworthy environment is the work of all and is a key to collaborative ministry.

To "co-labor" requires open, honest communication. The question is not only, "Does the leader have good communication skills?" but "Does the community have healthy communication patterns?" "We need to communicate better," cannot be a cliché that ends the conversation, but the beginning of mutual labor. We need to look at interpersonal dynamics in a fresh way. People need information so they are not just part of a meeting but an *informed* part. People also need to know why they are doing what they are doing and how they are planning to do it. A group needs good communication systems for use before, during, and between meetings. When are decisions made and by whom? Who will carry them out? Better communication through providing information, clarifying goals, planning the work, and establishing ongoing mutual accountability requires a commitment that facilitates shared, joy-filled work.

Patience and Respect
in a Time of Anxiety and Rudeness

We live in an age of anxiety where fear is exploited. Many people feel they have little or no control over terrorism, global warming, rising fuel costs, etc. (In truth, of course, we do have a voice and a calling to participatory democracy and can do something about such issues.) If people feel they have little control over the various arenas of their lives, they may try to exercise excessive control at church, even venting their anger and frustration in inappropriate ways to people who do not deserve it. Recognizing this problem does not alleviate it. But it does compel us as leaders mutually to create and work hard to maintain trustworthy places where people can use their voices responsibly and collaboratively.

That will require us to learn and use skills of patience, active listening, and clear, honest, and respectful speaking. This is difficult today. Civility is rare. The ridiculing quip and the mean snipe permeate the media—and are formative. We do not suggest turning off the television. By all means, we need to be fully engaged with all aspects of our context and culture. It does mean that sustaining healthy conversation will need to be modeled and taught. Interestingly enough, "manners" are once again being taught by some businesses. Many congregation members have never forgotten how to speak kindly to one another. But the very fact that it needs to be mentioned here indicates how deliberate we need to be in communicating honestly *and* respectfully. Together leaders need to act consistently in kind, respectful ways so that transformation, including transformation of the culture of daily life, is possible.

As a faith community faces change in leadership or anticipates moving forward by building on a newer church model, it becomes essential to check in with and re-establish trust between and among generations. To think of new forms of ministry for the future does not mean one has to negate the past. One generation's desire for a place with less adherence to authority may clash with another generation's preference for more traditional structures. But the commitment to Christ and need for caring community are indispensable no matter what. Helping generations trust one another is crucial *and* possible, but such trust among generations needs to be intentionally and creatively tended.

Trusting the People

Are people among whom we minister trustworthy? Yes and no. People within the church are no different from those in any other sector of society. At our best, we can be trusted to keep confidences, to work hard, to collaborate with others in direct, open, and honest ways. At our worst we are petty, jealous, and unreliable. We gossip, we betray, and we hurt each other terribly.

It may seem naïve to trust people, especially if we have recently been burned. To place ultimate trust in any one human being underestimates the sinfulness of the human condition. Even our very best friend may ultimately betray our trust. We do, however, have a trustworthy God. When we are let down, even abandoned, God is there. By resting in the arms of this God of covenant faithfulness, we are free from all that would enslave us, so that we can exercise trust even when we feel neither free nor safe.

What does it mean to trust the people? It means to trust that God has created each person and that there is potential in each person for faithful service, probably beyond what we know and possibly beyond what they even know about themselves. It means to trust that Christ has redeemed the very one we find most difficult to work with. It means that the Spirit is at work building and rebuilding community, constantly transforming us.

Practically speaking, it means that transforming leaders actively look for gifts in people, not just *some* people, but in the most unlikely of persons. They trust that each person has gifts, and that all gifts are needed in some way within the congregation (see chapter 13). It means that transforming leaders are committed to trust people with responsibilities that clearly have been given to them. To take back a task because we are afraid it will not be done to our liking undermines any future ministry (see chapter 5). Both the authoritarian leader and the leader who abdicates the full responsibilities of her or his office, display a lack of trust in the people. Authoritarians believe only in their own abilities and trust only their own judgment. Those who abdicate are afraid of the gifts of the members and threatened by their power. Transformational leaders are servant leaders who work hard themselves and trust people to become not only good followers, but gifted, transforming leaders themselves (see chapter 6).

We are called to believe the radical reformation concept that the church is the body of Christ. That means we have among us a priesthood of all believers. We respect and anticipate the ministry of all the baptized. The *laos*, the whole "people" of God, are engaged in ministry in daily life all week long (see chapter 16). We need not feel threatened by them but count on them to carry out transforming discipleship. Together we gather in a trusting community to be empowered for such ministry. Moreover, God is at work in the people among whom we minister. Because our trustworthy God is very much at work in the world, we can approach the people who are as yet outside the Christian community in a trustworthy way. We believe that God's actions of witness, faith, and love through us are not lost in the world. God transforms our love into mission[16] (see chapter 3).

Trusting the Called Leader

How important it is to trust pastoral and diaconal ministers. By virtue of their offices they have been called to serve faith communities as God's leaders. In the rite of installation, the people of God are asked whether they will receive the leader called to serve in their midst. The congregation is called to respect and trust their leaders.

In the current social context, lack of trust in leaders in general is rampant—and for good cause in many instances. Given the way some religious leaders abuse power, it is amazing that people still trust churches and leaders as much as they do. Having said that, however, today we often see uninformed judgment of leaders, groundless suspicion, and the consequent undermining of both mission and community. This eats away at the authority and personhood of pastors and other called leaders. For diaconal ministers there is the added burden of some people not trusting, or understanding, the very office of diaconal ministry. This erodes their calling to be a bridge between church and world.

True, the leader should not be given a blank slate. And, yes, trust must be earned, as mentioned earlier in the chapter. The faith community, guided by a trustworthy God, needs to work together intentionally so that leaders are trusted and empowered to consistently and accountably lead in trustworthy ways. To bear such a call is both a great privilege and an awesome responsibility.

How sad when trustworthy leaders become the target of abuse. Sometimes a faith community tolerates far too long the disrespectful, even sabotaging, actions by a troubled and trouble-making parishioner. When one person or a group is given free reign to shatter the trustworthy environment and, more often than not, to make the leader the scapegoat, the congregation's council needs the courage to say, "This must stop!" *and* consistently act on those words to reestablish trust and vitality in the community.

Ironically, sometimes people who are exhibiting mistrust of their leader still count on that very leader to fix what is broken. People's wounds and distorted attitudes toward authority lead them to make irrational demands of leaders, especially religious leaders.[17] It is at such a time that the leader needs especially to seek wisdom and support from a wise mentor, counselor, or spiritual director (see chapter 9) in order to continue to lead in the midst of suffering. When we are in such a situation we identify most closely with the denial and betrayal of Christ. It is important to remember that Christ's crucifixion is complete. His resurrection is real. We are not called to be martyrs or scapegoats. We are called to new life in Christ.

We need to remember who and whose we are. We belong to Christ and are called to Christ's service. How we behave under fire is crucial. Although people can take a lot from us, they cannot take our integrity. How we conduct ourselves in attempts to rebuild trusting relationships is crucial. Faith communities today need to practice careful discernment. They need to be biblically and theologically aware (see chapter 7), caring of the people, and aware of the missional needs of the world around them so that together leaders and parishioners can wisely engage in transformational ministry.

Trust of the Broader Church

Hans Kung wrote that we are not to place our trust *in* the church—because it will always disappoint us—but to believe that the church *is* God's redeemed people[18] (see chapter 3). We all need to be able to count on and work together so that the broader church body is a collaborative, mutually accountable body.

"We don't trust the national church anymore. They make us. . . . " So begins many sentences on challenging topics such as abortion, same-sex marriage, evolution, and more. So begins many budget-cutting sessions to justify keeping funds "at home" in the local congregation. Rarely do—or can—mainline churches "make" a local congregation do anything, but that is not the perception in a fearful or mistrustful congregation.

On one hand, fear and uncertainty in local congregations drive people to look to the broader church for answers to all their questions and to depend upon it to solve all their problems. On the other, people may believe judicatory leaders at synodical, regional, and churchwide levels cannot be trusted. Either perception is unhelpful. Judicatory leaders, often not known personally by congregations, are viewed as larger than life with enormous power. Disdain for them is revealed in how people refer to them. (In the case of our own denomination, the ELCA, the term "Chicago" or "Higgins Road" is often used rather than the actual names of people or their offices.) What is forgotten is that these are real people called to real positions and serving offices of the church. They are trustworthy resources for guidance, and neither gods nor demons. It is important for congregations to pray publicly for them and to use the magazines, resources, and study documents they develop. By discussing such documents (for example in an adult forum) people grow in understanding and are equipped to thoughtfully use their voices to respond to the study documents, rather than just react to the *idea* of them.

It is important to have a broad number of congregation members, of all ages and viewpoints, visit judicatory offices, attend assemblies, church-wide global mission events, youth gatherings, women and men's events, camps, and more. We can open youth to the possibility of attending church-affiliated colleges.

The closest expression of the broader church, the "neighborhood" of ten to twenty congregations in a conference or cluster (or whatever name is used in your area), provides a wonderful potential for extended community. Yes, pastors do get together for sermon text study, but what about other leaders and the laity? Youth need to be able to gather together to experience a stimulating challenge larger than a local congregation may be able to offer. The conference could provide joint teacher education. At one time this concept was strong in many places, but today it has been mostly lost and is badly needed. Choir exchanges and festivals, conference-wide appreciation banquets, and workshops for church council members are just a few of the possibilities for greater sharing.

Of course, people could say that they are too busy today for more "meetings" beyond the local congregation. But such wider involvement may actually save time in a sense by helping a congregation move beyond its own problems, providing new ideas, new vision, and mutual support. Transformative leaders will help build all sorts of bridges through multiple broader church involvements, including ecumenical and inter-faith gatherings that strengthen, enlighten, and enliven the local congregation. The church is an interdependent community of communities. In the fuller community we share in God's creation in prayer and love.[19]

When Trust Breaks Down

When trust is broken, is it gone forever? True, it is extremely hard to re-establish. A congregation cannot pretend things are okay. When trust is gone, a one-time-only confrontation or a surface "I'm sorry" will not suffice.

It may take a while for people to realize that trust is crumbling. They do not know how much has broken down until some, maybe many, have left. "Why did they leave?" people quietly ask. "We didn't know anything was wrong." But when we finally do see the naked truth, we want to glue things together quickly, or throw things—and people—away.

When trust breaks down in staff relationships, the council declares that one must go—often the lowest in rank. When a couple of people become upset with the pastor, they—not trusting that pastor enough to openly share the problem—call around to see how many other people they can find to add to their list of complainers, thereby multiplying the problem and more deeply dividing the congregation.

When trust is gone, the entire system becomes sick. The problems are complex. To quote an old nursery rhyme, after Humpty Dumpty fell off that wall, "All the king's horses and all the king's men could not put Humpty together again." After such a great fall, when trust is shattered, we cannot for all the world see how it can be rebuilt. We have seen it so many times, and we ache because of the tragedy. By all reason we say that trust cannot be restored.

But to give up hope is to say that we do not believe in the gospel, in the power of forgiveness or the promise of reconciliation. Christ died for the alienated, for the guilty, for the broken-hearted, for the hopeless. When we are most despondent, the resurrection is most real.[20] When we ignore each other's hurting cries, when our demands on each other are overwhelming and go unheeded, Christ has already restored our broken relationship with God and, even when we cannot yet experience it, our broken human relationships. Christ continually restores the church so that we can be his broken and resurrected body alive to serve all the world.

How then do we live in trust when trust has broken down? The problems or the pain will not automatically go away. Some of the broken pieces will never be mended. Still, even in the midst of the bitterness, there may be signs of God's unconditional love: although broken trust will not be restored, a layperson and pastor feed one another at the communion table; some people will not return to this congregation, but they do not leave the Christian faith; even though the trust will never be quite the same, two staff members forgive one another and do learn new patterns of communication.

When trust breaks down we need to trust in the unconditional love of a trustworthy God and call upon the help of the astute perspective and wise guidance of a church leader and/or a counselor from the broader church or community to help us deal with the anger, bitterness, and frustration of being a wounded community. They can help us set up new, healthier ways of communication and construct systems of accountability. We can learn to exercise respect even when respect has not been earned. We will need to check out frequently how our mutual accountability is going.

Christ's resurrection is complete and yet may not be experienced as complete. We live in the "already and not yet" of the reign of God.

We participate in God's trustworthiness while we learn again how to trust one another.[21] We live into that renewed relationship by being trustworthy, and yes, through caringly and carefully trusting. It is hard. In the midst of it all, God's mercy, forgiveness, and grace for transformation continues.

o o o o o o o o o o o o o o o o o o o o o

Personal Reflection

1. When have you lived freely in trustworthy relationships? What was that like?
2. When were you burned or broken by betrayal? What was the cost?
3. Where are you now in your ability to trust and be trustworthy?

Group Conversation

1. As a church council, call committee, judicatory staff, or any other small group, share your vision of what a "trustworthy environment" looks and feels like. What are impediments to such trust?
2. What factors contribute to establishing and sustaining a trustworthy environment? What could be your role in building trust?
3. What, in your experience, leads to a lack of trust in relationships or communities of faith?

Spiritual Practice

1. In the quiet of your own place of devotion, or in the company of a trusted spiritual companion or guide, pray out loud for those whom you do not trust, for those who seem threatened by you, or for those who seem to be undermining your ministry.
2. Pray also for those who do not trust you. Seek grounding in your trustworthy God.

Transforming Action

Select one arena (a committee, task force, council, etc.) that seems especially to be lacking in trust. Collaboratively with other leaders or potential leaders, develop a strategy for addressing the issue of trust and gradually building or rebuilding it. Practice listening skills. Use respectful conversation patterns. This may include taking time to listen to each other's faith stories.

Honoring the People:
Congregational Realities

chapter ●
two

THE MINISTRY OF THE CHURCH, according to St. Paul in 2 Corinthians, is "treasure" in "clay jars" (2 Corinthians 4:7). In the same way, the church is a fragile and broken vessel that carries the gospel and provides a context for our ministry. We are all too aware of the fragility of congregational life on many levels. Yet this fragile vessel is the very means God has selected to accomplish God's missional purposes. God entrusts the gospel to the hands of people like us. This is either one of the greatest mistakes God has ever made or one of the most amazing of mysteries.

Honoring Context

How does a transforming leader enter the scene of a new call in the most constructive fashion? How does a transforming leader accompany a people along the way? And how does a transforming leader relinquish leadership at the proper hour? We can draw basic wisdom about the nature of the church from the experience of those who have gone before us, including the insights informed by congregational systems theory. To explore congregational systems, we will be turning to the insights of family systems theory for transforming leadership both in this chapter and throughout this book.

Transforming leadership entails careful attention to learning and honoring the context of one's ministry.[1] As we explored in the previous chapter, trust is crucial for transforming leadership. Trust is established as one enters a new context with genuine interest in exploring the uniqueness of that place and its people. A new leader needs to be deliberate and thorough in becoming familiar with the contours of both the natural and spiritual geography. This necessitates using methods and tools appropriate to the task.

The discipline of ethnography provides a basic methodology for those who seek to study context in a systematic fashion.[2] Four avenues of investigation are available for consideration: participant observation, semi-structured interviews, material artifacts, and documentary evidence.[3] As one enters into a new context, there are many ways one can observe with the detachment of an ethnologist. One observes the customs and interpretive frameworks of people in virtually every setting. One compares and contrasts these with previous experiences. And one searches for the meaning of phrases, rituals, and behavior that are commonly used to interpret life.

Semi-structured interviews can be conducted with people both within and beyond the congregation. One is wise to visit with elderly members of the congregation and key leaders to have them tell you the congregation's story out of their own perspective. It is important to listen to the descriptions of times of celebration, times of conflict, and times of stability. It is important to attend to key names and key events in this narrative. Transforming leaders also do well to visit with people outside the congregation, both ministerial colleagues and community leaders. From these people one can learn about how the congregation is perceived by outsiders. One can also begin to gain perspective on factors that affect the entire community in which the congregation is located: economic trends, educational system, political tendencies, demographic characteristics, etc. One can begin to learn what gives people hope and what are the major challenges facing the community.

Material artifacts can lend keen insight into the context. One should do a survey of the church building itself. What does the architecture teach about the history and commitments of this people? What does the worship space teach about the local theology? What images are hung up on the walls, and what is their significance? Likewise, asking questions about artifacts in the local park, cemetery, or courthouse can reveal much about the values and history of this context.

Documentary evidence also is extremely important for understanding a new place. Within the church, reading the minutes from council and congregational meetings, reviewing annual reports, surveying newsletters, and studying any recorded history will be invaluable. These and other documents have much to teach about the ethos of this people, their loyalties, and their difficulties. Likewise, investigating local history through books, pamphlets, or videos provides a window into how life has been and continues to be experienced in this place. Reading books written by local authors can help build rapport with people as one demonstrates genuine interest in what makes this people and place distinctive.

As a new leader enters into the context through these avenues, he or she should pay attention to the people (those who are obviously in charge and those who are invisible), the location (how it is unique and how it reflects the larger region), the history (what is remembered and what is forgotten), organization (which groups are influential and how things get accomplished), activities (how people spend their time and what are recognized as significant events), and resources (what goods are available and what constraints are placed on their use). The emerging field of congregational studies provides helpful tools for investigating context that can be adapted to local use.[4]

As we have seen by our emphasis on paying attention to context, the key to building a climate of trust begins with honoring a people for who they are, who they have been, and who they will be.[5] The remainder of this chapter is organized around ten insights about the partnership between leader and people that can maximize team building and minimize frustration in every context. Each of the ten assertions is accompanied by a fundamental *theological truth* and a basic *leadership virtue*, consonant with the particular insight. For the fun of it, let's consider this a kind of top ten list: "The top ten insights a transforming leader should consider in honoring God's people in the congregation."

Honoring the Past

The first three insights begin by honoring where a people have been in the past, leading up to the present.

Insight #10: "The congregation was there before you were."

The exception to this, of course, is in the case of a new mission start. In all other cases, the saints of God have gathered for worship and the sacraments, lived through times of joy and sorrow together, and watched leaders come and go for "x" number of years before you arrived on the scene. Furthermore, the people of God have been sent out from worship to love and serve the Lord week after week in a variety of ways. Faithful ministry predates a new leader's own involvement in this place.

This insight affirms, too, that other ministers have labored in this field before you. New leaders honor the past by speaking well of those who have gone before them as ministers. Here "ministers" is used broadly to refer to ordained pastors and other professional ministry leaders. We need not be threatened by the past partnerships of ministers and people. Nor do we need to belittle those who are our predecessors. Rather, in the spirit of Luther's explanation of the eighth commandment, we are to "come to their defense, speak well of them, and interpret everything they do in the best possible light."[6]

A key theological truth here at stake has to do with *God's providential care for a people over time*. God is faithful and accompanies a people over the long haul. This leads also to a basic *leadership virtue*: humility. We humbly serve by honoring the footprints of those who have gone before us.

Insight #9: "There's a reason why things are the way they are."

The church is an all too human group. It consists of individual human beings who relate to one another in some predictable ways. Sometimes they get along with each other; sometimes they do not. Thus the "story" of each and every congregation consists of the complex series of human interactions that constitute its history. In congregational systems theory these interactions are called "emotional processes."[7] In congregational systems, like family systems, every relationship generates an emotional charge of some kind, some more powerful than others. How we react emotionally to other people is influenced by the kinds of relationships we have developed in formative relationships very early in life. For example, in talking to a certain church leader, I may find myself emotionally responding as I would to my own father. Or one may observe how the organist and the treasurer find themselves reacting to one another as they did with one of their own siblings, in rivalry to gain attention, although totally unaware that this is taking place. Or one may notice that an elderly man and one of the members of the youth group are bonding like grandfather and grandchild. These kinds of emotional processes are taking place all the time in ministry.

In this complicated set of exchanges, there are some predictable patterns. From these exchanges some people emerge as the powerful ones and others as the angry ones, the miffed. Some fall by the wayside, disappearing from view. "The way things are" is the sum total of all of these interactions. It may take a long time of careful listening in order to begin to discern the contours of this faith community's story. We listen by paying attention both to the congregation's story and to the stories of the persons who make up the congregation. We read church documents like annual meeting minutes, newsletters from previous years, or a formal congregational history to listen to the congregation's story. We meet with wise elders of the congregation who remember stories from critical incidents of the past to gain insight. And we spend significant time in the homes, schools, and workplaces of members to get to know them in their native settings. Without careful listening, one cannot assume to comprehend who these people really are.

There is a vital *theological truth* that emerges at this point: the ecclesial condition, like the human condition itself, is one of brokenness (i.e., sin). Dietrich Bonhoeffer wrote about the problem of "visionary dreaming" as one of the greatest dangers facing leaders in the church.[8] Instead of thanking God for what we have been entrusted, our visionary dreaming of what the church "ought" to be like instead leads to severe judgmentalism. Thus the *leadership virtue* accompanying this insight is simple: do not judge. There is much you yet have to learn about why things are the way they are.

Insight #8: "It is the congregation's job not to want to change."

In systems theory this is called homeostasis.[9] We live in a world of rapid change, most of which is out of our own control. Moreover, there is an essential serendipity to life that also renders life out of control: we get sick, accidents happen, people die. In the midst of a world that seems out of control, people seek security. We want to hold on to something unmovable, especially our faith in God.

The church represents God and the things of God. People desire to hang on to the things upon which they have depended in the past. They do not want these things to change, lest they lose their only anchor in life, i.e., their faith. We should not mistake this for an argument that all change in the church is to be avoided. Not at all. Rather take this as a plea for honoring the status quo in the process of implementing strategic change. Too often we simply do not understand or honor the good reasons why change is often resisted in the church. Sometimes there are good reasons why people resist change. In the best of cases, it has to do with preserving people's faith. In fact, by clearly understanding our histories, honoring what builds a solid foundation and what might have not been healthy, we will be more free to live together constructively in the present and move into the future with insight.

A *theological truth* to be deduced from this discussion is that the human condition is marked by fear of the future. We can be "peril"-ized by the prospect of difficult things yet to come. This summons forth a key *leadership virtue*: gentleness with God's people in contemplating change.

Honoring the Present

The next three items on our top ten list pertain to honoring the present congregational dynamics, as they likely will express themselves in ministry. There are certain realities that can contribute to fundamental wisdom about the developing relationships between a transforming leader and people.

Insight #7: "The congregation is divided roughly into thirds: one third will be 'inactive,' one third attend worship as primary or only activity, and one third are active beyond worship."

Each of these groups deserves something different from their pastor. First, regarding the "inactives": the reasons for their inactivity deserve to be honored. If one listens carefully, one will discover that a surprisingly high number of people who have become inactive in a church have good reasons for this being the case. Either there are family circumstances that they are struggling with and about which there is a measure of shame, or there is a history in the congregation that has led to their withdrawal. Pastoral concern for inactive members begins with making contacts with these people as positive as possible. It is self-defeating behavior to badger them for greater involvement. Rather, a ministry of inviting and waiting is the best policy. The day will come at some future moment when these people will need the church—for a wedding, hospitalization, or funeral—and this is the time to simply shower them with grace and kindness.

Those who attend worship as their primary activity deserve from their minister and other worship leaders the best possible worship preparation. If we indeed believe that God in Christ promises to meet us in Word and Sacrament, then leaders need to practice the finest preparation for presiding, preaching, teaching, and pastoral care at worship.[10] Do we still believe God's pledge that it is at worship where Christ promises to be powerfully at work? The time for worship, as the one place where the most people are present, affords itself as an occasion for ministering to the needs of people in a variety of ways. It serves as a moment for pastoral care as one addresses the human condition through the sermon, prayers, and sacramental ministry. Moreover, it serves as a time for engaging in serious Christian education, not only through the means of the sermon, but also through the use of worship aids like the bulletin, announcements, or interpretation of the liturgy.

Those who are active beyond worship (and sometimes even too active) deserve from their called leaders constant expressions of gratitude in response to the sharing of their gifts. Through written notes, brief phone calls, or email, pastors and other leaders can acknowledge genuine appreciation for the gifts shared that make ministry a mutual enterprise. Saying "thank you" does make a difference.

One *theological truth* informing this insight is that the body of Christ indeed consists of many members. Each has a particular place as a member of that body, however humble and underutilized. This leads also to a *leadership virtue*: graciousness to "sinners" and "pillars" alike.

Insight #6: "Your parents will be members of your congregation."
Of course, this will be rarely true in a literal sense. But in the manner of congregational systems theory, this will be virtually always the case. Systemically and symbolically there will be people in the congregation who will project their unresolved emotional issues upon you. After all, the leader does represent God and the things of God for many people. Thus you will be the recipient of anger and criticism and sometimes praise that has nothing to do with your own achievements.[11] Rather, people will employ you as a screen for portraying their own emotional baggage.

Not only this, however. There also will be instances when you yourself will (often unaware) project your own unfinished emotional business upon another person in your congregation. You will likely react in the same way you once (and/or still) respond to your own mother or father or sibling. The formal psychological term for this phenomenon is "transference." We all have what might be called our own "f.o.o.i." (family of origin issues). To the degree we remain unaware of our own "fooi" ("phooey") we will be liable to serious lapses of judgment in relating to other people, particularly those persons most evocative of our patterned emotional reactions.

The *theological truth* about ourselves that we may never fully transcend is this: the healer is also always wounded.[12] Each of us is finite and limited in our emotional capacities. This necessitates the *leadership virtue* of always seeking greater self-knowledge. In part this knowledge of self can be greatly enhanced by spiritual direction or therapy, particularly when emotional reactivity starts to get the upper hand in our lives as ministers.

Insight #5: "Some people will know how to push your buttons."
This is a corollary of the previous point. Not everyone is going to like you as a person or as a leader. In part this is because of what you represent to them in their lives, i.e., the church or God. In most cases, the negative reactions people will express toward you will have little or nothing to do with you personally.[13] This is generally the case, although those of us who are in ministry tend to take almost everything far too personally.

We need to acknowledge that we are authority figures in the eyes of other people. We represent to others God and the things of God. Many people have had difficult experiences in life that have prompted them to be angry at God or at the church. Those of us in ministry are in perpetual danger of overreacting to criticism or complaint. We live with the constant tendency to personalize every gesture or comment. The situation is especially volatile when your own transference meets the transference of another person in the church. Just watch for the chemical reaction and explosion!

The core *theological truth* that we need to reclaim each and every day anew: you are justified by grace through faith and not by the approval of other people. Those attracted to ministry are very prone to need personal affirmation and approval. Thank God that there is much of that to be had in the relationships of minister to people! But this also leaves many leaders extremely vulnerable to measuring their own lives according to how other people feel about them. For this reason, it is necessary for effective ministry that leaders cultivate a circle of support beyond the membership of the congregation, perhaps especially among colleagues in professional ministry. These relationships are crucial for lending the support and critical perspective we sometimes lose in the midst of the journey. For this reason we need to cultivate a key *leadership virtue:* self-differentiation. Beware of emotional enmeshment with the people you serve, in order to avoid over-investment or confusion of roles.

Honoring the Future

The final four items on this "top ten list" pertain to the emerging and future ministry partnership between pastor and people. We honor the people by wise and faithful accompaniment as we travel the road of ministry together. Transformation occurs not only through the initiative of the called leader but through deep and genuine relationships with the people that one serves. Leadership involves insight into the process by which we are enriched by mutually transforming relationships and awareness of the roadblocks that prevent the development of the same.

Insight #4: "The congregation and leader will identify other people to blame for their problems."

Human groups have a facility for resolving conflict by finding someone to blame. The cultural anthropologist, Rene Girard, has identified a deep pattern in the rituals and stories of ancient peoples that he describes as the scapegoat mechanism.[14] Whenever fear and anxiety levels are raised, human groups inevitably gravitate toward the identification of a specified individual or group as the cause of that fear or anxiety. Examples of this phenomenon range from the everyday "kick the dog" syndrome to genocidal actions on the part of societies, e.g., the Holocaust. Part of the mystification of this behavior originates in the fact that those who are acting out against the scapegoat are completely convinced that their actions are justified. They really believe the scapegoat is getting what is deserved.

Girard himself became attracted to the Christian faith when he discovered in the passion narrative of Jesus Christ the unveiling of this scapegoat pattern. In the Christian gospel we find revealed the sinlessness of the Crucified One. Scripture testifies to the fact that Jesus did not get what he deserved when he was executed. Unprecedented in human history is the Christian recognition and disclosure of the injustice of eliminating this scapegoat. This means that of all people on earth, Christians should be able to see scapegoating for what it truly is, the unjust displacement of fear and anxiety. Of all people on earth, Christians should be those who put an end to all scapegoating of individuals and groups, either within or outside of the church!

Far too often, however, Christian churches continue to find someone to blame for their problems. Conflict is all too common in congregations—conflict between individuals, conflict between the leader and certain members, or conflict directed at outsiders (e.g., the synod or the denomination). This leads to a crucial *theological truth*: Jesus Christ died as the final scapegoat. If you find yourself fearful or anxious and needing release, take it to the cross. The cross of Jesus Christ eliminates our need to turn other people into new scapegoats.

The *leadership virtue* related to this process is very simple: When you are wrong, apologize. Confession is good for the soul, including that of the leader. You need no other scapegoats than the Crucified One.

Insight #3: "Christ is God; you are not."

How often we get confused about this core issue! When we forget who God really is, the consequences are severe. This is the root cause for a number of serious maladies. Making one's own ministry into an idol leads to attempts at overcontrolling the church. After all, if I am God, then I need to be in control of everything. It leads to overworking.[15] Being God is more than a full time job. It can lead to addictions of various kinds. One needs more than a little help in order to live up to the divine job description. Trying to do so can finally lead to fatigue and burnout. Trying to be God for oneself and others is simply an exhausting and impossible undertaking.

The central *theological truth* is the recognition of a core temptation in the lives of pastoral leaders: idolatry. According to John Calvin, the human heart is a "a perpetual factory of idols."[16] We are tempted every day to try and take the place of God in our relationships with others. Thus the compelling *leadership virtue* is surrender. Let Christ minister to you through prayer, devotions, exercise, collegial relationships, and simply having a life beyond your congregation!

Insight #2: "People will tell you what you need to know, if you are ready to listen to them."

Paul Tillich once observed that the first duty of love is to listen. Listening to others is a great and rare gift. Listening is a tangible expression of love and care. It is the gospel embodied. While the whole world is ready to speak, where are the compassionate ears to receive and respond? The majority of pastoral care involves listening—to words, to body language, to affect, to nuances, to the whole story of a life.[17]

Entering into a new congregation in order to accompany this people into the future involves the fundamental responsibility of listening. We listen to the individual stories of members through strategic visitation that takes us into the realms of their daily life (homes and workplaces). We listen to the stories of the congregation itself through written and oral histories, mission statements, annual reports, statistical trends, budgets, architecture, and by talking with people inside and beyond congregational membership.

What is the "extant" (not just "professed") theology of this people? What are the operative theological concepts that are actually functioning in the life of the congregation? What are the most serious sins? The prevalent images of Jesus? The meanings of salvation? The reasons for hope? What is the mission of the church? The definition of good preaching? The status of the sacraments? The meaning of stewardship? The answers to these and a host of other theological questions are embedded in the communal life of this people. It is vitally important to spend significant time listening in order to discern how to appropriately and effectively lead this people into the next phase of its congregational mission at this moment in time. Such listening, above all, entails the readiness to be changed by what you hear. How do you correlate your own theological commitments to the life of these people, who already have their own commitments?

A clear *theological truth* to be honored in this context: this congregation already has a theology. The people are never a blank slate. And what is the related *leadership virtue*? Silence and awe in the face of so great a mystery! After all, it is always useful to be silent when trying to listen. Even in situations where there may be serious differences of opinion, it is important to enter into relationships with the posture of intentional listening as a first step. Only by doing so can one engage the other in understanding, rather than reactivity.

Insight #1: "The congregation will abide even after you leave."

Again, an important exception to this maxim is the eventuality that a congregation decides to close. Contrary to desire, this eventuality is being experienced by more and more leaders. Such leaders face the unique challenge of interpreting the closing of a congregation in a transformative way that opens a new path into the future. In every case, however, one must keep one's own role in critical perspective. Yes, the ministry of any single transforming leader will contribute greatly to the ongoing story of a congregation. The pastoral vision and energy shared makes a tremendous difference in partnership with the people. However, the day will come—often too soon—when you will again leave this people. Yet, the ministry will go on. Moreover, it is a good thing that the ministry goes on.

The degree to which ministry comes to an end when a particular leader departs a call is a key measure of that leader's ineffectiveness. We do not serve people well by setting up patterns of dependency relationships. Rather, we serve well by summoning forth a people's gifts and letting them loose in ministry initiatives.

This final item on our list also has ethical implications for how one leaves a place. When one relinquishes a call, one must entrust the ministry to those who become the next leaders in that place. One of the most complicated ethical dilemmas involves a pastor who has left a call, yet continues to meddle in congregational affairs. In such an instance, there is no honoring of the Spirit's nurture of the people through other laborers. Transformation, in the deepest sense, is the Spirit's work, and we need to trust that the Spirit both has guided the ministries of those who have gone before us and will continue to direct those who come after us.

The *theological truth* that informs this insight is the following: the harvest finally belongs to God. Particular leaders sow seeds, water the seedlings, and prune a few branches. But the final harvest is God's alone. Wilhelm Loehe wrote that "the church flows through the ages like a river."[18] This insight necessitates one final *leadership virtue*: "to equip the saints for the work of ministry" (Ephesians 4:12). The church flourishes best when the pastor takes the ministry of all the baptized with utmost seriousness, a ministry that transcends the service of any particular pastoral leader.

○ ○ ○ ○ ○ ○ ○ ○ ○ ○ ○ ○ ○ ○ ○ ○ ○ ○ ○ ○

Personal Reflection

1. What are the some of the biggest differences between the church where you are presently serving and your previous church experiences? What can you learn from these differences?
2. Thinking through the "Top Ten" list, what patterns do you see that might characterize your congregation? What patterns do you detect in yourself?

Group Conversation

1. Imagine you are introducing someone new to your church and community. What are the most important features you would tell them about your context?
2. Invite each person in the group to share some practical wisdom he or she has learned about the nature of congregational life through experiences of the church. If the group is large, share

in triads. Wisdom can be gained both from energizing and discouraging times. Discuss with each other what you have heard from each other to deepen that wisdom.

Spiritual Practice

1. Visit different spaces in the church building where ministry happens, such as the sanctuary, offices, classrooms, kitchen, and other gathering spaces. As you go to each space, pray for the specific people who enter these spaces serving in leadership and participating in activities.
2. You could extend this spiritual practice by visiting different places in the community context where the people of the congregation are serving all week long.

Transforming Action

1. Take one or more of the "Top Ten" and see how it could lead to a transforming action. For example, #10: "The congregation was there before you were."
2. Try to find out things you don't know about previous generations in the congregation and your predecessors in ministry. This might be through inviting conversation, by looking through old records, etc. How might you and the congregation build on that history?

Hearing the Wisdom: Twelve Ecclesial Foundations

WE NEED TO LISTEN CAREFULLY to congregational realities. Furthermore, we need to reflect on them in relation to ecclesial church foundations. "Ecclesial" comes from the Greek *ekklesia*, which refers to the "gathered people." In the church the gathered people are the "called out" ones who share one baptismal identity. *Ekklesia* can also refer to both the process of congregating and the congregated community. Our Creator God intends people to live together in healthy ways. Though we continually confound such community, we have been reconciled through Christ to live, transformed by the power of the Spirit, to be a "called out" people for service in God's world.

Throughout the centuries people have pondered the nature of this *ekklesia*, this "church." Though many more could be mentioned, here are twelve foundations for briefly considering what it means to be a transformed and transforming church. Each of the twelve is followed by some questions to probe transformative leadership in our own contexts. These classic voices are diverse and ecumenical,[1] as is the church.

1. Location: The Church Is Both Local and Universal

H. Richard Niebuhr wrote that the church is both local and universal. The localized church implies the global and historic. But without becoming localized and specific the church does not exist.[2] The New Testament often talks about the "churches" in the plural. The church is a community of memory and hope. It remembers Jesus Christ and the works of God among God's people through history while expecting the coming of the reign of God. Niebuhr said that the purpose of the church is the increase of the love of God and neighbor.

Churches are constantly being transformed, although often reluctantly. The whole church is real only in the local church. Yet, the local congregation is never the whole church. Congregations may need to be reminded of one or the other: "Remember, you, the people in this place, struggling together, *are* the church." Or "Remember, you are not the *whole church*." Churches need to pay attention to the needs of other churches so that they can learn from one another.

Where two or three are gathered in the name of Christ, Christ is present, but also present are all others in whom Jesus dwells. Even though there are spaces in the pews on Sunday morning, the saints from past years are there, too.[3] In fact, some people sit far apart as if aware of previous church members who sat beside them. In God's economy of time and space, they still do. With anticipation we also can envision those who are not yet here, preparing ourselves for their presence as we actively invite them to come.

How do we honor past beloved saints and eagerly welcome newcomers? How could we as leaders be transformed in our view of the church, both local and global, so that we might lead with vision?[4]

2. Nature: The Church Is Both Saint and Sinner

Jürgen Moltmann wrote that the church needs not adroit adaptation, but inner renewal. As with individual Christians, the Church is *simul justus, simul peccator,* both at the same time saint and sinner. But faith in the holiness of the church can no more be a justification of its unholy condition than the justification of sinners means a justification of sin.[5] The church is the community of justified sinners, who, liberated by Christ and experiencing salvation, live in thanksgiving.

What is the nature of the church? Benevolent or violent? Altruistic or egotistical? Generous? Self preservationist? Hans Kung wrote that the church is primarily here not to be admired nor criticized, but *believed.*[6] That does not mean we place our trust and belief *in* the church—because it will always disappoint us—but believe the church *is* God's redeemed people. Being and becoming a transformed and transforming church means not so much to find exactly the right paradigm, or structure, or program, or even leadership, as to *believe* that this people in this place *is* the church. Saint and sinner, caring and quarrelling, the church is both difficult and indispensable.[7] Confession is essential to transformation. Ecclesiology is grounded in Christology. The church is justified, not by its works, not by its history, not by it faithfulness, but by God's faithfulness as God engages the church in mission.

In what ways is our church both saint and sinner? When is it hard to believe that the people are the church? How is God's grace transforming our congregation, even now?

3. Redemption: The Church Needs Liberated Leadership

Rosemary Radford Reuther wrote that the transformation of society is the essential context for understanding the church. Redemption is not confined to the well-being of the individual, or to interpersonal relationships, or the ecclesial sphere. It is fundamentally the redemption of humanity and creation.[8] She calls for concrete engagement in the needs of the community and reading the scriptures in light of those needs. That allows room for the continual rebirth of the Spirit and the recreation of Spirit-filled community in its midst.[9]

The church has a prophetic role in the world. Reuther calls for this prophetic role to include a critique of patriarchal hierarchy, and any other form of exclusion and oppression. However, the Spirit-filled community deludes itself by imagining that it can live without any historical structure at all.[10] There is no one right structure; all church structures are to serve the purposes of a liberating God. Reuther calls for being an exodus community, an exodus not from the church, but from sin and evil, exclusion and domination, so that all might be involved in liberating leadership for the sake of mission. Transforming leadership is liberating leadership. In every age we are called to claim the liberating power of the resurrection that sets people free not simply for their own personal salvation but for the courage to speak boldly and to create communities of inclusion, justice and shared power.

How do patriarchal hierarchy and other forms of oppression and exclusion harm and hinder the church today? What does transformed, liberated leadership look like? What does such a liberated church look like?

4. Shape: The Transforming Church Gathers All People Around

Letty Russell wrote that the church in the round describes a community of faith and struggle working to anticipate God's new creation by becoming partners with those who are at the margins of church and society. This metaphor speaks of people gathered around the Eucharistic table and at all kinds of tables in the world in order to connect faith and life. The transforming church is struggling to become a household of freedom, a community where walls have been broken down so that God's welcome to those who hunger and thirst for justice is made clear. Such a church works for justice in solidarity with the oppressed, welcoming everyone in God's global house as partners.[11]

If the table is spread by God and hosted by Christ it must have many connections: it must serve to connect people to Christ in transformative ways. God in Christ is shaping the community of faith, transforming the lives of people and the worlds in which they live through the power of the Spirit.

For those whom society (including the church) has marginalized, the first step is getting through the door to find a place at the table, the Eucharistic table, the council table, the serving table. While some do find their way in, they may find that little has changed. The shape of the table needs to change in order not only to accommodate new people, but to welcome them fully and use their gifts. We have yet to move beyond mere toleration to a genuine learning from one another, which results in the people being "loved into roundness." Such transformation will mean redefining, redesigning, redoing, and rebirthing the church itself.[12] This *is* mission.

Metaphorically speaking, what is the shape of our church? Who is still not at the table? What are the fears? How are people new at the table changing the shape of the table?

5. Ministry: The Living Saints Who Are Your Neighbors

"Thank God," Martin Luther wrote in 1537, "a seven-year-old child knows what the church is, namely, holy believers and sheep who hear the voice of their Shepherd." The church's holiness consists of the Word of God and true faith.[13] Luther did not begin his reform of the church on the basis of pious leaders, but through a transformed concept of the church itself.

Luther's definition of the church as the communion of saints is the basis for his definition of ministry. He said that the living saints are our neighbors, the naked, and the hungry. We should direct our help to them. He transformed the definition of sainthood in scholastic theology and substituted "service" for merit. The priesthood of Christ and the priesthood of all believers belong together. Every Christian is a priest in the sense of servant. The common priesthood of all believers is one of the most revolutionary doctrines in church history (see chapter 16).

By 1539, with papal authority repudiated and new patterns of reform emerging throughout Europe, Luther repeated his early emphasis that God's Word cannot exist without God's people and conversely, God's people cannot exist without God's Word. Neither the universal church nor the local congregation is ever perfect; instead they are always in a state of becoming. Reformation means ongoing transformation.

As a church, who is our neighbor? In your particular setting, how do congregation members understand the priesthood of all believers? How do they live that mission out in transformative ways?

6. Vocation: The Church Is Set Apart to Be Sent Forth

Suzanne de Dietrich wrote that in an individualistic age, everywhere there is a hunger for community, but what is meant by "community" is not always clear.[14] The search can easily be superficial. A single person at a given moment may be the embodiment of the group, but that one never stands alone. That one carries a message that is meant for community or that will call a new community into being. Faith means responding to God's mighty deeds by commitment. The immediate result of God's redeeming action is the coming into being of a community of believers.[15]

"The church has to rediscover again and again it vocation, its *corporate vocation* as the witnessing community taken out of the world, *set* apart for God, but set apart in order to be again sent to the world."[16] Therefore, two temptations that hinder mission are either to consider the separate life inside the church as an end in itself or to succumb to a slow process of assimilation in the world by which we lose our identity as God's people.[17] The transformed and transforming body of Christ is an organic unity. A church living in isolation is in constant danger of losing sight of God's claim. God transforms the church through each community of faith listening to and learning from the voices of other churches around the world. This is one way the local church is held accountable to its mission in the world.

Which danger is most tempting to your congregation—isolation or assimilation? How is our church listening to voices of other churches calling it back to its vocation? How can transformed leadership empower people to be a set apart and sent people of God"?

7. Mission: The Church Is Something to Give Away

Juan Luis Segundo wrote that Christianity is something to give away. The church was not instituted to save only those within, but to serve all humanity. The church's very mission is concern for people beyond the walls of the church. The transformative question is: How are Christians to live and to serve in order that the people beyond the church are to receive from the ecclesial community that which God is intending to give? Every act of love is an act of faith, trusting that in God's hand this gesture is not lost in the world. God transforms our love into mission.[18]

Jürgen Moltman says it this way: "It is not the Church that has a mission of salvation to fulfill to the world; it is the mission of [God] that includes the Church, creating a church as it goes on its way."[19] The church does not cease to exist, but rather, while participating in God's acts of love and justice in the world, God transforms, strengthens and shapes the church for yet more service. Our mission begins, not with what we create, but with what God is already doing through the liberating activity of the Spirit in Jesus Christ.

Wilhelm Loehe wrote that the entire church is on a pilgrimage. It flows through the ages like a river. The church is not a territorial church, but a church of all people that has its children in all lands and gathers them from every nation. Mission is nothing but the church of God in motion.[20]

What does it mean in our context that by participating in God's mission, God is transforming the church? What missions are we already engaged in? How do those challenge and strengthen us? What statement can we make about what God is doing in our midst?

8. Confidence: Self-Negation Blocks Real Courageous Service

Carol Lakey Hess speaks to the apathy that blocks God's transforming power. She writes about the prophetic torpor and diminished capacity of congregations to care about and respond to injustice. Too often they fall into feeling sorry for themselves or wallowing in what they are not. She believes that mere surface niceness or overemphasis on self-abnegation blunts a person's—or a congregation's—prophetic voice.[21] Congregations often underestimate themselves, or unnecessarily apologize for themselves, failing to see the ministries in which God is already using them and through which God is developing their skills.

Care for others that is diminished by lack of self-confidence, whether on the part of an individual or a congregation, turns inward. Hess quotes Elisabeth Cady Stanton who was fond of saying that sometimes self-development is a higher duty than self-sacrifice.[22] Intended ministry is not real ministry. Care must be understood as

God's concern for human wholeness and widespread justice. Spirituality is much more than a call to humility. Spirituality is a call from the Holy Spirit to human spirits to participate in and be transformed in relation to community with others. This calls for courageous, caring, and conversational leadership that fans embers of concern into action for justice. This is transformation!

Is there apathy in our congregation? What are its signs—lack of interest in opportunities for mission; lack of self-confidence; judgment of self and others? With the help of the Spirit, how can transformed leaders build both confidence and courage to transform apathy into action?

9. Inclusivity: The Church As a Company of Strangers

For strangers, the church needs to be a place of safe ground, so the church must resist being a tight little circle, a "family." Parker Palmer warns against turning the stranger too quickly into friend. The foundation of life together in a faith community is not the intimacy of friends, but the capacity of strangers to share a common place, common resources, and common problems.

Transformation does not mean turning strangers into people "just like us," but providing a place where they can face their fears of being the stranger and deal with those fears. According to Palmer, the church then becomes a place where scarce resources are shared and abundance is generated, where conflict occurs and is resolved, where opinions become audible and accountable. Such a church is a place where people are empowered and protected against abusive power and where people of vision attempt new projects.[23]

Harold Wilke writes about dealing with the one who is stranger to us because of difference. He says that people are afraid of the unknown—particularly a disability—because it reminds them of their own weaknesses or inability. He says, "I do not understand how the threat exists; I only know that I am afraid."[24] In the caring congregation, the concept of wholeness itself is transformed. Wholeness is not a matter of health or perfection. In fact, all of us are only temporarily "able-bodied." Christ imputes wholeness and salvation. It is a matter of believing that the church is whole even while it is broken. The Body of Christ is not whole unless all are a part and using their gifts to serve.

How does our congregation try to turn the stranger too quickly into "friend" (someone just like us)? What are our fears about the stranger? How can we help provide a safe place that is accessible to all and where we can really ask and learn about each other?

10. Strength: The Church Is a Suffering Servant

Dorothy Soelle decades ago prophetically described people building a wall of weapons and succumbing to the dictatorship of capital. Seeking such total self (or national) security depends upon becoming a culture of acquisition and of analgesics. This anesthetizing of life is, in fact, the enemy of human community. When we deny the existence of suffering or seek to alleviate it from only our own lives, Soelle says, the goals of truly loving the neighbor and bringing about justice are subordinated to the goal of getting through life "well," unscathed, and untouched by the suffering of the world. This is to seek a Christian utopia. Freedom from suffering is not the value Jesus Christ strove for. Neither was it passive endurance, but rather productive suffering for the sake of justice, ministry, and mission.

Soelle assumed God is not a sadist. Nor is God a contriver of suffering, an originator of it, nor merely a spectator to it. God is not cynical. God is the liberator, the ally of the poor. Jesus is the oppressed victim, the man of sorrows. At the beginning of his work he renounced both power and freedom from suffering when he was tempted by Satan. He did not want to be stronger than we are collectively. He did not want to be strong except through the solidarity of the weak.[25] Believing in Jesus Christ, the transforming church will not have as its goal "life without suffering." It will not forget the needy once television producers have determined their viewers have compassion fatigue. Trusting in a suffering God, a transforming church can overcome narcissism and replace apathy with empathy.

Who is suffering in our congregation? In our community? In our world? How do each of us, in our own suffering, meet each other through the suffering of Christ?

11. Challenge: A Global Church Will Face Idolatrous Promises

Karen Bloomquist of the Lutheran World Federation asks: What are the challenges to the church today given the huge gap between those who benefit from and those who are harmed under forces of globalization? Churches that see social issues as merely outside their concern will sacrifice their very soul or become increasingly irrel-evant. Churches cannot remain silent because competing gods are at stake. It is a matter of idolatry.

Bloomquist writes that justification by grace through faith is at stake when people are tempted by the allure of other "salvific" prom-ises—consumerism, technological wonders, and the prosperity hoped for under economic globalization.[26] This global transformation is based on "neoliberal" theory that assumes equal partners with equal access to information, technical expertise, and trade conditions. But that is a far cry from the harsh disparities in the real world, where the three wealthiest people in the world have more than the GNP of the 48 poorest countries, where over three billion people try to survive on less than two U.S. dollars a day, where the world's large econo-mies are not governments but large corporations unaccountable to the public.[27] The *ecclesia* as the assembly of God is in danger of being replaced by the global market. The question for transformational leadership is, "Can a wealthy church be on the side of the poor? Can there be rich Christians in an age of hunger?"[28]

How is leadership in our congregation preaching, teaching, chal-lenging, and empowering people to interpret and to understand global challenges? How might congregations and members act for justice?

12. Gift: The Church Is Not a Claim but a Gift

Dietrich Bonhoeffer knew the dangers of being the church in a danger-ous world. He wrote that the nature of the church can be understood only from within, not from a disinterested standpoint. The individual exists only in the other. It is only in God that the claim of the other resides. A faith community is a concrete unity; the center of action does not lie in each member, but in all members together.

There is perhaps no greater loneliness than in community. We make demands on one another. We fail to hear the other's cries of pain. We wear each other out in conflict. We become literally sick and tired of one another. The joy of fellowship dissipates into feel-ing alone, abandoned. God takes on such loneliness. To create a new transformed reality Jesus calls us to repentance. Christ knew what it meant to be truly alone. He bore the ultimate abandonment on the cross, crying, "My God, my God, why have you forsaken me?" (Mark 15:34).

As the love of God restores communion between God and humans in Christ, so too, the human community is transformed into a living reality in love. The Holy Spirit approaches each of us, strangely enough, *deepening* our loneliness, making us even more aware of the ways we are estranged from one another, so that we know we need to turn to Christ. Each of us is justified and sanctified in the midst of ultimate loneliness. As the love of God restores communion between God and humans in Christ, so, too, the human community once again becomes a living reality in love. Then the Spirit places us within the divine community. Then members of this community no longer see one another as claim (demand) but as gift.[29]

How is the Spirit transforming our faith community from loneliness to restored community? How can we move beyond only putting demands on one another to seeing each other as a gift in Christ?

Life Together

God's love wills community. The church that is built on Christ's work of forgiveness, reconciliation, restoration, and renewal will become not only our "wish dream," but God's transforming community. Dietrich Bonhoeffer's classic words about life in community resonate today:

> Innumerable times a whole Christian community has broken down because it had sprung from a wish dream. Serious Christians, set down for the first time in a Christian community, are likely to bring with them a very definite idea of what Christian life together should be and to try to realize it. But God's grace speedily shatters such dreams. Just as surely as God desires to lead us to a knowledge of genuine Christian fellowship, so surely must we be overwhelmed by a great disillusionment with others, with Christians in general, and, if we are fortunate, with ourselves.

> By sheer grace, God will not permit us to live even for a brief period in a dream world. . . . Only that fellowship which faces such disillusionment, with all its unhappy and ugly aspects, begins to be what it should be in God's sight, begins to grasp in faith the promise that is given to it . . . Those who love their dreams of a community more than the Christian community itself become destroyers of the latter, even though their personal intentions may be ever so honest and earnest and sacrificial.

> God hates visionary dreaming; it makes the dreamer proud and pretentious. . . . Because God has already laid the only foundation of our fellowship, because God has bound us together in one

body with other Christians in Jesus Christ, long before we entered into common life with them, we enter into that common life not as demanders but as thankful recipients.[30]

o o o o o o o o o o o o o o o o o o o o o

Personal Reflection

1. With which of the above foundational principles do you reso-nate? Why and how?
2. Which challenges you to think some more or to transform your thinking?
3. What other classical voices provide wisdom for you?

Group Conversation

1. As leaders, what wish dreams of your vision of the church has God graciously shattered? What gifts of being community is God giving you?
2. How is God forgiving, reconciling, restoring, and renewing trans-forming leadership in your community?

Spiritual Practice

1. Read (or read again) one of these classic works, chapter by chapter, as part of your daily study. You are not compelled to "master" the book; nor will you be tested on it. Rather, let such reading be a spiritual discipline.
2. Be open to the Spirit's transforming not only your mind but also your heart.

Transforming Action

By yourself, or, better, with a few others, visit another congrega-tion, perhaps of another denomination. Observe, converse, and inquire about how they are "church." Think about the gift you are or might be to each other.

Leading for Mission:
Problems and Practices

chapter ●
four

TRANSFORMING LEADERSHIP IS THE RESPONSIBILITY of the whole group, not just the power of persuasion by a single person with a vision. Leaders come in many shapes and sizes: quiet and boisterous, organizers and influencers; those who are out in front, those who lead from the middle, and even those who nudge from behind. Transforming leadership is ministry that guides the people of God, helping them fulfill their calling and purpose. Leaders help to organize the church so that maximum use is made of all its resources, motivating people to work for the renewal of church and world. Leadership—grounded in trust in God, liberated by the love of Christ, and empowered by the Spirit—gathers, nurtures, teaches, and inspires the church to be the gifted people of God in mission. God is creating, redeeming, and renewing the people of God to plan and to be mutually accountable for action.

Defining Leadership

In one very helpful definition, Ronald Heifetz articulates leadership as the art of "mobilizing people to make progress on the hardest of problems."[1] This chapter will explore the varied dimensions of this definition. Three aspects of this definition are particularly useful for those seeking to engage in transforming leadership.

First, leadership is an "art." Leadership is not primarily about what Heifetz calls "technical solutions." Leadership is not primarily about implementing programs or following set formulas. It is not about knowing the right answers or developing organizational charts, although good planning is part of leadership. Rather, leadership is about a range of relational practices that need to be engaged with flexibility and adaptability in given contexts and situations. As an art, leadership summons forth originality and creativity as one seeks to imagine, embody, and serve God's transforming purpose of establishing life-giving relationships. The exercise of these practices requires wisdom and adaptability in navigating an ever-changing organic system.

Second, leadership is about "mobilizing" or "empowering" people." It is necessary but not sufficient that the leader him/herself is committed to God's purpose of creating life-giving relationships and engaging congregations in mission. Most leaders are people of deep conviction about the missional purposes of God through the church. But the personal commitments of the leader are only a starting point for congregations actually becoming missional communities. Most Christians in congregations believe God has called them to mission. However, it is crucial that leaders engage in *transforming practices that empower people* to participate in this ministry and mission. This chapter will articulate key transforming leadership practices.

Third, leadership seeks to engage the hardest of problems. All congregations perennially face two particular problems: (1) Remembering and claiming its true *identity* as the people of God in Christ Jesus, and (2) Moving outward from that identity as the body of Christ sent in *mission*.[2]

Claiming our true identity in Christ and becoming a people who participate in God's mission are the two most difficult challenges faced by leaders of congregations. This is true because no matter how well we may have resolved these challenges yesterday, they must be continually reengaged today and in the future.

So many identities compete for the allegiance of the people in congregations, including things like personal success, accumulating things, maintaining an image, winning, or being patriotic. We are constantly tempted into idolatry by clinging to false identities or suffer amnesia about our true identity. One ongoing, even daily, leadership task involves returning to our own core baptismal identity, dwelling in God's Word, partaking of Christ's Supper, thanking God as the Giver of all gifts, and remembering whose we are. By the power of the gospel of Jesus Christ we are set free *from* all false identities (idolatries) that hold us in bondage.

We are likewise in constant temptation of avoiding or undermining God's missionary purposes for the church. The Triune God is a missionary God who sets us free by the power of the gospel and sends us out by the power of the Spirit. Yet, sin clings so closely that avoidance, resistance, and destructive conflict threaten to separate us from the mission God seeks to accomplish. (Should it surprise us that the power of Satan is most intense in seeking to divert the church from claiming its true identity and thereby blocking its participation in God's mission?) We are easily distracted; we become embroiled in destructive conflicts; we direct our best energy into blaming others, both within and beyond the circle of the church; we undermine fundamental trust and destroy relationships. Only the power of the gospel sets the church free *for* recognizing the needs of a world of neighbors.

Ten Leadership Practices

Building on the previous chapters, here we propose and describe ten leadership practices for mobilizing congregations to address their two most difficult problems: claiming identity and engaging in mission.

1. Form and preserve an environment of trust.

In many ways this is the foundational practice. For this reason Chapter 1 elaborated in great detail the importance of establishing trusting relationships and fostering a climate of trust. This is necessary from the very beginning of one's ministry in a place and remains an ongoing task. As one begins to develop trust between leader and people, there is a significant shift in how people perceive the leader's authority. Over time in a trusting environment, the authority of the leader begins to shift from the formal authority that belongs to the office and call to the acknowledged authority that belongs to the leader by virtue of trustworthiness and competence (see chapter 5).

2. Draw on the deep values of the people.

Each Sunday at worship the assembled congregation rehearses their deep values—through the confession of sin and absolution, songs of praise and thanksgiving, the proclamation of law and gospel, confessing the creed and praying the prayers, at the font and the table, in sharing the peace and by being sent. Likewise through the ministry of God's Word—through preaching, lifelong catechetical instruction (catechesis), and regular Bible study—the people are immersed in their heritage and values, continue to deepen their faith, and grow in their ability to be ministers in daily life. As ministers of the Word, pastors and diaconal ministers have at the center of their call the responsibility to bring God's Word into every aspect of ministry—not only at worship or in classes but also at committee meetings and in conversations throughout the week. Through worship and the ongoing ministry of the Word, the leader reconnects people with the deep values of the faith. In this way transforming leadership summons forth theological clarity about questions of identity and mission.

In leading a congregation in mission, the leader needs to excavate these deep values and explore how they are already embedded in the lives of the people, learning to draw upon these deep values creatively in ministry. Too often leaders will assume an oppositional stance in relation to their congregations, instead of listening profoundly and searchingly for how the deep values of the faith are already present as a resource for mission and outreach. Congregations are rooted in heritage and traditions that are informed by the deep values of the faith: love of God and love for neighbor. They are engaged in all sorts of ministry within the congregation and to the families and neighbors. The question is: How can the extant values of the faith become an asset and resource for envisioning and implementing mission and outreach in the future? It is crucial for people to learn to connect and reconnect what they are doing explicitly with the central tenets of the faith and missional purpose in order to reach out even further, maybe beyond their comfort zones. A congregation already has a sense of purpose deeply ingrained in its way of being. One key practice for a leader is to identify that purpose and to ask: What about this purpose needs to be affirmed and drawn upon?

3. Imagine God's future together.

When we consider the teachings of Jesus, especially his parables of the kingdom, Jesus appeals in colorful ways to the human powers of imagination. Through telling stories, Jesus had an amazing capacity to help his listeners imagine the world otherwise, to imagine themselves as if there really were a kingdom of God more compelling than any other power on earth. In many respects imagination is the lost dimension of faith. Typically when we explain the meaning of faith, we refer (rightly) to two aspects: faith as trust (*fides qua*) and as a content to be believed (*fides quae*). However, there is a third aspect of faith that is palpable in the gospels, that is, the stirring of the human mind to imagine a world where God is ruling, transforming the world, and changing people's lives.[3] How can leaders, appealing to the biblical witness to the inbreaking kingdom of God and the way of the cross, stir our imaginations to begin to imagine the world other-wise, cross-wise? Robert Greenleaf writes:

> As a leader one must have facility in tempting the hearer into that leap of imagination that connects the verbal concept to the

hearers' own experience. The limitation on language, to the communicator, is that the hearer must make that leap of imagination. One of the arts of communicating is to say enough to facilitate that leap.

What changes people finally, even more than the will or reason, is the power to imagine their lives otherwise!

4. Identify the assets of the congregation and build on them.

Powerful tools for congregational leadership are available for transforming leaders in the methods of appreciative inquiry and asset-based congregational development.[4] How can we begin to approach organizational leadership by identifying the spiritual gifts of the people and congregational assets, thanking God for these, while constructing ministry and mission starting from the gifts God has bestowed? This approach is dramatically different from one that instinctively problematizes every situation. Moreover, it is an approach that summons us to expand our horizon regarding the meaning of the stewardship of gifts. (see chapter 13 on Asset-Based Congregations). While congregational conflict is often very real, and congregations do face real problems in resources and relationships, the posture of appreciative inquiry can help to reframe reality in a more constructive lens.

5. Understand systems and the certainty of avoidance behaviors.

A leader can easily become stymied by the seeming intransigence of congregational life. Especially when one interprets congregational life only or primarily in terms of the influence of individuals, one can become deeply frustrated about the prospects of change. Systems thinking breaks open the limitations imposed by focusing only on problem persons and difficult relationships. One of the basic concepts in systems thinking is the profound reality of homeostasis. Why are we ever surprised that people and congregations are unwilling to change? In our world, change is rapid and relentless. No wonder members want their congregations to be places of stability in the midst of the hurricane! Interpreting congregational life from a systems perspective can allow the leader to gain perspective on the status quo and provide a vantage point from which to envision effective strategies toward change. (chapter 14 will elaborate implications from systems thinking for transformational leadership.)

6. Maintain sufficient differentiation to see the big picture through the development of an adequate support system beyond the congregation.

Heifetz refers to the importance of being able to see things from "the balcony."[5] By this he means intentionally disciplining oneself to see congregational dynamics from a more objective point of view. We are tempted as leaders in many ways to become so emotionally invested in our ministry and work that we lose perspective on the whole. We may begin to focus on particular irritations to such a degree that we fail to interpret systemic changes accurately as they unfold. For this reason, it is utterly necessary that congregational leaders maintain an intentional support system beyond their own congregations. Such support networks often may include professional colleagues, continuing education events, spiritual director, coach, therapist, mentors, and/or prayer partners. The neglect of the basic stewardship of one's own life leads to depletion or depression, on the one hand, and to controlling behaviors or addictions, on the other. (chapter 9 will more fully elaborate the necessity for an intentional support system.)

7. Focus on appreciating and developing the leadership of others.

Transforming leadership is, in this book, a function both of particular leaders and the entire community, living in symbiotic relationship. No single leader has every needed gift. Rather, there are complementary gifts among the members of the body of Christ. In leading a congregation in mission, it is vital to identify, appreciate, and give thanks for the gifts of others. Ministry and mission occur in partnership with the people of God.

In developing the leadership of others, there are many useful tools that exist as established programs, such as small group ministry, Stephen Ministry, coaching techniques, or congregation-based community development. The development of other leaders is a key factor in the process of transformation into missional church. Transforming leadership engages people to address their most difficult problems (identity and mission). This means summoning forth the best energies of others and avoiding over-dependency on a single leader.

8. Recognize that transforming leadership as difficult and challenging work.

At our school we listen intentionally to the joys and frustrations in ministry that our graduates share at their three-year reunion. Each year we hear them talk about the difficulty of the task: congregations embroiled in destructive conflict, financial crises, communities experiencing profound losses (unemployment, closed medical care facilities, consolidation of schools, adult children moving away and never coming back), and intolerance from ministers of some other Christian traditions. Nevertheless, in the midst of such honest sharing, God allows a spark of hope to glimmer:

> But we have this treasure in clay jars, so that it may be made clear that this extraordinary power belongs to God and does not come from us. We are afflicted in every way, but not crushed; perplexed, but not given to despair; persecuted, but not forsaken; struck down, but not destroyed; always carrying in the body the death of Jesus, so that the life of Jesus may also be made visible in our bodies. For while we live, we are always being given up to death for Jesus' sake, so that the life of Jesus may be made visible in our mortal flesh. So death is at work in us, but life in you." (2 Cor. 4:7-12)

The way of the church in mission is the way of the cross.

9. Accompany people over time.

It takes far longer to become a missional church than we would like to believe. It takes approximately three to five years to establish a climate of trust in the congregation under the best of circumstances. Developing vibrant contextual ministry—including active evangelizing, ecumenical partnerships, global connections, and social ministry—takes even longer. How can we develop structures (social and economic) that promote longevity of leaders for strategic missional purposes in alignment with the mission of God? (See chapters 1 and 9).

10. Remain rooted in the gospel above all things.

The First Commandment, as interpreted by Martin Luther, remains primary: "We are to fear, love, and trust God above all things." It is the gospel of Jesus Christ, the message of God's grace and love for the world in the cross and resurrection, that sustains us in our weariness, sets us free from our captivities, and keeps us hopeful about

God's future. Foundational for transforming ministry is a spiritual life that centers us each new day in the gift of grace, given freely and abundantly, in Christ Jesus. Transforming leadership is not measured by how I am feeling on a given day or by how people seem to be responding, as much as we long for such positive signs. Transforming leadership is a gift of God under the cross through the power of the Spirit. We need to continually ask: How can we abide in this power by engaging in vital spiritual practices that sustain us as transformed and transforming leaders?

Leadership for Mission

If leadership is the art of mobilizing a congregation to tackle its most difficult problems and if the most difficult problems faced by congregations are those of reclaiming our identity and mission, then transforming leaders need to maintain clarity in articulating what the mission of God for this people might look like. As we think about the mission of the church, we need to return to Jesus' core teaching summarized as the Great Commandment:

> "Teacher, which commandment in the law is the greatest?" He said to him, "You shall love the Lord your God with all your heart, and with all your soul, and with all your mind. This is the greatest and first commandment. And a second is like it: You shall love your neighbor as yourself. On these two commandments hang all the law and the prophets." (Matt. 22:36-40)

According to the Great Commandment, the core mission of the church is twofold: We are called (1) to love God and (2) to love our neighbor. Loving God engages us in worship and spiritual practices that cultivate our *identity* as the people of God. Loving our neighbor sends us into the world to live out God's mission as the church. Within the theological tradition, there exist a variety of "great" metaphors that are employed to describe the church in mission. The following chart maps out the terrain covered by six of these great metaphors that describe God's purposes for the church: mission, justification and justice, witness, evangelizing, discipleship, and stewardship.

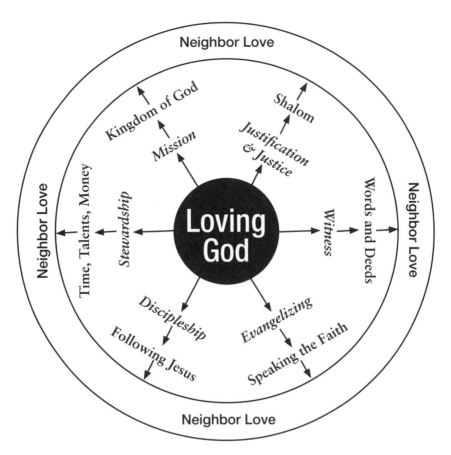

Figure 1. Six Great Metaphors for Interpreting God's Work

In imagining God's missionary purposes for the church—purposes to which the church seeks to be faithful—transforming leaders can appeal to each of these great metaphors in proclaiming what God has in mind for the work of the church in the world. Each metaphor accents differently God's purposes. But each of the six great metaphors also complements all of the others. Taken together these six metaphors help the church to maintain its bearings in the swirl of distractions that threaten to take it off course. Each of the metaphors articulates a slightly different aspect of how the church is to navigate between its central identity (loving God) and its central purpose (neighbor love).

Mission accents the apostolic character of God's work. The people of God are a "sent" people. Jesus sends forth his disciples to proclaim the good news of the kingdom. The Holy Spirit blows the church out of the sanctuary and into the world as God's agent of bringing God's kingdom to all. This is why the very last element of the liturgy is called "the sending." God's eschatological purpose is to bring the kingdom of God in its fullness (1 Corinthians 15:24-28). The Triune God is a Missionary God.[6] The *missio Dei* is to usher in God's saving kingdom. God's mission is to bring life—true, authentic, everlasting—to the world.

Justification and justice belong together as elements of God's purpose for human life. Taken together the metaphors of justification and justice underscore the restoration of right relationships as central to God's intention for human beings. Justification describes God's act in Christ on the cross to bring us into right relationship with God. Justice describes the ideal for how human beings are to live in relationship to one another. The Scriptures witness clearly to both God's act of justifying sinners and God's expectation that human beings demonstrate justice in relationship to one another. Shalom (salvation) describes God's intention for humanity, when we live both in right relationship with God (justification) and in right relationship with one another (justice).

Witness, as a metaphor, refers to testifying to others about God and Christ through one's words and one's deeds.[7] Witness is a term that encompasses the notion that our entire lives are intended to point to Christ. "I appeal to you therefore, brothers and sisters, by the mercies of God, to present your bodies as a living sacrifice, holy and acceptable to God, which is your spiritual worship" (Romans 12:1). The martyrs are those who have laid down their lives as such a witness. The word *martyr* means "witness." A witness gives account to others of the faith that lies within. We witness to the hope that is in us (1 Peter 3:15) by what we say and what we do.

Evangelizing is used in a very specific sense. Evangelizing refers to *speaking* the faith.[8] Often evangelism is a term used to describe any form of outreach, from placing yellow pages ads to putting a bumper sticker on one's car. But the New Testament words, *euanngelion* (noun) and *euanngelizo* (verb), both describe the verbal sharing of the good news with others. Evangelizing involves proclaiming or speaking the message so that the other comes to faith: "So faith comes from what is heard, and what is heard comes through the word of Christ" (Romans 10:17). We share the love of God not only implicitly by how others view our lives but explicitly by learning to speak the faith to other people.

Discipleship is a key term in the Gospels that refers to "following after" Jesus. The disciples were those who were called to be Jesus' followers. The German word *Nachfolge* makes this explicit. Bonhoeffer helped to reclaim the centrality of this basic New Testament idea for the life of the church today when he wrote his classic commentary on the Sermon on the Mount, *The Cost of Discipleship*.[9] In contemporary parlance, discipleship means the commitment to follow after Jesus in all of one's life. Thus there is a close relationship between the meaning of discipleship and the practices one follows in all of life. This includes how one follows after Jesus at home, work, and in recreation—all of daily life.

Stewardship is a metaphor that describes how one manages the household that belongs to another.[10] Several of Jesus' parables refer to slaves or servants who have been given responsibility to care for the affairs of the master (for example, Luke 19:11-27). Because God is the owner of heaven and earth (Psalm 24:1), human beings are those who have been entrusted with life and goods that belong to Another, not to us. For this reason, we are called to be stewards of what God has entrusted to us as gift. All of life is to be understood as stewardship, not only our money but our time and our talents. We are finally accountable to God for how we make use of the things that have been entrusted into our care. We confess in the Apostles' Creed that Christ will come again to judge the living and the dead. We will be called to account for our stewardship.

Together these six great metaphors help to keep the church oriented toward its missional purpose. Each metaphor provides unique accents. But finally each of the six metaphors is complementary to the others in helping us imagine what God has in mind by the Great Commandment, that we are to love God and love our neighbor as oneself. Transforming leaders are adept at drawing from these metaphorical fields in order to interpret God's purpose in calling the church into existence in the first place.

○ ○

Personal Reflection

1. What are the most important qualities in good leadership you bring to ministry? Where have you seen these practiced?
2. What are some of your own frustrations, doubts, and worries about your leadership role? What helps you tackle the most difficult leadership challenges you face? What helps you maintain your focus?

Group Conversation

1. Consider current local, national, and global arenas. Give some examples of leadership in crisis, contention, or confusion. How do these connect with people in the local congregation?
2. In giving leadership in your congregation, how can you draw upon the deep values and assets that are already present in the congregation?
3. In what ways have you helped people appreciate and develop their leadership within this faith community? How can this faith community more fully raise up its leadership?

Spiritual Practice

Read Martin Luther's explanation of the meaning of the First Commandment in the Large Catechism, which includes the passage, "A god is that to which we look for all good and in which we find refuge in every time of need. . . . True worship is that the heart should know no other consolation or confidence than in God." How does this conviction provide you counsel as a transforming leader in the midst of turmoil?

Transforming Action

Contact a colleague and invite conversation about where you see your congregations in relationship to matters of identity and mission. Or, invite the church council of another congregation to have such a conversation with your council.

Identity
Claimed
section two

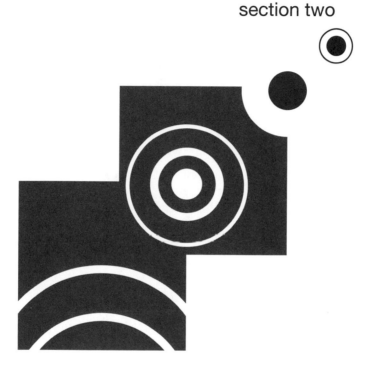

THE ISSUES OF IDENTITY, POWER, and authority—when clarified, claimed, and lived out—define transforming leadership. Authority has to do with the responsible exercise of power. Exercising authority means neither domineering in authoritarianism nor abdicating under the guise of pretending to serve, but rather being shaped in the cruciform shape of a strong servant leadership that empowers others. Transforming leadership involves clarity about the ministry of the Word, which provides theological vision in all aspects of congregational life. Claiming one's own power and authority does not need to negate the power and authority of others. In the midst of oppressive systems, our very concepts of power can be transformed so that collegial, collaborative partnerships can emerge.

Leading with Authority

chapter
five

HOW DOES A TRANSFORMING LEADER both claim rightful authority and remain accountable to the people being served? One of the
most challenging aspects of pastoral ministry is to walk the tightrope
between claiming too much authority for oneself and claiming too
little. Both the authoritarian self and the humiliated self are dangerous alternatives. Authority has to do with the responsible exercise of
power. It involves remaining grounded in one's call, claiming one's
gifts, and sharing those gifts with others in a way that builds mutual
ministry. In this chapter we will describe the contours of pastoral
authority, reflect on the experience of claiming one's authority, consider what it means to be called into an office, and examine how
authority becomes exercised in relationship to others.

What Is Pastoral Authority?

The two concepts, power and authority, are closely related. Power
can be defined concisely as "the ability and means to get something
done." In our typical use of the term *power* we acknowledge that
some people have more power than others. For example, presidents,
generals, CEOs, movie stars, and professional athletes are afforded
great power in our society. These are among the "movers and the
shakers," the people who have the power to accomplish just about
anything they want.

From a theological perspective, however, there is only one who
has all the power: Almighty God. In the Christian faith, one of the
core attributes of God is *all-powerful*. Ultimately, all power derives
from God. God is the Creator of heaven and earth, the All-Mighty.
All the energy of the universe finally flows from God. Apart from
the energy that flows from this God, there would be no power. Furthermore, this Almighty God has chosen in Christ to be revealed in
weakness, incarnate in human flesh, humbled by death on the cross
(Phil. 2:5-8).

Although it is commonplace and useful to employ the term *power* to describe human interactions, there is a real sense in which we human beings are dependent upon God for any power that we claim as our own. All power finally belongs to God, and any power we might have is related to the power bestowed upon us. This means that, properly speaking, what we have in life is "authority" and not "power" (see chapters 6 and 8). We make this formal point as an attempt to norm and check abuses of power, although we will also speak of the exercise of power in the more conventional sense of the concept in the remainder of the book. We have authority that derives from God and is accountable to God. We have authority that has as its norm the crucified, servant authority of Jesus Christ. Those who serve in positions of pastoral authority do well to understand that the exercise of the office of ministry is always held accountable to the revelation of God's authority among us in the person of Jesus Christ.

The New Testament word that describes Jesus' own authority is *exousia*. Matthew 7:28-29 reads: "Now when Jesus had finished saying these things, the crowds were astounded at his teaching, for he taught them as one having *authority*, and not as their scribes." The word translated as "authority" is the Greek word *exousia*, which can be broken down into its component parts of *ex-* and *ousia*. *Ousia* is the noun meaning "being" and *ex-* is a prefix meaning "out of." The word *exousia* thus refers to someone who relates to others "out of the core of one's being." *Exousia*, or authority, is always exercised in relationship. Out of one's inner sense of identity and being, one relates to others authoritatively.

Notice how the inner and outer aspects of authority are reflected in the contributions of two important authors, Jackson W. Carroll and Celia Allison Hahn. Carroll defines authority this way: "Authority is the right to exercise leadership in a particular group or institution based upon a combination of qualities, characteristics, or expertise that the leader has or that the followers believe their leader has."[1] Celia Allison Hahn describes authority as the consequence of three contributing factors. Authority is an "inner reality" that is "exercised in speaking and acting," which is "recognized by others."[2] Both of these descriptions of authority recognize that the leader exhibits a particular inner quality and that others are receptive to that ability. For example, a pastor may have excellent skills in seeing the whole picture of what needs to be done at a meeting and by setting an agenda, but unless those at the meeting trust his or her ability and receive that leadership, little will be accomplished. "We are all active participants in authority."[3]

Transforming leadership is exercised in the interplay between the inward authority possessed by that leader—charisma, skills, wisdom, and knowledge—and the acknowledgement of that authority by those who are led. Both dimensions are crucial to the process of leading authoritatively. The challenge is lived out in discovering the proper balance between these two aspects. Excessive claims about one's internal authority lead to oppression. Exaggerating the emphasis on how one is accepted by others can lead to a dependency relationship. Herein lies the challenge: How does one learn to live in the tension between operating autonomously as a leader and becoming overly dependent upon what others think?

Claiming One's Gifts

Those who seek to serve as transforming leaders in the church come with many innate gifts as well as with skills honed by significant experience. Moreover, those who enter into ministry are unique individuals, whose configuration of gifts and skills is like no one else's in the world. Consider the factors that contribute to the uniqueness of your identity as a leader in the church: gender, body type, personality type, ethnicity, race, experiences, strengths, liabilities, voice, language abilities, age, birth place, etc. The characteristics that shape who you are as a leader are unlike any other person in the church. Yet it is exactly the person you are—in all your peculiarity—whom God has called to the service of leadership in the church. Transforming leadership begins with acknowledging and giving God thanks for the gifts and skills that have been assembled in a unique package that is you.

You are a unique person, with particular gifts and specific experiences, whom God has called to transforming leadership in the church. For many people, the experience of call begins with an inner experience by which they sense God has set them apart for some particular form of service. Sometimes it takes years of discernment before an individual is ready to acknowledge and affirm the *inner call* from God. This may especially be true for women who for centuries were barred from consideration as public leaders in the church because of their gender. Understandably, some women have internalized this external resistance and thereby also experience inner struggle with their sense of call. Yet even those—both women and men— who at one point seemed crystal clear about their sense of inner call may later discover themselves caught up in a crisis of unanticipated discernment, long after the time when they believed their call was already a settled matter.

We are stressing at this point that every candidate for public ministry has a unique combination of gifts and skills, as well as a unique call story.[4] It is essential to transforming leadership that no one despises the gifts, skills, and call that God has provided. While your gifts and skills exist in a unique configuration, that does not mean they are inferior to the configuration of gifts and skills that belong to another person in ministry. God employs each and every one of us in our own particularity. The call of God is extended to you as a person who incarnates the world in a unique way. No two ministers on earth are exactly alike. That is a good thing. Thanks be to God!

Called into an Office

One of the most difficult adjustments made by those recently consecrated as diaconal ministers, ordained as pastors, or installed in some other form of leadership in the church, is to comprehend the concept that *people are always going to relate to them in terms of the office they hold.*[5] This never means that one sacrifices the unique configuration of gifts and skills that make up who you are. But it does mean that one's uniqueness is put in service of the office to which one has been called.[6] With one's office comes a set of expectations that affects both one's own self-understanding and what others rightly may expect to receive from this person as minister.

The contours of the office are well described in the rites that accompany consecration as a diaconal minister, ordination as a pastor, or installation into another calling in the church. By way of illustration, we will look at the offices of diaconal minister and pastor as they come to expression through the appointed rituals for these offices in the Evangelical Lutheran Church in America. To what is a diaconal minister consecrated?

> The Church calls diaconal ministers to speak God's Word, the gospel and the apostolic faith to God's world. It also calls them to speak for the needs of God's world to the Church. This call is a call to public witness and service that exemplifies Christ-like self-giving and leads the Church and all its baptized members to witness to Christ in the world.

Diaconal ministry reflects the historic call of deacons to serve those most in need on behalf of the Church. You have been called to the diaconate to give leadership in the Church's mission to proclaim the gospel through word and deed. Therefore serve the needy, care for the sick, comfort the distressed, and through words and actions witness to God's love for all people.[7]

As sign of the office of Word and Service bestowed upon a diaconal minister, a basin and towel are presented as signs of Christ-like service.

In the ordination rite for pastors, the office of Word and Sacrament is well described in the four questions that the ordinand is called upon to answer:

Will you assume this office, believing that the Church's call is God's call to the ministry of Word and Sacrament? Will you therefore preach and teach in accordance with the Holy Scriptures and these creeds and confessions? Will you pray for God's people, nourish them with the Word and Holy Sacraments, and lead them by your own example in faithful service and holy living? Will you give faithful witness in the world, that God's love may be known in all that you do? After each question, the ordinand is to reply, "I will, and I ask God to help me."[8]

Through prayer with the laying on of hands, the candidate is ordained, receiving a stole as a sign of the office of Word and Sacrament.

By the rite of consecration or ordination, the person so vested now assumes an office through which others will relate to her or him. Just as those entering into professional ministry each have an inner call from God, so the *outer call* is extended through the process leading to consecration/ordination. This outer call is understood to be from God, extended by the action of the church. To bear such a call is both a great privilege and an awesome responsibility. One of the most significant adjustments to be made by a newly consecrated/ordained minister is to live into the reality that other people now will relate to them through the office that has been assumed. Even if one meets people at the grocery store or high school musical, one meets them as a minister. There is now no relating to others apart from one's office. This becomes part of the burden one bears on behalf of the ministry of Christ. And it also becomes the source of great joy as one is received in Christ's name (John 13:20).

Living into One's Authority in Relationship

We hold our authority as a trust from God. We serve as leaders who have a particular set of gifts and shortcomings, experiences and skills. Beginning with a very personal sense of inner call, transforming leaders have also received an outer call from God mediated by the Church. The receipt of this outer call has entailed a process of preparation for service in the church and has been marked by the ritual through which the office is bestowed. Now as an office holder, we relate to others through the auspices of our particular leadership office.

Transforming leaders will experience all sorts of expectations from others, including expectations that are often based on their experience of authority figures in other settings. Sometimes these expectations have little to do with the particularities of one's own person. Rather, people bring to the new leader their good or bad experiences with other authority figures that they have experienced in their lives, beginning with their parents and including other leaders in the church. Not only does the leader bring along "fooi" (family of origin issues, p. 22; see also chapter 14) out of the past, but every person in the congregation also has "fooi" to bring to the encounter.

In this way, already from the beginning, one person will relate to the leader in terms of dependency, having learned this posture of relationship from other authority figures in life. Another will bring to the new leader a great deal of hostility, directed at earlier authority figures—or even at God—but transferred in the direction of the new leader. Others may bring feelings of guilt or fear. It is crucial that the transforming leader not overreact to such emotional transference, for it often comes by virtue of the office one bears. Instead, the transforming leader apprehends such dynamics for what they are, expresses genuine care for the person, and establishes the relationship on a new and more sound basis. By taking the time to listen actively to each person and to relate to each according to the unconditional regard that belongs to the gospel, most relationships can soon transcend the unrealistic expectations and projections that first encumber them. Only by listening and acting authentically in a relationship can transforming leaders help people see the new minister for who she or he really is and leave behind the associations that connect the leader with one's predecessor.

The vast majority of people in the church desire to trust their leaders. This means that those in authority have an initial investment of social capital that is theirs to employ, unless it is somehow squandered away. For example, most people want to trust their pastor and confide many of the most precious life experiences in conversation. This is why, as was stated in Chapter One, that significant time must be devoted in a particular setting to building relationships by visiting with people and listening to their stories. Transforming leadership establishes the foundation for all else by building trusting relationships between leaders and people, as well as fostering trust between the people in the community itself.

The exception to this formula—and it is an exception that tragically is affecting more and more congregations—is the circumstance in which conflict has marred the communal life to such a degree that the capacity to trust has been dramatically undermined. In such settings, a deliberate process of healing must be undertaken, probably through the intervention of an intentional interim minister and an extended process, such as the "Bridgebuilders."[9] For those leaders who find themselves embroiled in a high-level conflict situation, particular attention must be directed at reestablishing a climate of trust before one can hope to engage the congregation in a process of transformation. Many leaders underestimate the length of time needed to resolve endemic conflict before a congregation will be poised to enter into a visioning and transforming process. One probably needs to think in terms of years (rather than months) for healing to take place in contexts where conflict has undermined one or more previous leaders. In order for a leader to be sustained for such a lengthy period of healing, it is imperative that there be an adequate support system beyond the congregation itself, a commitment to stay the course, and resources to equip leadership for conflict resolution.[10]

As one leads with authority and people live into trusting the person who inhabits the office, steadily one moves from relying primarily on the "formal" authority of the office to gaining "acknowledged" authority. *Formal authority* is what people are willing to ascribe to one based on the office one holds. *Acknowledged authority* is based on the trustworthiness and skill one has demonstrated in building solid relationships with the people one serves.[11]

Toward Integrative Authority

Celia Allison Hahn makes several astute observations, based on extensive research, about how different leaders operate according to four different styles of exercising authority. She distinguishes between 1) received authority, 2) autonomous authority, 3) assertive authority, and 4) integrative authority.[12] Moreover, she notes a significant difference between men and women in the exercise of leadership. We will build on her findings in the concluding section of this chapter.

Leaders always begin with "received authority," that is, the authority that others are willing to grant them based on the office they hold. This is a passive form of authority, which simply receives whatever others are willing to yield. Men tend to be granted a higher measure of authority based on the higher status of men in patriarchal society, quite apart from any actual competence. Women tend to be granted relatively little authority, based on societal socialization and cultural expectations. For this reason, many women have been forced to operate with little acknowledged authority, whereas men tend to readily operate according to a second style of exercising authority, "autonomous authority."

"Autonomous authority" is authority exercised with little regard for the context or for a sense of partnership with others. Women have been socialized to avoid claiming autonomous authority; and so ironically they are expected to rely on received authority while received authority is often withheld from them. Autonomous authority operates primarily in relationship to one's own judgments and sensibilities, imposing these on others under the conviction that "I know best" what is good for the whole. In many cases, people are willing to abdicate their own responsibility to an autonomous leader, especially insofar as the decisions of the leader have positive consequences for the group. One might refer to this as "benign" autonomous authority. In some contexts, congregations have grown accustomed to, even dependent upon, generation after generation of autonomous leaders. In such a context, people may experience any form of authority other than the autonomous type with frustration.

Hahn found that men and women are quite different in coming to exercise "autonomous authority." Men, for example, tend to be socialized into autonomous authority by their culture. Many men operate according to autonomous authority as their default position. This is the kind of authority that society has come to expect of "real" men. Should another man challenge such authority, the situation easily degenerates into a power conflict, whereby the contest is framed in terms of "winners" and "losers." For many it is unthinkable, however, that the autonomous authority of a man be challenged by a woman. Sacrificing one's autonomous authority to a woman is tantamount to losing one's masculinity, both in one's own perception and in the eyes of others. Many men thus find themselves "stuck" in the autonomous authority mode and have a hard time moving beyond it.

Women, on the other hand, tend to be socialized into and found to remain at the level of received authority. While women give high regard to partnership, society wants to confine women to received authority, dependent particularly upon male validation. Furthermore, society regards autonomous authority as more valuable than partnership. Women, therefore, have a dilemma. Do they try to break out of received authority into autonomous authority? When they do so, either their leadership might be seen as more valid, *or* others may experience their autonomous authority as anger, aggression, or trying to exercise illegitimate control. Because of the societal pressures seeking to confine them to this kind of authority, some women break out of received authority into autonomous authority with a great deal of emotional force. Because it is contrary to the standard arrangement, society may react negatively to such an autonomous exercise of authority on the part of a woman. A woman exercising autonomous authority may knock men off balance, although this autonomous style would be totally acceptable if exercised by a man.

For those operating according to autonomous authority, the next natural progression is "assertive authority." While assertive authority shares some of the independence of autonomous authority, what begins to emerge is a greater acknowledgement that one's own authority is always exercised in relationship to the authority of others. In the case of assertive authority, one is not limited to a single way of engaging authority but begins to assert oneself authoritatively according to the appropriate authority also being asserted by others. One begins to be able to relinquish the need for control that belongs to autonomous authority and adapt to the proper exercise of authority in relation to other persons. With assertive authority, others do not experience the aggressiveness of autonomous authority. One operates as an authoritative member within a system rather than an authority over others in the system. For women, this is experienced as a healthy form of partnership, devoid of unhealthy dependency. For men, this is a breakthrough into learning to share authority with others.

Women and men both attain to the fourth (and highest) level, "integrative authority," by learning to exercise authority contextually. This is the goal for transforming leadership. Instead of being fixed on a single mode, those with integrative authority are able to select from a repertoire of authority styles to fit the present context. This means that some situations call for the leader to operate in the mode of received authority, for example, by affirming others in the development of their own leadership capacities. An occasional situation still may call for the strong and clear contribution of autonomous authority, particularly when core values seem to be at stake. More often, one will choose to exercise assertive authority, as one learns to lead in concert with the gifts and authority of other people.

What is unique about integrative authority is that the leader is self-reflective and cognizant of making choices about the best style of authority to fit the present context.[13] The leader is aware of and has developed a variety of authority styles and has learned the wisdom of when to draw upon each of them. With the exercise of integrative authority, the leader is most concerned about maximizing the gifts of each and every person so that a servant community might arise.

Finally, the goal of a transforming leader is to operate with integrative authority. This style best honors the gifts of other people, building community in such a way that the gifts of the leader are also appropriately honored. To lead with authority is to transcend the dangers of either the authoritarian or the humiliated self. Affirming one's own gifts and experiences, the transforming leader accepts the responsibilities of the office to which one is called.[14] This transforming leader then lives in trustworthy relationship with others until a community of mutual ministry is established in which the gifts and authority of every member are honored.

o o o o o o o o o o o o o o o o o o o

Personal Reflection

1. Who have been role models for you in exercising authority? Reflect on specific characteristics that you may have adopted (or adapted) for yourself.
2. How might you work to expand your repertoire of authority styles? To what degree are you able to exercise integrative authority as described in the chapter?

Group Conversation

1. How do you define power? What is the relationship between power and authority? Share your ideas with one another and listen carefully and respectfully to similarities and differences.
2. What factors contribute to the development of moving from formal authority to acknowledged authority? What can block that process?

Spiritual Practice

Do a Bible study on Jesus' exercise of authority. Dig into the text and explore the meaning of authority in Matthew 7: 28-29.

Transforming Action

Visit the Healthy Congregations Web site at www.hcongregations.net. Consider putting some of the ideas into place in your setting.

Transforming Servant Leadership

"I DON'T WANT TO BE the kind of pastor who needs to control every-thing," said Kevin.

"I've been burned by authoritarianism so many times." responds Kristi. "I'd like a new kind of leadership that could avoid playing a power game."

"But, on the other hand, I hate it when people see me as not being strong," Kevin goes on. "I'm worried they will trample all over me."

"Yes, I know what you mean," Kristi agrees. "I want to be a 'servant leader,' but that seems to give some people permission to treat me like a door mat; and then I begin to feel like one."

Servant Leader: The Paradox

The term *servant leader* is a paradoxical image, often verbalized, though less frequently exercised.[1] Some leaders who have adopted that term for themselves discover that people seem confused by what it means. It is hard to picture a "servant leader." Years ago a reli-gious leader holding a position of authority was often unquestioned.[2] Today, people frequently resist such authority but are not able to describe what should replace it.[3] "Strong leader" often tops their list of characteristics they seek in a new pastor. But do they ask where that person is going to lead, or what "strong" means?[4] Likewise, a congregation may call a diaconal minister to "serve" among them. But does having a servant as a leader mean that man or woman is at the beck and call of all of the members, doing whatever anyone wants at any hour of the day or night? Such servanthood may feel like subservience.[5] How does being a servant of Christ translate into transformational leadership, particularly given the complexities of congregational life today?

Leaders themselves seem to err either by abusing power or by abdicating authority. Servant leadership is leadership that transforms communities for service. To be a servant leader holds great promise if we take a new look at—even "transform"—the concept "servant leader." Can we grasp its power and potential? We need to fully claim the authority and responsibilities of the office to which we are called without veering over into authoritarianism.[6] Furthermore, we need to be willing to be a servant, being clear that this does not mean we doubt our gifts and sink into abdication of our roles. We need to explore more deeply the problems caused by authoritarianism and abdication, and the freedom God promises for healthy servanthood and authoritative leadership.

Exploring the Deeper Issues of Faith

In "The Freedom of a Christian" Martin Luther wrote: "A Christian is a perfectly free lord of all, subject to none. A Christian is a perfectly dutiful servant of all, subject to all."[7] Luther goes on to root such freedom in the Word of God. We do not become servant leaders simply by trying hard. We will, on our own, in all of our relationships fall away from truthfulness and righteousness into suspicion and contempt. We are not able to live in trust; we continue to design for ourselves relationships of domination and dependency. Each of those in its own way is idolatry.[8] Nor is it a matter of trying to be a better and better Christian. Even our best attempts at "servant leadership" will injure us—and others—if we believe we are justified by them. In such self-justification, we will continue to discover new ways to dominate others (nicely, of course) or to demean ourselves in unbelief and allow ourselves to be dominated. In the Deaconess Litany, the community prays that "we no longer think of ourselves more highly than we ought to think, nor deprecate ourselves in unbelief, calling common what God has called clean."[9] Christ Jesus "did not regard equality with God as something to be exploited but emptied himself, taking the form of a slave" (Phil. 2:6b-7). In this Christ we have been justified, liberated for vocation, and called to serve the neighbor. This is the nature of God's transforming life among us.

When we trust in a God who liberates us from oppression, we are freed from having someone "lord" it over us—whether a church council member, a troubled and troubling parishioner, or a staff partner—and from the temptation to "lord" it over another—a church council member, a troubled and troubling parishioner, or a staff member. Only one is Lord (*dominus*); collaborative servant ministry is the antithesis of domination. Christ's victory over death and all oppressive powers—even, perhaps especially, those within ourselves—frees us to serve.

This service is not to be confused with subservience, which operates under the domination of another. Our relationship to one another is changed because our relationship with God is changed, transformed. "As servants of God (*doulos*, being under someone's total control), live as free people; yet do not use your freedom as a pretext for evil " (1 Pet. 2:16). We are no longer slaves of systemic sin, oppressive systems that idolatrously enslave people. We have been set free from enslavement of one another so that we can become "slaves of righteousness." "Now you have been set free from sin and are [becoming] the slaves of God" (Rom. 6: 18, 22). Trusting the gift of new life in Christ, this service (our *diakonia*) is life-giving. *Diakonia* builds and heals and provides others freedom to claim their own power.

One can test whether the oppressive relationships have been buried in Christ and if we believe we have been raised to new life. Do I unnecessarily defer in the presence of a bishop, a district superintendent, an elected official, or a doctor or lawyer? Am I frequently condescending towards those whom I "help"? Do I catch myself testing out the authority ladder? Feeling myself on a low rung, I first subjugate myself. Then, if I discover that the person above me does not have the power I imagined, I skip right past the step of partner and peer, to be higher than the one I formerly feared. Such a hierarchical view of leadership will result in an endless race to an elusive top. We have been freed in Christ from all such enslavements.

In a time of changing roles and relationships, it is difficult to achieve healthy partnerships while maintaining appropriate leadership. But it is time for transformation. We have come a long way in discovering the joy of discerning gifts and empowering the saints to use all their gifts for ministry in the world. We believe in the concept of shared power. But when things do not go well, we may resort to a "back-up"—unbecomingly familiar—leadership style in the midst of conflict. Such an unhealthy style serves neither ourselves nor others.

People have caught a glimpse of participatory decision-making, so we simply cannot go back to earlier styles of hierarchical authority. But in the midst of complexity and conflict, the temptation *is* to go back. It is as though we are swimming across a river. We can glimpse the distant shore, but we are weary. We panic and want to turn around. But it may be even further than we think back to the familiar old shore of one person dictating decisions. Can we trust that in working together we will arrive at that new place where servant leadership and healthy partnership is a way of life?

We will need to trust deeply, rather than simply say, "Swim harder." Our false gods of self-aggrandizement and self-negation have died with Christ and we are raised to new life in the Spirit. We can trust the God who created us for interdependent servanthood. Those whom we fear cannot ultimately harm us. And when we are trampled, or trample, we can remember that through the forgiveness of sins we are freed for servanthood. We can trust the Spirit's power, which is unlimited. If my colleague grows, becoming more skilled and powerful, that does not automatically mean I have less power. If my gifts are enhanced and I grow in power that does not have to mean I will hold my colleague or congregation down. Their growth in ability and skills for leadership does not mean my leadership is no longer needed. The very concept of leadership is transformed. Trusting in the power of the Spirit, which is not a limited commodity, we can trust each other to grow in power without diminishing ourselves. That is a radical statement, but it is true. We can trust the Spirit's power in the other whom we serve and whom we are called to lead. And when we do, we are surprised by the grace that ministry is multiplied.

Trusting in the new life in Christ, we also may see signs of servant leadership emerging. For example, do we find ourselves receiving an insight from a child, rather than simply giving a pat on the head? Rather than avoiding a "superior," do we one day turn around and offer concern for that person's own well-being? Have we already experienced transformation within ourselves? Have we discovered our subservience turning into genuine servanthood? Are we leading in new ways with courage?

The paradoxical terms servant and leader do go together and can enhance each other. It is good to claim the Spirit's power, exercise our proper authority, and lead! It is good to receive the mind of Christ in order to be a genuine servant, compassionate and empowering. When the terms coalesce, keeping roles and relationships clear, surprising new grace-filled possibilities for partnership emerge.

In order to put flesh on this paradoxical concept, we shall look at seven aspects of servant leadership: *power, presence, knowledge, roles, relationships, decision-making,* and *proclamation.* For each aspect we first see a description of an effective leader and then a description of an effective servant. Next follow two opposite distortions: on the one side, the authoritarian (one who requires complete obedience, exercising control over the will of others); on the other side, the abdicator (one who pretends a servant stance but is actually unable or afraid to lead). Pride that is self-righteous is the sin of idolatry of self. However, we can never overcome pride simply by denouncing the proud. We also must empower those who would be victims.[10] The human condition (sin) is complicated. Self-negation that leads to abdication is also a problem of belief, a bondage from which one needs liberation.

There are many reasons one could slip back into authoritarianism or abdication (see chapters 9, 12, and 14). For example, picture yourself walking a servant-leader path, with the distortions as ditches on either side. Some will be more likely to veer off the path to one side, and some to the other. Or one could veer off either side, depending upon the circumstances. It might be helpful to think about times when you are under stress. Which direction is your "back-up" (unhelpful) leadership style likely to take? In better understanding ourselves, our insecurities, and our stress points, we may be more able to recognize when we fall into an unhealthy backup leadership mode. Dialog with a trusted friend or colleague about the following also could be helpful.

Power

One who leads understands power and uses it effectively.
One who serves empowers others.
Abuse of power is authoritarianism.
Refusal to claim one's own power is abdication.

Power can be defined many ways. Power, simply put, is the ability to make something happen. When power is abused, things happen to people without their consent. Authoritarian people, unable to trust in a gracious God, try to play god at the expense of others. Under the guise of leadership, they deny the humanity of those whom they lead. Abdicators are afraid of power, believing it to be evil.[11] They deprecate themselves in unbelief. In refusing to be God's Spirit-led, power-filled leaders, they block the work of God in the church and in the world. Servant-leaders understand power and are not afraid to lead in making things happen, empowering others also to do the work of the Spirit. Barbara Jordan, who served as congresswoman and educator, said that we cannot give another person power, but we can act in ways which allow and encourage others, particularly the powerless, to claim their own power.[12] Sr. Marie Augusta Neal wrote about a theology of relinquishment.[13] Freed from needing to hoard power and lord it over others, we can lead with open hands, rejoicing in sharing power so that mission and ministry happen. Servant leaders use power to become change-agents for justice in the world.

Presence

The leader is aware of his or her own physical size and presence and uses them well.
The servant sees differently-abled people and meets them where they are.
The authoritarian tries to be larger than life.
The abdicator tries to hide out or vanish.

Most of us believe there is something wrong with our appearance. If only we were taller, thinner, nicer looking or more vigorous, we could lead more effectively. History shows that leaders come in all sizes, colors, ages, and in both genders. "There are some quiet leaders and leaders one can hear in the next county. Some find their strength in eloquence, some in judgment, some in courage."[14] We are unconditionally loved by a gracious God, but when we are unable to accept Christ's acceptance, it is hard to accept ourselves. The authoritarian tries to compensate by appearing larger, louder, or stronger. Reluctant leaders may try to be smaller or hide their gifts. Society, including the churches, has often refused to accept people as leaders because of their color, gender, class, or disability. We may internalize that rejection. Such a tragedy! The servant leader sees Christ in the mirror, as well as his or her own face. Made in the Creator's image, God transforms us in Christ but does not fit us for service by changing our size, appearance, voice, or personality. (We are the ones who are more likely to try to make over those whom we would lead.) The Spirit raises up leaders among unlikely people, giving them presence in history and self-presence to lead.

Knowledge

The leader is knowledgeable and gives clear direction.
The servant asks and finds out where people are in their thinking.
The authoritarian assumes he or she knows everything and is unwilling to learn for fear of losing face.
The abdicator believes he or she cannot know and therefore is unable to learn from or about others.

Many people believe leadership is simply a matter of giving directions and having people follow. When faced with leading people through a crowded city, one quickly finds that giving directions is no easy matter.

It is hard to pay attention to where you are going and, at the same time, check to see if the followers are still behind you. Leadership takes ability, skills, and knowledge. A person may be overwhelmed by what they do not know and try to hide their lack of knowledge. It is fine to simply say, "I will need to find out." But then we should make sure that we do it. Servanthood does not mean being inept. It takes much knowledge, wisdom, strength, and skill.[15] Servant leaders know they are not God and do not need to be, but they believe God is teacher as well as servant and creator. With a curious, adventuresome spirit, servants will search the Scriptures to teach and proclaim them. Servant leaders also will learn from the people among whom God has called them to lead and serve. They will visit and watch and take notes. They will search out the history of a place and its people. They will reflect theologically with the faith community. Then, and only then, will they, as leaders, be able to provide vision and help people dream their own dreams.

Roles

The leader claims the authority of his or her office and respects the roles of others with whom he or she serves.

The servant moves freely among people, able to serve in a number of roles without losing identity.

The authoritarian claims authority for him or herself in every situation.

The abdicator too easily surrenders authority and role.

To exercise appropriate authority is essential. Role and identity must not be confused. Our identity is rooted in Christ. This frees us to serve and be served, to follow and to lead. The authoritarian confuses role and identity, thereby needing to be in control in every situation. When worth is not measured in status, there is the potential in the church for an amazing fluidity of roles (role clarity, however, is important in each particular situation). Blessed are those who fill the office they hold. Blessed is the church where people respect one another and perform their specific tasks. Some roles will be assumed for a lifetime, others for a week. The church is transformed when people are able to be in roles according to gift, rather than other characteristics such as gender or ethnicity. No longer are some labeled followers and others leaders; we collaboratively participate in leadership for mission. The person with Down's Syndrome can be given the authority to lead a song in worship. The president of a corporation is free to serve coffee.

The leader of leaders and equipper of saints will help people find their identity in Christ, claim their gifts, and help the community exercise role clarity and mutual accountability.

Relationships

The leader is assertive and able to interact with people.
The servant considers each person important and listens carefully to each one.
The authoritarian ultimately becomes isolated.
The abdicator through dependency deprecates him or herself.

If power corrupts, then absolute power corrupts absolutely. People caught up in their own power begin to cut themselves off from ordinary people, particularly during times of conflict, surrounding themselves only with those who bolster their ego. They may think they lead, but they become feared and even hated by those whom they would lead. Meanwhile, dependency is the cloak of the pretend servant. Their mere would-be service makes others uncomfortable. Their "help" feels more like a burden. Relationships become guilt-ridden and soon no one is free to serve. There is growing enmeshment and co-dependency. Servant leaders are clear in identity and therefore able to relate with a wide range of people, seeing each as gift. They seek out relationships to listen and learn. While the number and frequency of relationships may vary with personality, servant leaders are secure in their relationship with God and comfortable with people. Most of us can think of people who have been mentors or role models for us. We remember those persons not only because of their leadership qualities but because they were able to relate to us in a way that both made us feel special, and also let us grow to become the people we have become.

Decision Making

The leader manages well and is decisive.
The servant consults, links, and facilitates mutual decision-making, using the gifts of all.
The authoritarian controls.
The abdicator is "humbly proud" of not being able to make decisions.

The one who believes that leading is "calling the shots" has control but also takes on an unnecessary burden of trying to play God. No one but God has the wisdom to decree what is and shall be. The authoritarian who believes it must be "my way" at any cost, through direct or manipulative means, often pays a high cost of fatigue, stress, and sometimes loss of the position itself. The one who abdicates authority under the guise of humility, feeling insecure, may actually feign inadequacy. People, waiting to be led, become confused and frustrated by the person's lack of organization. Then decisions are not made, or made inadequately, by a few people who step in to fill the vacuum. Servant leaders know their own mind and opinions but also know when to speak and when to refrain from speaking. Their silence is an active silence, however, as they seek out the mind of all. They facilitate through providing resources and empowering those who did not know they could speak. They help people listen to each other and then guide the group to seek more information and to weigh possible consequences. They seek out wisdom from unlikely sources in the community beyond the church. Rather than pitting people against one another in win-lose situations, they patiently help transform a congregation by working toward consensus.

Proclamation

The leader proclaims with conviction.
The servant proclaims with a listening ear.
The authoritarian pontificates.
The abdicator speaks hesitantly or not at all.

In both authoritarian and abdication modes, one does not really hear. If a leader learns to love only his or her own voice, the leader will speak louder from the pulpit and more frequently at meetings or in ordinary conversation. The speaking one, with gifts exercised, becomes more facile. Those silenced in awe or obedience begin to doubt their own ideas. Meanwhile, the leader wonders why no one seems interested any longer. The abdicator, lacking confidence to speak, may mistakenly confuse not speaking with genuine listening. Such a person needs to learn to gain confidence to use their own voice as well.[16] While we each have a different role in the community, the leadership of proclamation of the Word is a communal calling. Yes, people learn by careful listening, and they also learn much as they hear themselves speak for the first time. All God's people need not only to be hearers of the Word, but skilled in sharing it. The servant leader develops a rhythm of listening and speaking. The wise leader, like a midwife, will assist people in giving birth to their own ideas, rejoicing in God's good news as it is spoken by all the people.[17]

○ ○

Personal Reflection

1. Where did you find descriptors of yourself in the seven aspects of leadership (power, presence, knowledge, roles, relationships, decision-making, proclamation)? When are you more likely to act in authoritarian ways? When are you more likely to abdicate?
2. Where do you find strengths for servant leadership in yourself? How might you develop those strengths? Who or what helps you?

Group Conversation

When congregational leaders (or newly-selected or potential leaders) are gathered, discuss the following:

1. What do you think a servant leader looks like? Acts like? Name some specific characteristics.
2. When have you been hindered in your own ministry by authoritarianism? What effect did it have on your personal growth and development? On the community's growth and development?
3. Think about a time when you, or someone with whom you worked, abdicated their leadership role. Tell about the incident (changing the names and places if necessary). What effect did that have on people?
4. Think of mentors or role models who are servant leaders. Name some particular way in which you have become, are becoming, or would like to become like them.

Spiritual Practice

Read Mark 10:17-52. Focus particularly on verses 32-45.

1. How is Jesus' servant leadership rooted in his death and resurrection? Note that Jesus does not say, "Try hard" to be a servant, but says about his followers, "It is not so among you" (v. 43).
2. How is this connected to Christ's baptism? What does this have to do with our baptism and our servant leadership?

Transforming Action

1. Building on the reflections and discussion above, put into action a strategy for the next six weeks . . . or six months . . . to trace growth in being a servant leader, either by yourself, or as a group.
2. Reinforce transformational behaviors when you see them.

Leading Theologically

WHAT DOES IT MEAN TO be a minister of the Word? Those who serve as diaconal ministers are ministers of *Word* and Service, while ordained pastors are ministers of *Word* and Sacrament. What would it mean to take with utmost seriousness the calling to be a *minister of the Word*? Notice the centrality of the ministry of the Word in this charge given to Timothy:

> These are the things you must insist on and teach. . . . Until I arrive, give attention to the public reading of scripture, to exhorting, to teaching. Do not neglect the gift that is in you, which was given to you through prophecy with the laying on of hands by the council of elders. . . . Pay close attention to yourself and to your teaching; continue in these things, for in doing this you will save both your-self and your hearers. (1 Tim. 4:11, 13-14, 16)

Transforming leadership requires that ministers of the Word see preaching and teaching as core responsibilities of this calling. The church is adrift today in a sea of confusion about its identity and mission. Threatened by a tidal wave of biblical literalism on the one side and by the whirlpool of postmodern uncertainties on the other, ministers of the Word face the monumental task of steering the vessel through the storm. Yet, in how many settings do ministers of the Word understand teaching to be at the core of what they are called to be and do? Repeatedly, I observe how ministers of the Word are scarcely involved in matters of teaching adults and immersing them in the living Word of God.[1] Instead, they are engaged in many other worthy involvements, but by so doing they neglect the one thing needful (cf. Luke 10:42). By neglecting the ministry of teaching the Word, in many and various ways all week long, we are in the process of sacrificing an entire generation to the trends of the times or to literalist legalisms.

This chapter will hold up the calling of the rabbi as an image of ministry for the transforming leader. We advocate that the transforming leader must be a committed servant of the Word in all that she or he does. One perennial task of the church is to pass down the riches of the Christian tradition to the next generation. This is at the heart of the church's apostolic mission. Taking the ministry of the Word seriously means reorienting one's time in relationship to the centrality of this calling. This chapter provides both theological grounding and practical implications for this task.

The Minister of the Word as Rabbi

Jesus was sometimes called "*Rabbi*," most often in the Gospel of John (1:38, 1:49, 3:2, 3:26, 6:25, and 20:16). Because John's Gospel derives from the period toward the end of the first century, this title, attributed to Jesus, may reflect the growing importance of the rabbi within Judaism in the Diaspora, following the destruction of the temple in 70 C.E. Once the Jews were scattered, without temple rituals to unify them, their very identity as a people was severely threatened. In this crisis, a new form of Judaism emerged: Rabbinic Judaism. Instead of being a people centered on the sacrificial cult of the temple, the identity of the people was defined by the gatherings of Jewish people in synagogues around the Torah—the law, the instruction, the teaching of God. The rabbi became the guardian and steward of this gift.

Torah should be understood not so much as the Hebrew Scriptures or a book but as the teaching—a way of living, a way of being and doing. Torah means instruction and wisdom. The goal of life is to immerse oneself in this teaching: "Keep these words that I am commanding you today in your heart. Recite them to your children and talk about them when you are at home and when you are away, when you lie down and when you rise. Bind them as a sign on your hand, fix them as an emblem on your forehead, and write them on the doorposts of your house and on your gates " (Deut. 6:6-9). Of all the words in the world, this Word of God is the one that can give orientation for navigating our way through the vicissitudes of life. For example, God's Word of promise made to us in baptism remains true no matter what losses life may bring our way.

A wonderful model of the living Word can be visualized by considering a page of the Jewish Talmud. At the center of the page are the words of Scripture. Surrounding this Word of God is printed the commentary of the early rabbis on the biblical text, called the Mishnah.[2] Next, printed on the borders of the page, are the comments of later rabbis who interpreted the Mishnah's commentary on Scripture.

These comments are the Gemara. Finally, the contemporary reader comes to the text, seeking the living Word of God. Often in the Jewish tradition, Talmud study is carried out in pairs. So imagine two contemporary students of the Word, discussing vigorously the meaning of the Gemara comments on the Mishnah commentary on the Bible. This is to underscore that we stand in a great traditionalizing process. The living Word of God has been handed down from one generation to the next. It is the responsibility of this generation to ensure that the next generation inherit this living Word of God for its own life and, furthermore, that this next generation be equipped to pass down the Word to the generation following. This underscores the vital importance of catechesis as an indispensable dimension of transforming leadership.

The rabbi is one whose calling is to be devoted to the Word, the teaching. The rabbi undertakes this calling not in the place of the community, but on behalf of and for the sake of the community. The rabbi is called to a threefold task: 1) to *study* the Torah and vigorously engage it; 2) to *do* the Torah by living a holy life in discipleship and prayer; and 3) to *hope* the Torah, clinging to God's promises in spite of the suffering and complexities of life. This calling of the rabbi is in a sense to *become* the Torah, a living embodiment of Torah devotion. Yet again, this is not an end in itself. The rabbi serves as a minister of the Word *in order that the people themselves become the Torah*, a people immersed in the Word of God, until each and every one becomes also a rabbi. Could we imagine here the priesthood of all believers as the rabbinate of all? (See chapter 16.)

The Minister of the Word in the Christian Church

Martin Buber once wrote: "What matters is that time and again an older generation, staking its entire existence on that act, comes to a younger with the desire to teach, waken, and shape it; then the holy spark leaps across the gap."[3] What does this awesome responsibility mean for Christian ministers of the Word? It means, first of all, reconfiguring the center of gravity of the ministerial office.

Joseph Sittler once lamented the "maceration" of the Christian minister.[4] Maceration refers to being chopped up in small pieces. Sittler's analysis of the ministerial office is as fresh today as when he first wrote it. The professional model of ministry has led ministers of the Word to be divided into myriad activities, all good in and of themselves, but collectively leading to disintegration. According to the professional model, the minister of the Word finds on the desk not only the Bible and books, but more importantly "a roll of blueprints, a file of negotiations between the parish, the bank, and the Board of Missions, samples of asphalt tile, and a plumber's estimate."[5] Today we might add to this list software for keeping church records, a DVD on church management, Web page addresses for new communion ware, a musical score for the praise band, and the schedule of the church's softball team. While these items are each useful in their own right, the collective effect can be that the minister is a jack-of-all-trades and centered in none. It is core to transforming leadership that the minister be centered in the Word above all things. Ministers of the Word need to place the Word at the center continually, each day, each year.

Consider the variety of images that frequently can depict the minister's work: professional, counselor, manager, social worker, wounded healer, chaplain, financial officer, musician, janitor, etc. While no one of these activities is intrinsically wrong, collectively they point toward the "maceration" of which Sittler wrote. Is there any single image that can center and guide those called to transforming leadership in the church? We propose that the appropriate and necessary service that gives order to all the other activities is that of a *Servant of the Word*.[6] This resonates with the name of the very office that is held, i.e., Word and Sacrament (ordained pastor), or Word and Service (consecrated diaconal minister). It is this service that is most needful within the Christian community, in spite of the myriad other things people want to assign priority. Ministry of the Word thereby constitutes the core identity of transforming leaders.

Servants of the Word are called upon to interpret all of human experience—one's own and that of others—habitually in relationship to God's Word. Ministers of the Word operate according to a thoroughgoing action/reflection method through which one is constantly asking about what God is doing in the world. The servant of the Word accompanies people along life's journey, helping to clarify and name the core questions that we all face: "What are you afraid of?" "What holds us in bondage?" "What is separating us from others?" "What does life mean in the face of finitude and death?" Through astute listening and caring speech, the minister of the Word assists people in deepening their questions and searching for God's presence and God's purposes. In this way, transforming leaders invite spiritual reflection. Connie Kleingartner, Professor of Evangelism and Congregational Ministries at Lutheran School of Theology at Chicago, teaches leaders to ask, "How is it with your soul?" Servants of the Word live out the calling as those who witness to the truth: "Your word is a lamp to my feet and a light to my path" (Psalm 119:105). The minister of the Word accompanies people as they search for answers to life's mysteries and dares to announce the Word of promise and hope.

The ministry of the Word is what is distinctive about the calling of those entrusted with the office of Word and Sacrament or Word and Service. Ministry of the Word means one's life is always engaged in attentiveness to God's Word. This attending begins with one's own life of prayer, devotion, and study (see chapter 9). But it also means that ministry of the Word is what one intends to provide in every relationship, every committee meeting, every public act. Finally, God is the primary agent of all transforming ministry. It is God's Word that accomplishes the transformation for which our hearts long:

> For as the rain and the snow come down from heaven, and do not return there until they have watered the earth, making it bring forth and sprout, giving seed to the sower and bread to the eater, so shall my word be that goes out from my mouth; it shall not return to me empty, but it shall accomplish that which I purpose, and succeed in the thing for which I sent it. (Isaiah 55:10-11)

Centered in the Word, our range of daily tasks is transformed. We search out the most effective software for keeping church records because we know that each person in the parish is a member of the Body of Christ. We work with blueprints and plumber's estimates, asphalt tile, and the bank, understanding how buildings are not idolatrous ends in themselves but that they are shelters of sacred space for the proclamation of God's Word, centers for missional outreach and service. We work together with other leaders in selecting music and communion ware. And we become tangled in differences of opinion, which can lead to conflict. But searching the Word, we find pathways towards reconciliation so that we might truly worship together and, yes, even play softball together. On any given day, we will serve as counselor, manager, social worker, wounded healer, chaplain, financial officer, musician, janitor, and who knows what else, but we will do all things as transforming leaders grounded in the Word.

Ministry of the Transforming Word in Practice

Among the many images of ministry that compete for the leader's time and attention, understanding oneself as minister of the Word, as rabbi, has much to commend it. This image of the ministerial office grounds one's identity and service in a life that begins with prayer and study of God's Word, not as ends in themselves but as devotion to those matters that finally are of the greatest value to the life of the community of God's people.[7] The danger of putting such a concept into practice is that it may conflict with the disintegrated approach to ministry that is based on the people's multiple competing expectations regarding how the minister should be scheduling time. It is only by entering into ministry humbly, accompanying God's people faithfully, and gently leading them to expect to be fed by God's Word that the church can reclaim the centrality of the ministry of the Word on the part of its leaders. The ministry of the Christian leader can regain its proper center only as the people learn to expect the living Word of God to nourish their lives. In very practical terms, this may mean that the minister redefines how his or her ministry is perceived, or makes changes in ministry activity.

1. The Minister's Study.

For example, one way to raise these expectations is think of how one describes the space in which the leader's desk is located. It has become far too common to call this place an "office." Rather, in the spirit of the ministry of the rabbi, this space properly serves as one's "study." For it is in this place that the ministry of the Word begins. What would it mean for the people to learn that their minister spends devoted time every morning to prayer and the study of God's Word? Thinking of the minister's space first and foremost as a place of study and devotion may not only re-center the service of the minister, but perhaps the ministry of the entire congregation.

2. Holy Conversation.

What would it mean for the minister to invite people who "come by the church" to join him or her in the sanctuary for a time of prayer and listening to God's Word? Thereby the church's greatest spiritual resource regains its privileged place. A minister of the Word is called to be a speaker of the faith. This certainly includes ritualized speaking of the faith through formal times of preaching and teaching.[8] But it also means that one's calling as minister of the Word summons one to bring God's Word into every encounter and relationship. This does not mean quoting Bible verses on every occasion. Rather, it means that God's Word becomes a living Word through the shaping of relationships and conversation around matters of the heart and soul.[9] Each person is made in the image of God. Each one has been redeemed by the work of Christ. Each one is precious in God's care. God's Word becomes newly incarnate in the genuine care shown by the minister for the souls of the people. In this way, ordinary conversation is transformed into a form of God's Word. The minister of the Word is called upon to relate the things of God and the presence of Jesus to the lives of this people by modeling speech that reclaims God as a natural dimension of daily life. For those with the eyes to see and the ears to hear, God is as present as their next breath. The ministry of the Word can make explicit what is implicit. We speak God "present" until the people themselves also begin to speak of God alive and active in their midst.

3. Expanding the Use of Lectionary.

Transforming leadership in the Word takes with utmost seriousness the lectionary texts assigned for the week—not only in preparation for Sunday but for the life of the congregation and the life of the world. Mark Olson described an approach to ministry that organized the entire life of the congregation around the meaning of the lectionary texts for daily life.[10] At every church gathering or committee meeting, in every act of pastoral care or visitation, the same texts that are assigned for worship become the lens for interpreting all of life in a given week. The congregation comes to dwell in God's Word with reference to the meaning of these texts.

For example, the lectionary texts assigned for the first Sunday in Advent in Year C are Psalm 25:1-9, Jeremiah 33:14-16, 1 Thessalonians 3:9-13, and Luke 21:25-36. Starting with Sunday, what would it mean to bring this set of texts to everything the congregation does? What would it mean to invite the congregation council at its monthly meeting into a conversation about the meaning of Psalm 25:4-5?

> Make me to know your ways, O LORD: teach me your paths. Lead me in your truth, and teach me, for you are God of my salvation;, for you I wait all day long.

What would it mean to invite the women in the Martha Circle to reflect on the significance of Jeremiah 33:15 as they prepare for the coming Christmas holiday?

> In those days and at that time I will make a righteous Branch to spring up for David; and he shall execute justice and righteousness in the land.

What would it mean this week to bring 1 Thessalonians 3:12-13 to a dying member of the church whose family gathers around the bed?

> May the Lord make you increase and abound in love for one another and for all, just as we abound in love for you. And may he so strengthen your hearts in holiness that you may be blameless before our God and Father at the coming of our Lord Jesus with all his saints.

Finally, what would it mean to engage the youth group in conversation about the meaning of Jesus' words in Luke 21:32-33, especially in relationship to the apocalyptic predictions about the end of the world that recur in the message of many dispensationalist churches?

> Truly I tell you, this generation will certainly not pass away until all these things have taken place. Heaven and earth will pass away, but my words will not pass away."

The lectionary is a treasure of God's Word that we have not begun to value deeply if we only reference it on Sunday morning. What would it mean to orient all of congregational life to this treasure? Ministers of the Word are called to connect all of life to the living Word of God.

4. Teaching the Word.

New occasions continue to arise in ministry that are unprecedented in the leader's experience. Each of these can be viewed as an occasion for study and learning. A building project gives rise to studying God's Word about what it means to be a church. A diagnosis of multiple sclerosis gives occasion for learning about this disease and how to minister to people and families who suffer with it. A question raised in the adult forum leads to directed study that can be shared with the class on a subsequent week and with the whole congregation through the sermon. A meeting of the local food pantry provides the impetus to return to God's Word on the justice issue of feeding the hungry. One of the wonderful gifts of ministry is the possibility of relating every occasion to the study of God's Word and to share the life connections one is making.

Formal occasions for teaching provide ready-made opportunities for dwelling in God's Word and preparing one's insights in a form that can enrich the lives of others.[11] Teaching confirmation classes can be real occasions for examining the meaning of the Bible and

Catechism for the lives of these particular young persons. To do this well requires serious preparation, more than following the directions in the leader's guide of a curriculum resource. The invitation to lead the Bible study at a circle meeting can be the opportunity for exploring the assigned texts in depth and relating them to the lives of these women. Above all, the minister of the Word should engage in regular teaching of adults in a Bible class that meets on Sunday morning, as well as perhaps other times during the week.

While sermon preparation is clearly necessary for the ministry of the Word, setting aside time to prepare and lead Bible studies for adults is also vitally crucial and a core calling for ministers of the Word. Neglecting this core calling has contributed mightily to the cultural assumption that television preachers provide the normative interpretation of Scripture. Ministers of the Word need to teach regularly on Sunday mornings because that is when the largest number of people gather at the church. It is an insufficient excuse to say that schedules are too tight or that there are not enough people interested. Even when multiple parish responsibilities *do* make Sunday morning teaching impossible, alternative scheduling needs to allow communal study of God's Word to take place. Teaching ministry is core to the office of one trained as a minister of the Word. By attending to the teaching of the Word with diligence and devotion, all of ministry returns to its proper center.

5. Meetings and Special Occasions.

Ministry of the Word entails bringing a connection between life and God's Word in virtually all of the multiple tasks of congregational leadership. Meetings are great occasions for teaching and Bible study. Rather than offering a perfunctory prayer before proceeding to business, engage the people in a few minutes of reflection or discussion around one of the week's lectionary texts. This is a way to help people establish priorities for decision-making based on the highest priority: God's Word. In the written communications from the church, such as weekly bulletins, monthly newsletters, or emails, many connections can be made between the life of the people in the congregation and God's Word. For example, one pastor made it a priority to connect the pastor's message in the monthly newsletter with the centrality of worship in the life of the congregation, always pointing to God's promise that Christ will be present for us in Word and Sacrament. All of the routine administrative tasks of ministers, whether making phone calls, preparing mailings, planning youth events, or keeping church records, can be revitalized by seeing them as occasions for the ministry of the Word.

6. Continuing Education.

It is essential that ministers of the Word keep growing in their own intellectual and spiritual lives. Continuing education, whether done as personal study or as study in the presence of others, is a must. Reading provides one of the best avenues for personal study.[12] Consider an array of reading materials, books, and journals for different kinds of growth: 1) something related to the Bible as a whole or to an individual book of the Bible; 2) something in an area of personal interest or ministerial strength to deepen existing knowledge; 3) something in an area unfamiliar that introduces new learning; and 4) some diversionary or recreational reading, completely for the joy of it.

Reading selected journals (in print or on-line) can also be very useful for keeping current on recent scholarship and new publications. Continuing education events provided by one's church body or educational institutions can also provide a wonderful setting for personal growth and professional development as a minister of the Word. Even more useful is to develop a colleague group of two to four persons from one's denomination or beyond, who covenant to meet together regularly to discuss common readings, attend lectures together, or watch videos. Often such groups can become the lifeblood of one's ministry, providing opportunities for ecumenical relationships to flourish and where insights can be gained from colleagues who share your commitment to a ministry of the Word.

Transforming leadership is relational leadership that is intent on connecting the lives of people to the living Word of God. Ministers of the Word are called to inhabit the Scriptures in such a way that others are themselves invited to dwell in the Word as the source of life.[13] Ministers of the Word are called to be agents of transformation by linking people to the One whose Word finally has the power to transform them. This is a service that hearkens transforming leaders back to the calling of the rabbis who helped to preserve the identity of God's people in the times crisis that threatened the loss of that identity. May ministers of the Word serve to deliver the church in this generation from the spiritual amnesia that threatens our identity and mission today!

o o o o o o o o o o o o o o o o o o o o o o o

Personal Reflection

1. In your experience as a life-long learner what have you discovered are the qualities of good Bible study leadership? How can you continue to grow in your range of abilities in order to help people be centered in God's Word?
2. Which Bible texts have the most significance for your life? Why? How do you "inhabit" the Scriptures through these texts?

Group Conversation

1. How is the image of "rabbi" helpful or not helpful as you think about giving leadership in the ministry of the Word today?
2. How is your congregation handing down the Word of God from one generation to the next? How are you together reaching out beyond the congregation through teaching ministries with the precious gift of God's Word?
3. How are the lectionary texts used in the life of your congregation beyond the worship service? How might they be used?

Spiritual Practice

Practice *Lectio Divina* on Isaiah 55:10-11. Read the text slowly and contemplate its meaning for your life. What words or images are prominent? Read it a second and third time and concentrate on other aspects that had not come to mind before. What is God saying to you through these verses?

Transforming Action

Live into the image of yourself as servant of the Word more deeply. Trace how your actions might be transformed in the course of a day, or a week. How might you for one day intentionally seek to practice ministry of the Word consistently in each and every relationship and ministerial activity?

Transforming Power for Partnership

chapter eight

IN THIS CHAPTER WE FOCUS on leadership, power, and partnership.[1] The oppressive systems of sexism, racism, classism, nationalism (particularly militaristic nationalism), and other "isms" are interrelated.[2] Shared power in relations, be they equitable gender relations, interracial relationships, etc., is vital for embodying and modeling transforming leadership. Inequitable power relationships create dissonance and need to be negotiated if leadership is truly to be transforming.

In most sectors of public life women and men and people of various racial and ethnic backgrounds are now visible together, often sitting side by side at the news anchor desk or on church councils. However, they are not present in equal numbers as corporate CEOs or as senior pastors of large congregations. So where are we now in regard to power and partnership? The questions are deep and involve us all in our personal and professional relationships. We all have been changed and are changing. However, issues of patriarchy, white privilege, economic entitlement, control, and oppression remain. Full partnership is elusive, but it is possible!

It is important to realize that, given the nature of human sin and brokenness, oppressive systems do not just cure themselves, nor fade away. They hold both oppressed and oppressor captive. The nature of patriarchal oppression, for instance, is so much a centuries old system, so much a "reality," that it is hard to imagine otherwise. Church and society may make progressive changes only to see oppression re-emerge in new, perhaps more subtle, forms. Each of us is racist, sexist, classist, and more, because we have been socialized into and participate in the human condition of inequitable power systems. Rather than debate or defend, human beings do well to confess. Only through confession of systemic and personal sin are we free to examine root causes and claim new life in Christ in order to be empowered for transformative change. The people, different from ourselves, who most threaten us are the ones we need most to understand. We are called to take a serious look at ourselves and at the oppressive systems in which we all participate, and to be genuinely open to transformative ways of being in relationship for the sake of mission.

The power of the Holy Spirit is unlimited. Ministry is not a competitive sport. We sometimes fear, "If you have more power, I will have less." That may be true in the world's economy of power, but God's unconditional love, new liberating life in Christ, and the power-filled Spirit transform our very concepts of power and partnership (see Galatians 3:21-29 and 5:1). There is a direct connection between justification and justice. By God's grace the potential for genuine partnership leads to transformation in congregations and in global relationships. When *you* are fully empowered, I am more empowered as well.

Frequently in this chapter we will focus on gender, not because it is more important than issues of race, class, etc, but because the authors are of the same race and different genders. By looking at one expression of the power systems, it is possible—and important—to discover the problems and potential in all. We write as radical feminists. By "radical" we mean going to the "root" of the issues and taking seriously the deathly bondage of *all* oppressive systems. When we confess our participation in these systems, we take them to the cross. In the power of the resurrection, we are freed for powerful servanthood and Spirit-filled partnership.

We write as a woman and a man, realizing that we cannot speak for all men and women, nor for all male-female relationships. We write as a man who, because he is part of the male system, knows he would be presumptuous to simply claim to be feminist, (just as a white person cannot claim to understand the reality of a person of another race), and as a woman who has said to this man, "I have seen, heard, and experienced you seeking to understand and working to change. *I believe you* when say that you are a feminist." Realizing power differences that exist in almost all human relationships, we write deeply committed to transforming partnerships for the empowerment of all people in a just and peaceable world.

The Power Cycle

When we consider oppressive systems of exclusionary power, we observe a cyclical movement wherein the oppressor (intentionally or not) seeks to keep the oppressed in an inferior position in the system.[3] This power cycle is real, strong, insidious, and so commonplace we often don't notice it, particularly when we are in the power position. We refer to "oppressor" and "oppressed" systemically, not personally. People may find themselves as the "oppressed" in some regard and as "oppressor" in some other regard, e.g., gender, race, global economics, or educational opportunities. Readers are invited to enter this conversation from wherever they are, opening themselves to the ongoing growth that is needed by us all as we work toward a more just, equitable society and transforming partnerships. Even in places where official exclusion on the basis of race, ethnicity, gender, or sexual orientation is no longer operative, vestiges of old prejudices and oppression remain. People oppress and are oppressed. Looking at the power cycle can be helpful (see figure 2 and explanatory paragraphs that follow):

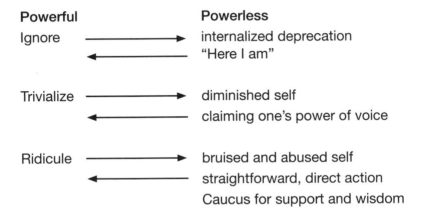

Figure 2: The Power Cycle

If change does not take place, the power cycle continues with "elimination" leading once again to ignoring powerless people and the problem of powerlessness. However, at *each* stage there is potential for systemic change resulting in transformed power relationships and true partnership.

Ignore

When those in power hold that power clearly and firmly, they feel they can afford to ignore the powerless. The powerful are publicly named, while those without power are referred to as "others"— nameless, anonymous, and seemingly insignificant. In not noticing, in not really seeing, much less knowing, the name, story, or gifts of the "ignored," it is the powerful who remain ignorant. A patriarchal congregation leader who relates to people in a condescending fashion may feel in control but is ineffective if he or she does not know, really see, or understand the people the leader is called to serve.

Ironically, those historically victimized by oppressive systems who were thought to be ignorant because they were kept from full access to education—women, people of color in this country, and people in the "servant" class economically—often were more aware, more astute, more savvy than their oppressors. This is because they had to know two systems: their own as well as the dominant, white, male system in order to survive. Likewise, powerful nations (whose people may speak only one language) are a danger when they remain ignorant of other languages, cultures, and of the multi-lingual people living in other nations.

Those ignored may remain in that state for years, but if they should arise and say, "Here I am." "My name is . . ." "I am somebody." "You cannot ignore us, for we will exercise the indirect power we have" (including "riots" or "terrorism"), the powerful must take note. And they may be extraordinarily surprised. "Where did that (they) come from?" "I thought the little lady was happy all these years." "Why aren't those 'underdeveloped' nations happy with the benevolent aid we give them?" After a natural disaster such as Hurricane Katrina when television cameras show African Americans and poor people ignored, the country is surprised that racism and classism still exist.

At this point, as at many points in the power cycle, there is opportunity for mutual knowing and partnership. Transformation in the relationship is a real possibility. There is opportunity for men to ask, "What is it like for you as a woman?" for a Euro-American to say to an African-American, "I would like to understand how the vestiges of slavery still have ramifications today," and for a super-power nation to learn the language and history of the nation it does not understand and feels is a threat. When such learning begins, the oppressed—now acknowledged—will have opportunity to finally ask in return, "What is it really like for you as a man?" "What is it like to always be put into the 'oppressor' category?" "What is ordinary life for you like in *your* country?" This dialog would not have been possible before, because the oppressed person's view of the oppressor also was only partial. They viewed the oppressor from afar primarily as powerful, rich, or privileged. Mutual knowing takes time, genuine (not superficial) interest, and, most of all, respect (see chapter 10). When a congregational leader is able to relinquish control, transformed leadership can lead to healthy, mutual, and informed partnerships.

Even though the power differential may remain, the relationship will have been transformed. In genuinely learning from one another, each is changed. This does not mean that circumstance and appropriate designation of roles are erased. A nation will remain its own size. Pastor will remain pastor and organist will remain organist. But the ability to respect, to really *see* the other and to receive each one's gifts fully in the congregational or global community is changed. Once this relationship is transformed, fear is lessoned, the potential for more just distribution of resources is increased, and growth in partnership is exponential.

Trivialize

If the formerly ignored succeed in becoming visible but the relationship is not transformed into partnership, or if the formerly ignored are present "at the table" on board and committees but the "shape of the table" does not change to fully incorporate the change in power relationships,[4] the powerful may attempt new strategies to return things to the *status quo*. A clergywoman is trivialized when she is introduced as "Tammy," though her male counterpart is addressed as Rev. Johnson. An African American man during slavery was trivialized when not addressed as Mr. Jones, but as "uncle" or "boy." Such trivialization continues in racist stereotypes and slurs. A person from another country is trivialized when seen only as a foreigner, not as a person with a history, a story, and wisdom.

In a congregation, a staff member who is beginning to be noticed for making a contribution to ministry may be marginalized when he or she is perceived as a threat to the one "in charge." In the power cycle it is tempting for the oppressed to remain in a diminished light, which may seem safer. But they often work very hard to be accepted. Trivialization seems such an insignificant, benign tactic. But it works!

Trivialization may take the form of humor that might be intended to be good-natured but actually puts one in a trivialized position.

Dealing with such humor is difficult. If one's person or ideas are trivialized "humorously" and one speaks up, the response is often, "Can't you take a joke?" In order to transform the moment, one could try to claim one's power of presence and voice and respond straightforwardly, as though it is not a trivial, humorous matter. This can diffuse the situation, opening the way for respectful discussion. However, if the one trying to hold on to power responds with dismissal or anger, the opportunity for partnership is delayed, and the powerful may hope such delay is permanent.

An oppressed person or group may be trivialized through lack of full attention. When "they" start to be noticed, the controlling one may diminish or "forget" them.

At a committee meeting people with prestige of age, gender, or status may pay attention only when the issues in which they are interested are being discussed and give their attention to "important" personal work when the discussion turns to items the new-to-the-table people have placed on the agenda. Such trivialization diminishes people and hinders mission.

Trivialization may take the shape of reference to someone's "little" projects, or through adjectives describing their person or gender as "cute" or "quaint." At this stage of the power cycle, the less powerful person's words and ideas are often not heard until they are repeated a second time at a meeting—as though they were not ever originally said—by someone who is regarded as having stature.

Even saying, "I'm trying to be sensitive," can be a way of keeping the other small, as if they are so fragile that they cannot possibly deal with anything of substance. A characteristic of genuinely transformed partnership is *mutual* sensitivity and care—which means respect, curiosity, and openness to change.

One danger of trivialization is that the person with new position but less than full power may internalize such trivialization and fail to use full voice. To be inside a structure and trivialized may be more frustrating than exercising power from outside the institution. This tactic of reserving power for the group traditionally in control will continue as long as the newcomers accept their trivialized position.

If the power cycle is to be broken and shared power achieved, the formerly powerless will need to claim their own power. The powerful need to recognize the important role of relinquishment of power.[5] The powerful can refrain from trivializing remarks, checking their attitudes as well as their actions. They will need to consciously "pay attention," learning to listen to different voices and respond positively to different ways of running a meeting, or running governments. This may include public apology, even if long overdue, in terms of entire groups of people who have been trivialized and suffered from oppressive actions.

While working together in a congregation, leaders of different roles, genders, ages, or racial and ethnic backgrounds will need to take time to recognize and talk about power dynamics. Setting and maintaining a trustworthy environment—for everyone—(chapter 1) is crucial. That will not be easy, but such transformation is possible, necessary, and, ultimately, transformative for the entire community so that it can fully engage in mission and ministry. However if partnership at this stage is not achieved, and if the powerful perceive trivialization is not working in their favor, in order to retain power they may resort to ridicule.

Ridicule

At this stage, leaving someone out is more intentional and purposeful. Comments become more crude, for the one in power is becoming more desperate. The need to "level" someone who seems to have become more prominent than they deserve is bewildering to the one being leveled, but the powerful, in trying to retain power, may go to ridiculous means to do so. Ridicule, in any form, is not only disrespectful and demeaning but often dismissive and mean. It is meant to be, because in the insidious power cycle, the goal of the powerful is to preserve their full, complete positions of exclusive power. (Likewise those who believe they *should* have power because of some privilege may resort to demeaning tactics.) The powerful find it hard to imagine that a transformed realm also would be a good thing for them. Those who are seen as a threat to the system are seen as too "uppity." They should not presume real equality; they need to be put back in their place.

The term "politically correct," at best trivializes; when said with disdain, it ridicules. It takes the guise of being appropriate, but is most often used to defend oneself and one's position and therefore to dismiss. People who start a sentence, "I'm trying to be politically correct," or "I *have* to be politically correct" usually are saying of themselves, "I really don't get it yet." They implicitly say, "I know they have to be here—by law or by virtue of a changing society—but I do not yet acknowledge the legitimacy of their presence and do not intend to engage their personhood and their gifts."

Ridicule may be overt through racial slurs or macho power blocking. Women may be dismissed if they are not believed to be strong or gutsy enough to "take it." A temptation for women is to adopt patriarchal uses of power, believing they need to do so in order to "make it." When the very concept of leadership has not yet been transformed, women who have become strong leaders are perceived to be "bossy."[6]

The power of ridicule for women, when internalized, keeps them from exercising leadership in their own style. It also deprives those trying to hold on to power of benefiting from new forms of liberating leadership that would be more collaborative. Ridicule is a form of violence that has long been endured by women.[7] Men who have been abused as children, or as adults by those with more power, are also victims. Coming to grips with such victimization may be difficult.

Issues of power are always present. Those formerly holding power by virtue of white privilege or economic or military "superiority" may try to regain that position, assuming that those finally gaining *some* power of their own will next want to take *all* the power. Such people and nations have not yet experienced the benefits of shared power and equal partnership wherein people exercise power in mutually transformative ways. To successfully reduce someone's or some group's significance through ridicule is to make them irrelevant.

Although this stage of the power cycle is very dangerous, it may hold the most potential for transformation of the entire system. Partnership is possible. Both parties can help this transformation happen by promising to respect one another. They can talk "with" rather than merely "about" one another. When congregational relationships have disintegrated to the point of ridicule, transforming leadership will need to work hard not only to tolerate but to value and appreciate the diversity of gifts and opinions.

In order to change the dynamics, those facing ridicule can try to maintain composure, not going "one down." This is not easy, particularly on the spot, because ridiculing remarks often come out of the blue. But one can try to maintain one's integrity (something others *cannot* take away) by looking the ridiculing person in the eye, making a clear statement of fact, and strongly but calmly refusing to accept the ridicule. That can break the power cycle and open new possibilities for partnership. The key is to believe in oneself, not the ridicule.

Because we are each made in the image of God, because Christ has died and is risen, and because the transforming Spirit is at work, we can—we must—regard each other in new ways. Letty Russell wrote, "I find that one educates for partnership by the method of participation in that partnership with God, with the world, with self, and with others. We learn through entering into the process of partnership itself. Secondly, we educate for partnership by being partner; by providing the context of community where people can experience partnership."[8] The way toward transformative sharing of power is to act in admiration even when we do not yet truly admire one another (see chapter 10). There is some truth in that adage that we can act our way into a new way of being. We live as though we are already partners, because in Christ, we already are.

Caucus

When trivialized and ridiculed, it is not easy to continue in one's work, especially when such attitudes and actions are internalized. It is necessary to gather with others who do understand, who have seen what happened (or who will believe one's account) and devise alternative responses. People caucus by race, ethnic group, gender, class, sexual orientation, age, and more. We use the example of gender here.

Women have a strong history of sisterhoods, quilting circles, book clubs, and mission organizations. Excluded from the public sphere, they gathered in the private sphere. Today women still find such groups helpful for nurture, understanding, and mentoring. Such gatherings need not frighten, but they often do. Fear brings out comments—perhaps said in a jovial manner—such as, "You must be getting together to talk about us" or "I'm going to have to break this up." "Caucus" *is* a political term, used in instances where there is intentionality about gaining and strategizing power. Circles and some other same-gender groups are not overtly about seeking power but are more a natural form of empowering. Men may perceive any gathering of women as a caucus that is plotting to upset the given ordering of men and women.

Even at this point in the power cycle, there is the potential for full partnership. Transformation takes place for men as they learn by working with women as equal partners. Men, too, may want to gather in all-male groups. How is this different from "the old boys' club"? When women were—are, in some cases—excluded from ecclesial roles and groups, they were (are) deprived not only of access but also of decision-making and networking opportunities. But once such groups are open to women and men equally, there is also room for some healthy groupings by gender.

Men will need to support one another, to learn from each other how they can deal with a world that seems to have changed out from under them. They may feel captive to an old paradigm and not know how to move into a new one. On the way toward transformed male/female relationships in a patriarchal system, some may have to deal with the question of how one deals with a sense of guilt over centuries of domination and a feeling of shame in being a male, when that is what one is. Wise feminists do not simply want men to feel guilt or shame. That is not their goal; it may be men who are most helpful to other men in the process of change. Men may need such a group and male mentors for their own "nurture," even though that word would probably not be used.

Likewise there is a danger of men abdicating realms that are becoming more equal between women and men (e.g. fewer men attending some colleges and professional graduate schools) and retreating to a realm that is more clearly still "of men." This also is not the goal. During a time that is still transitional, being together as partners and sharing leadership in equitable ways is something we need to discover and foster together.

In congregational leadership when difficulties in sharing power emerge, it may be important for those who have not yet made the transition to talk with others, e.g. a struggling senior pastor speaking with a senior pastor who may have healthier styles of partnering, seeking to gain perspective and courage to change. We all need to continue to seek wisdom on the journey of transformation.

The Token Stage

Whereas full partnership of more equal numbers of women and men may seem threatening, ironically the token stage may be the most dangerous because it is most artificial. Remaining at the token stage is dangerous for the individual, who may feel isolated. Groups which have traditionally held power may fear growing numbers of the previously excluded, but the presence of only a few can create fear of "what could happen if all those people are allowed in." Decades after civil rights legislation on school integration and housing discrimination, there are few truly integrated, racially balanced schools or neighborhoods. Likewise today one sees wealthy people of all hues, but the great challenge of inner city poverty remains.

There is great value in moving beyond the token stage. A larger number of diverse people creates more potential for greater use of many gifts and a rich multicultural experience. There is less sense of "over-against," which the powerful may view as political strategy in the caucus stage. A greater presence of breadth and variety of people means that the "token" does not feel burdened to represent all women, or all Latinos, for example. Members of different groups, now becoming more equitable, can truly get to know each other, thus transforming partnership.

The predecessor bodies of the Evangelical Lutheran Church in America, as many mainline churches, were at the token stage in the early 1980s. When the ELCA formed in 1988, it used representational principles for all decision-making groups from the regional to church-wide level. Surprising to some, that large, over-night change did not produce more fear, but a feeling of "this is natural." Full representation of men and women has made significant differences in agendas, policies, and leadership style. Today it seems strange when only one woman (or one man) is at the conference table. However, the ELCA still has much room to grow in full partnership with regard to broader racial and ethnic diversity.

Once again, we see that there is potential for breaking out of the power cycle and experiencing the joy of shared power and transformed leadership at any stage. It takes work and deliberate positive action to change old systems and to continue to work on partnership. Those holding the power, whether we speak of sexism, racism, or classism, usually will not magnanimously give it up. If the fear continues, they may go even further to return things to their original—those used to patriarchy or white privilege might say "natural"—state.

Eliminate

Fear of the one who is different—especially when that one is gaining in power (whether it be in numbers, money, or "weapons of mass destruction")—can escalate to the point that the powerful believe they need to shun, fire, or exterminate the one who still has less (but growing) power. Full, healthy partnership is thwarted; because it has never been experienced (nor can it be imagined), it is feared. The final, now desperate, action of the formerly all-powerful is to get rid of individuals, programs, or institutions where the formerly oppressed now enjoy some power and place.

In a congregation there may be some visible, noticeable signs of the emergence of transformation, but resistance can still raise its head. When conflict arises, frequently it is the one with the least power by virtue of gender, or race, or status who is asked to resign. So the youth worker or the diaconal minister quietly takes a position in another church, while the senior pastor decides, "I will assemble a new staff of 'my' people." By eliminating a position or hiring someone more docile, the congregations can go back to the *status quo* and return to dependency, thereby underutilizing or not recognizing the talents of many gifted people.

Mary, the mother of Jesus, was called by God to exercise power, through her own body, in a way that was socially unacceptable. Joseph, with all good reason, "planned to dismiss her quietly" (Matt. 1:18), but he did not. And she did not refuse to use the power she was given to bear the one who would turn power upside down. Actively receptive, she said, *ad sum,* "Let it be with me according to your word" (Luke 2:38). God's will through Jesus Christ would bring down "the powerful from their thrones" and lift up "the lowly," to fill "the hungry with good things," and send "the rich away empty" (Luke 2:52-53).

A patriarchal system keeps leaders from seeing why people with less power do not feel safe. Although the associate pastor sees the long-established senior pastor as having plenty of power, that pastor may feel threatened by the associate. The super-power nation may not be able to understand why other nations, towards whom they have been so "benevolent," do not love them. Surprised and threatened, that nation may decide it needs to do away with leaders or nations who challenge its global position, announcing that it is for self-preservation. The super power often either over- or under-estimates the power of the less powerful. Not understanding the power-dynamics, the "safe" way seems to be to get rid of the one with emerging power.

In regard to gender, women (even after they have access to positions of authority) may not appear to be using the power they have, due in part to women's style of leadership that is more often relational and non-hierarchical. Many are reluctant to take more than "their turn" or to take credit for work others "under" them have done. They do not like the term "under." Schooled for years in using indirect or even manipulative power because they did not have access to direct, legitimated power, they may be hesitant to formally speak up. For example: a woman raises an idea at a meeting, but ends a declaratory sentence with a question mark. "We should open the doors of the church to the homeless coalition?" (Her voice goes up at the end, orally signaling doubt or question.) Not surprisingly, her request is turned down. She assumes it can be no other way.[9]

The reader by now has no doubt recognized the similarities of the power cycle to the abuse cycle in domestic violence. The abuser trivializes, belittles, and tries in every way possible to diminish the self-esteem of the abused. Escalating ridicule and verbal abuse follow. The abused is often isolated, shamed into staying at home, cut off from friends and any assistance that would validate the abuse and offer support. (The "caucus" opportunity is missing.) Finally, the cycle reaches the violent stage, resulting in either physical, sexual, or emotional abuse (or a combination thereof). When the abused is "beaten down," the power cycle returns to what may seem like a period of calm, but it actually provides the abuser with restoration to power and the ability to "ignore" the personhood of the abused. The abused one, returned to bondage, longs for a normal relationship; she or he may try to imagine it will not happen again. It will take courage to once again assert oneself. With the cycle of abuse habitually in place, the victim is actually accused of triggering the violence, even without overt action or self-assertion. The abuser, fearful of loss of control, will escalate the violence periodically. The victim is most in danger of severe violence when she or he threatens to leave and break the cycle of power.

Transformed Power Relationships

In order for full partnership to be realized, the formerly powerful and the newly powerful need to listen to each other certainly, but they also need to use power in new, mutually respectful, and energizing ways. This will mean a radical transformation in relationship, both in the personal and the global spheres. This means powerful nations fully supporting global organizations, such as the United Nations, where partnership among large and small nations can be actualized. This means changing the "shape of the table,"[10] using new strategies so all voices are actually heard, and adopting fully participatory methods of decision-making. It will mean the oppressor relinquishing power and the oppressed, now with new choices, claiming an identity other than victim. Both oppressor and oppressed truly need to want and to persistently move toward healthy partnership.

In many parts of society such new shared power and energizing partnership is being realized. However, on the way towards this new promised life together, we sometimes feel afraid (the powerless) or threatened (the powerful) and long for a return to old familiar systems. If people allow themselves once again to be silenced, or let themselves be put away silently (for their "own good"), or participate in their own co-optation,[11] the power cycle returns. Patriarchy, white-privilege, and neo-colonialism prevail. Once again, stripped of emerging power, people and their oppressive condition are subject to being ignored. If the governments whom the powerful assume to be a threat are annihilated, not only is healthy global partnership thwarted, but the powerful are left with the idolatrous burden of occupying the conquered under the guise of liberating them.

Two other dangers threaten full partnership: de-valuation and abdication. Women and people of color have entered previously all-white, male institutions in large numbers. The opportunity is now finally here for men and women and for people of diverse races to share power. Men entering previously all-female institutions, e.g., women's colleges, the nursing profession, or day care is another story. Some men feel they will lose status by entering such professions. Note the lower pay scales of previously all-female professions, even when society says it values nursing, care giving for the elderly and pre-school education. To keep the women's sphere from becoming power-ful, society may de-value the entire enterprise, even with some men in it. Men's entrance into previously all-female groups needs to be done with full awareness of power dynamics, lest women participate in their own co-optation with men quickly "rising to the top" in leader-ship roles, or the institution loses its power and identity altogether.

Likewise, full sharing of power is thwarted when, rather than rejoicing about equal numbers of women and men in previously male-dominated institutions, men begin to abdicate. It is as if the organi-zation or profession is now tainted with too many women's voices. Men—those who have not yet had the opportunity—will need to learn the value of partnership. It is likened to Euro-Americans dismissing the transforming quality of encounter with people of other back-grounds. Even in the absence of outward racist acts, racism reigns. Even in the absence of a women's "take-over," men leave an institu-tion or organization where some women have begun to fully exercise power. It is not that the newly liberated want men—or whites—to leave. The result of getting rid of those who are newly claiming power or of abdication by the formerly all-powerful is a return to the first stage of oppression and the power cycle starts all over, just in a dif-ferent way.

However, just as women are learning how to not let themselves be ignored, trivialized, ridiculed, or eliminated, men who have seen new liberating ways of sharing power have an obligation for advocacy. They may be tempted or goaded to revert to patriarchal gamesmanship. But, freed in Christ from such internal or external threat, they can speak a prophetic word. Likewise women can show appreciation for transformation they have seen in men. Together we need to continue to uphold one another.

We may be much further along the way toward full partnership than many church communities realize. But we still have work to do. We have glimpsed alternatives to the old ordering. We have experienced shared power and real partnership. God is transforming the church and the world. To believe we are created for interdependence, to radically examine the systemic problems can open the way for redemptive possibilities, for the grace of reconciliation, new life, and Spirit-filled empowerment for ourselves, each other, and for transformational, collaborative ministerial leadership.

o o o o o o o o o o o o o o o o o o o

Personal Reflection

1. How have you experienced women exercising power? Men?
2. How do *you* exercise power? How does that change in your different roles, e.g., when you serve as a leader or when you are following someone else's leadership?
3. Reflect on some examples of leaders whom you believe have exercised power wisely and justly (examples in history, globally, or in your own context). Reflect on, or write about these leaders who share power well.

Group Conversation

1. How have you experienced oppression? As a man? As a woman? How are you oppressed? How are you an oppressor? Listen carefully, trying not to be accusatory, or defensive.
2. Theologically, systemic sin is frequently manifest in strategic oppression of entire groups of people because of their gender, race, or ethnicity. What are some blatant or subtle examples in your context? Globally?

3. Share a brief story of ineffective, misguided, or abusive leadership you have experienced. Listen carefully to each other. Tell some of your stories of leaders who share power well.[12]

Spiritual Practice

1. Pray for the power of the Spirit to transform one relationship you are now in, whether as oppressed or oppressor. Consider a new vision of shared power.
2. Pray for strength to act on that vision and to share it with another.

Transforming Action

1. Develop a strategy to work towards change in an ecclesial institution of which you are a part.
2. What are the differences if you are inside or outside the power structure?
3. With whom would you work? Where do you start? What are some realistic steps you can take—together!?

Integrity
Tested
section three

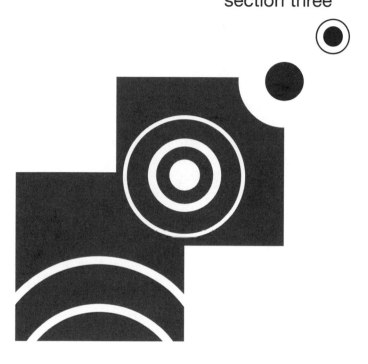

THE SPIRITUAL LIFE IS INDISPENSABLE for transforming leaders. Maintaining boundaries and cultivating classical spiritual disciplines provides a center for leadership in the midst of complex currents that can unsettle leaders and communities. Integrity requires navigating relationships amid the dynamics of the life-giving relationships of admiration, affection, and respect. Respect is central to professional ethics. Furthermore, ethical leadership is demonstrated through the stewardship of confidentiality, collegial relationships, and finances in the everyday work of ministry. Given all the responsibilities faced by leaders, tremendous stress can emerge in a time-urgent, multi-tasking society. Our very concepts of time need to be transformed.

Stewardship of Life:
Spiritual Practices
for Sustainable Ministry

chapter
nine

FOR THOSE CALLED TO PUBLIC ministry, one of the deepest sources of joy is the opportunity to enter into life-giving relationships with God's people. This is at the heart of transforming leadership. What a profound privilege to be invited into people's lives exactly at times of celebration and crisis! What a privilege to be able to minister when a new child is born, at a wedding, or during times of anniversary remembrance! What a privilege to be invited into people's lives when they suffer loss and grief, struggle with an addiction, or face anxiety and depression! Where trust has been established as the foundation of ministry, transforming leaders will discover marvelous opportunities to contribute to human health and flourishing. One of the most satisfying aspects of ministry is the ready access into people's lives when they are most vulnerable and thereby open to the Spirit's presence.

Yet, these times of privileged access are simultaneously the very occasions that require conscientiousness and vigilance on the part of the minister. Integrity may be tested in many ways. On the one hand, the demands of ministry place extraordinary stress on the minister as caregiver. Insofar as the minister is a finite human being, there is the need for times of re-creation and renewal as a regular part of the rhythm of life. Such times do not occur by happenstance. Rather, the minister needs to take responsibility for the stewardship of his or her life, treating it as a precious and finite resource that must be handled with care. On the other hand, such times of vulnerability require the careful and deliberate establishment of professional boundaries to guarantee clarity of role and purpose on the part of the minister. Too often where clear boundaries have not been observed, and the result can be misunderstanding, at the very least, and devastating harm in the most tragic cases. This chapter begins by stressing the need for transforming leaders to be stewards of their lives by attending to "family" (not only biological relations but all those who have become familial by close association), the health of their own souls, and the development of an intentional support groups beyond the congregation. It concludes with exploring some of the delicate boundaries that ministers must learn to negotiate. Stewardship of one's own life and observing boundaries are both essential to transforming leadership.

Self-Care As Stewardship of One's Own Life

The person called to ministry, either as pastor or diaconal minister, needs to grasp how this is *a call to service in a public office.* Unlike occupations where one punches a time clock, or has clear distinctions between when one is "on" or "off" duty, there is a way in which the minister is always on duty, regardless of the time of day or place of meeting. This places a burden on the shoulders of the minister (and often also on family members!) that seems both weighty and unavoidable. Depending on the size of the community where one serves, one can seemingly never escape from publicly representing not only the church but also the things of God! The minister is a public figure, not only in the congregation and among church members, but in the surrounding community—at the grocery, the bank, or the high school football game.

People pay attention to the demeanor and behavior of ministers and hold them to a higher standard. Insofar as the aura of the minister also casts a shadow of expectations on family members—spouse or children—the burden of the office can be heavy. While the public character of the office opens many unanticipated opportunities for ministry among people beyond the life of the congregation, the burden of the office can be relentless. How should the minister think about establishing and navigating the necessary boundary between one's public ministry and one's personal space?

There is much talk these days about "self-care." There has been a burgeoning literature on this subject, also directed at those who work for the church.[1] The themes of "workaholism" and burnout have become familiar. It is all too evident that pastors, diaconal ministers, and other church professionals are vulnerable to these maladies. Whenever our own self-worth becomes dependent upon the practice of ministry—even more, our success in ministry—we are in danger of falling into dangerous patterns of overwork. Those who enter into church vocations may be particularly susceptible to these patterns in their desire to "do something helpful." The problem is that the needs of the world, even the needs of people in a particular congregation, are infinite. If we measure our worth by how much we are needed in helping others with their needs, there will be no end to our workload. Recall the scene from the film *Bruce Almighty* where the divine Bruce is overwhelmed with email cries for help!

While the intention of the self-care movement is very salutary, the description of this very activity as "self-care" seems problematic. Self-care as a term sounds very self-indulgent, even selfish. It does not resonate positively with the ministry as a servant vocation. Far more accurate and preferable is to describe the need to care for one's own life and well-being as a form of stewardship. My life and your life are finite resources that require careful and caring stewardship, if they are to be available for service to others in the most beneficial way. Many questions emerge: If I am not a good steward of my life in relationship to the Word of God, how will I offer sustenance to others from the Word? If I am not a good steward of my emotional and social life, I will become resentful and harsh in ways that undermine the life of the community. If I am not a good steward of my physical life, I will become subject to illness and exhaustion that finally detract from my ability to minister to others. When talking about self-care, we do better to think about it in terms of the stewardship of one's own finite life. Such stewardship is a *sine qua non* for transforming leadership.

How does one begin to manage the stewardship of one's own life? First, one must take seriously the degree of freedom that ministers have over their daily schedules. Most ministers have a great deal of freedom in setting their own schedules, far more freedom than most other working people. The primary responsibility for overwork and exhaustion belongs to the minister who fails to pay attention to all aspects of one's health, which includes the emotional, social, intellectual, vocational, physical, and spiritual dimensions (see chapter 12). The Wholeness Wheel (Figure 3) connects all aspects of personal health and well-being under spiritual well-being.

The transforming leader needs to attend to all of these dimensions of spiritual well-being—the emotional, social, intellectual, vocational, and physical dimensions—in order to lead renewal and change in a congregation and in the lives of individuals. Three aspects of one's personal life need proactive attention in order to steward one's life wisely: care for family, care for one's soul, and nurturing a community of support beyond the congregation.

The Wholeness Wheel

Figure 3: The Wholeness Wheel

Copyright 1997 InterLutheran Coordinating Committee on Minsterial Health and Wellness of the Evangelical Lutheran Church in America and The Lutheran Church—Missouri Synod.

1. Care for Family.

All ministers are members of a "family." We use this term in a broad way. For those who are single, "family" may mean family of origin or extended family. It may be a close network of friends, either locally or at some distance. This "family," consisting of select trusted friendships, sustains us throughout a lifetime. These relationships are not limited just to the current location of service. Family can, of course, mean spouse. It can mean children, small or grown and living on their own. It can mean parents and other relatives. Families and our relationships with them change over time.

Some families live together in close proximity. Other families live dispersed, with members at a considerable distance from one another, often due to the contingencies of the call process. In either case, the care of and for family is vital for ministerial well-being. Family is the primary social unit in which each of us has been formed. Families may be the most wonderful or the most difficult place to live—often both at the same time. The quality of relationships among family members contributes much to one's own well-being or state of dis-ease. High priority must be given to nurturing these formative and supportive relationships. For those who live at some distance, regular contact by cell phone and other electronic media is essential. Scheduling days off and vacation time to spend time together takes careful planning. The danger of isolation and loneliness for any one of us—particularly for those who live alone—is high.

For those who live in a local family unit, the most precious commodity to be shared with one another is time. The minister needs to set aside hours of the day for quality interaction with members of one's family and supportive friendships. One of the greatest assets of the minister's vocation is the ability to schedule one's own days. Often, it is possible to schedule time according to the activities of other family members. Planning ahead to set aside particular dates and times is imperative.

Throughout the centuries, those called and set apart by the church for ministry had a variety of expectations and restrictions placed on them. For example, until recent decades deaconesses usually could not marry. Some chose to live in deaconess communities. Today there are many diaconal communities across the globe. Commitment to community provides lifelong support and calls for lifelong mutual accountability. Members of the community serve in all sorts of ministries and locations. They tend relationships in their community and among immediate and extended family.

In regard to clergy, only in the last generation or so have the expectations placed on the pastor's spouse ("wife" was the word) gradually begun to change.[2] Years ago men who attended seminary (when men only were allowed) were expected not to be married as students, but they suddenly needed to be married when working as pastor in the parish. At that time, the pastor's wife had a specific role. The old stereotype of the "pastor's wife" as assistant pastor is in many places a thing of the past, although echoes may remain. In recent decades, the role of the "pastor's husband" has emerged and is less defined. In spite of that, or perhaps in part because of it, men married to women clergy are finding their own ways to define themselves and to serve.

Spouses of both genders frequently hold their own full-time jobs with all the responsibilities that go along with that. The life of a minister's family has grown increasingly complex. When ministers are married to each other, there is the joy of shared profession but also the complication of multiple roles, ministry sites, and expectations. All of these changes have in many ways increased both the freedom and the stress on ministers' families, which results in an urgency for intentional stewardship of family life. Ministry remains a very stressful vocation, as the minister commonly deals with rising expectations and decreasing status.

The importance of intentional family care has never been greater. Multiple issues related to family emerge, including the issue of being a "trailing spouse," economic strains, worries about health care for parents living across the country, and the complicated question of who will be pastor to the pastor's family. Ministers' families need interaction with those who can provide unconditional support and wise counsel. Denominational leaders, such as bishops, seldom have the time to provide ongoing pastoral care. Furthermore, relationships with bishops can be complicated by issues of authority and power. Perhaps the best solution is to covenant with a trusted pastor colleague who would pledge to interact with one's family in a pastoral way. In addition to this, it may be very important to develop relationships with counselors who can provide therapy both for those who minister and all those who belong to the constellation of family as they deal with challenging issues. Emotional and mental disease deserve the same kind of healing treatment as the physical ailments for which we go to the pediatrician or family practitioner.

2. Care for One's Soul.

The recent and intense interest in "spirituality" has challenged the church to reexamine its fundamental core. Given the proliferation of Christian churches and other religious communities in our society, how could spiritual "seeking" have become such a widespread cultural phenomenon? What has been missing from people's lives, so that books and self-help programs in the area of spirituality have become so prevalent? As we have noted, the Christian conviction, articulated once so eloquently by St. Augustine, is that "you [God] have made us for yourself, and our heart is restless until it rests in you."[3] Human beings are created for life-giving relationship with God, and human life is diminished until this relationship with God is addressed. Human beings are spiritually hungry, so hungry that they attempt to feed their souls not only with nutritious food but also with spiritual junk food.

If those engaged in ministry are to be physicians for the souls of other people, it is urgently necessary that ministers engage in life-giving spiritual practices that care for their own souls.[4] Their experience with a wide range of spiritual disciplines not only provides nurture for their own inner life, but also broadens the range of spiritual experiences that can be offered as a resource to others. Ministers who are called as servants of the Word of God must devote themselves to lives of prayer and study (see chapter 7). Interest in spirituality in recent years has led to the retrieval of many ancient spiritual disciplines that are proving themselves valuable for mediating the presence of God among us. Some of these spiritual disciplines include spiritual direction, contemplative prayer, centering prayer, *lectio divina* (spiritual reading), journaling, meditation, and fasting.[5]

Many pastors, for example, have begun to engage in spiritual direction with qualified spiritual directors. (In the ELCA, spiritual direction is required for formation of diaconal ministers.) It is a requirement of most diaconal communities. Sabbaticals, retreats, celebrations, and commemorations are times for refreshment and renewal. These must be scheduled to punctuate the rhythm of life. As leaders of spiritual communities, pastors have an ethical obligation to keep their own spiritual lives in order. While it would be legalistic to dictate which spiritual practices need to be in place in the life of the minister, devotion to some aspect of the spiritual disciplines needs to be an essential part of the vocation. While this chapter cannot provide an extensive description of matters related to spiritual disciplines, many resources for more full development of the spiritual life are readily available.[6]

Care for the soul also entails a readiness to engage in personal growth through the assistance of a qualified counselor or therapist. One would expect ministers to be capable and ready to refer people in need to an appropriate professional in mental and emotional health. Yet there remains stigma and shame that sometimes prevents ministers themselves from seeking such help.[7] The journey of life is filled with deep mystery, both within and without. One of the deepest mysteries of all is self-understanding. So many things about our own lives are hidden from our own eyes. Family of origin issues (see chapter 14) can remain a lifelong challenge to wise and constructive ministry. Destructive secrets can take a toll on the life of the minister and need resolution. Virtually every human being would benefit from occasional visits to a counselor or therapist; so also the minister. The damage done to self and others is multiplied when the minister resists engaging in routine mental and emotional health.

3. Nurture a Community of Support Beyond the Congregation.

As emotionally close as one might become to certain members of one's congregation, there remain boundaries that need to be observed. One can never confide all of one's struggles and fears to even the most trusted members of a congregation out of respect for their need to have a minister. There are certain confidences that, once shared, might make it difficult for those members to be able to relate to the minister in a pastoral way. Furthermore, there is the perpetual danger of showing favoritism to an "inner circle" in relationship to other church members who stand outside that circle. While different ministers may choose to negotiate this boundary between pastoral ministry and friendship in different ways, the need for a community of support beyond the congregation should be clear.[8]

It is vital for emotional and social well-being for transforming leaders to have a circle of care beyond the faith communities where they are called to serve. We need personal affirmations that derive from our "being" rather than our "doing." We need arenas where we are able to be a "self" rather than being inextricably tied to our public ministry role. We need outlets where we are able to process our emotions in a trusted environment (yet without betraying confidences). We need a place of refuge that is best found among those to whom we relate mutually as friends.

Upon entering into a new ministry setting, one cannot assume that a community of support will simply appear on the scene. Developing a community of support requires intentionality on the part of the minister and may itself be hard work. The obligation to make friendships and nurture a community of support belongs to each us, even when we are the new person in a new setting. Others will already have their own familiar circles and patterns of relating. One truly must initiate friendships in order to have friendships.

Frequently, the most cherished friendships may develop with other colleagues in ministry. Out of text studies, ministerial alliances, and denominational gatherings, relationships with colleagues can grow into deep friendships. One should be open to the possibility that these friendships might be with ministers from church traditions other than just one's own. Especially in smaller communities, some of the most life-giving relationships are ecumenical relationships with colleagues from other denominations. One's community of support might also include other professional people who are new to a local community. Often those who are in "helping" professions, like social workers, teachers, or medical staff, share many of the same joys and frustrations of laboring closely with other people in their daily work and will have empathy for the work of ministry. The crucial point is that you must take initiative in developing such friendships that can be vitally necessary for surviving the pressures of parish ministry.

Who Are the People in Your Circle of Support?

God uses many people in a variety of roles to care for, challenge, nourish, and invigorate us for a transformational spiritual life. The following list underscores the point that we need multiple people in our circle of support. Having just one person in our life upon whom we depend to fill all our needs simply will not work. To rely on a single support person—including one's spouse—places an undo and unsustainable burden on that person. Moreover, such a pattern is neither healthy nor sufficient for our own health. With this in mind, who do you have in your life that serves your well-being in the following roles?

Mentor: A person you regard as wise and who, in turn, sees promise in you. A truly mentoring relationship cannot be merely assigned (although it could begin that way), but is mutually chosen.

Pastor/Diaconal Minister: A person who proclaims to *you* the Word of God, particularly if *you* are a pastor or diaconal minister. Leaders need opportunities to worship while not leading, to receive the sacraments, to grow in the Word, and to receive *diakonia (service)*.

Spiritual Director: A person who will pray with you and who will guide you in your own life of supplication, intercession, praise, and thanksgiving. Transforming leaders need multiple ways to dig deep into the well of refreshing spiritual waters.

Colleagues: People with whom to work, co-labor, and share leadership. Even if you are in a position of solo leadership, you can seek out colleagues in neighboring churches, church bodies, or community professions.

Companion/Intimate Friend: A person you deeply trust, who is willing and able to hear your joys and pains, who will listen to the profound and to the mundane, and who asks questions and challenges you to think, even while offering steadfast acceptance.

Extended Support Circle: People with whom to laugh, relax, and do fun things. Friends may be nearby or a phone call away. To be truly at ease and for the sake of role clarity, leaders need to sustain a community of support beyond the place where they lead.

Family: This may mean spouse, children, parents, siblings, communal order, or extended relationships. You are part of a family by birth and by choice. These relationships nourish us and place responsibilities, and sometimes burdens, on us. They share with us each chapter of our lives.

Confessor: A person who can hear our private confession. Leaders need a regular time to be truly open about their own sins. A confessor is a person who provides complete confidentiality and offers admonition, comfort, conversation, and absolution.

Counselor: A person trained to help you deal with issues that arise from being in stressful situations as well as long-standing personal issues. A professional counselor can provide help not only during a time of crisis but at regular check-in times.

Medical Doctor: A person with medical expertise who cares about and serves our physical and emotional health.

Exercise Partners: Persons with whom one cares for one's physical health through regular exercise. These are people with whom you covenant to hold you accountable for diet, sleep, and physical fitness.

As stewards of our own precious and finite lives, we need to perform a regular audit of the human resources available to us and to check whether we are living in healthy relationships with those who can help sustain us for healthy living. Only by doing so will we also be able to thrive in ministry, especially over the long haul.

Honoring Boundaries

Education about boundaries in ministry has become urgently necessary.[9] Chiefly due to the prevalence of clergy sexual abuse, clarity about sexual boundaries has become a basic and fundamental point of instruction for pastors and those engaging in pastoral ministry. Because ministers have access to persons in situations of acute vulnerability and because ministers *always* bear the burden of responsibility to ensure that no harm is done, the maintenance of strict sexual boundaries is entirely the ethical obligation of those in professional ministry.[10] In the relationship between a pastor and parishioner, the power relation is never equal.[11] Therefore the burden for honoring sexual boundaries belongs always to the minister. Where a violation of the sexual boundary occurs, it is always the fault of the person in ministry.

While it is also true that men occasionally have been victims of sexual abuse and that women and other men have been predators, the vast majority of predators are men and their victims women. In reflecting on years of teaching on the topic of sexual boundaries, one phenomenon has been very striking. Men and women respond dramatically differently to the theme. The discussion of sexual boundaries for men very soon raises the question about the possibility of being falsely accused. Even though such instances are rare, men live with the fear that words, gestures, or touch could be misinterpreted as violations of the sexual boundary. The fear of false accusation is existentially very acute for men in ministry. The response of women, however, is quite different. For women the reality of becoming the victim of harmful sexual advances is immediate. Many women have already been the victims of men who have violated sexual boundaries, including many women who have had this experience in their role as ministers.

The contrast between these experiences leads to two very distinct mindsets about sexual boundaries. Both genders approach the subject in fear and trembling, but for quite distinct reasons: men out of fear of false accusation, women out of fear of becoming a real victim. As the church continues to strive to become a community of women and men in mutual ministry, this dynamic requires far more attention and discussion as education about boundaries continues.

How does one monitor oneself in relation to sexual boundaries? There are several considerations.[12] First, know thyself! Recognize your own finitude and human neediness. Where there are issues that require professional attention, it is important to enter into therapy. Second, engage in conscientious stewardship of your own life. Already this chapter has provided much guidance on this topic. Both married and single people have sexual needs that require appropriate care. Married persons need to attend to marital health and single persons to the danger of isolation. Third, know the law! It is important to know both the ethical expectations of the church and the legal requirements of the state. One must be clear that the consequence for violating sexual boundaries are very severe. The church, recognizing that this is a matter primarily of justice and not forgiveness, functions with a virtual "no tolerance" policy. The law is a gift for curbing our temptation into sinning. Fourth, enter into a covenant with trusted colleagues with whom we can engage in honest self-evaluation and mutual critique. Colleagues and others in our circle of support who can tell us when we need to attend to our own well-being or see a therapist are a true gift from God.

Fifth, avoid compromising situations. Ministry is a vocation that will never be free of all risks, but one can avoid putting oneself in a compromising situation. For example, know the limits of one's own professional competence in counseling situations and be ready to refer in such cases. Also, meet with church members (especially of the opposite gender) as much as possible in structured environment: in a church office (either the door open or a window that makes visible the parties inside), at times of the day when a church secretary is in the building who knows about the appointment, in the church sanctuary, or in a public setting such as a restaurant. Certainly, there are times when ministry is necessary in less structured settings, but practice vigilance regarding whether a particular meeting is in accord with "normally accepted practice." It may be very useful to publish for congregational knowledge a set of guidelines for meeting with the pastor. Such procedures help to establish an ethic for pastoral counseling relationships. One's ethic of sexual boundaries also necessitates great intentionality about the use of touch in pastoral ministry. While the absence of all touch would be a diminishment of pastoral care, one has to be circumspect that touch is understood and interpreted by all parties as appropriate. All demonstrations of affection need to be undergirded with respect (see chapter 10). *How* one hugs or holds hands in pastoral care makes a difference. Asking permission beforehand can be a healthy practice. Refraining from touch in certain situations may be the best decision.

Lastly, it is wise to avoid "dual relationships" in ministry. This means that one's primary relationship with members of the church is the relationship of pastor to member. This is why friendships of full mutuality with congregational members can be problematic. When the boundary shifts to a level of mutuality it will be difficult for the minister to maintain his/her professional role.

These are but a few guidelines for honoring sexual boundaries. This chapter has already made reference to a number of other important boundaries necessary in ministerial practice: the boundary between one's public ministry and one's personal life, the boundary between a community of support outside the congregation and the relationships with members of one's congregation, the boundary between the normal struggles of human life and the need to visit with a counselor or therapist. The following chart (Figure 4) depicts several of the critical boundary issues faced by those in public ministry.

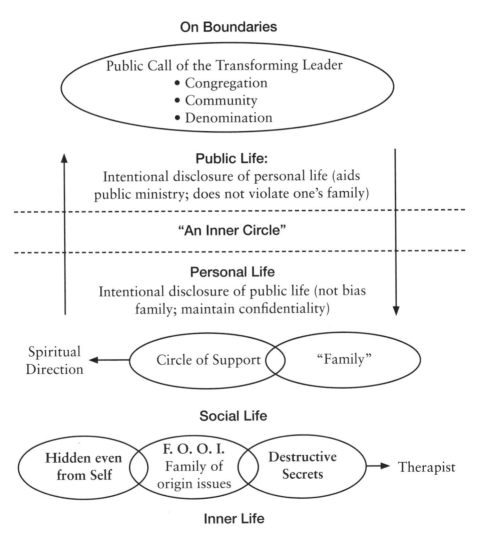

Figure 4: On Boundaries

A final boundary consideration involves the movement between the minister's public ministry and the realm of personal life. This boundary involves what one discloses from one's personal life in the arena of public ministry, on the one hand, and what one brings home out of public ministry into the realm of personal life, on the other. In disclosing information about one's personal life (family and friends), it is imperative that one do serious reflection about whether such a disclosure is actually serving to enhance one's ministry to others, or whether one is making such a disclosure out of some unexamined personal need. It is a useful practice to seek permission from those persons who are the subject of such disclosures, especially family members, to make sure that the stories shared are not in some way inappropriate. Surely, ministry would be impoverished if the minister makes no personal disclosures about his/her life. But it is very important that such disclosures never be at someone else's expense.

In a parallel way, great intentionality is required in deciding what information should be brought into the personal realm out of public ministry. Immediately there are issues of confidentiality at stake in bringing into the personal realm matters that have been shared in the confident trust that they will not be divulged. (Chapter 11 will take up the theme of confidentiality at greater length.) But there is also the crucial matter of not bringing home all of the "garbage" from church in such a way that it poisons the participation of one's family in the life of the congregation. Ministers do well to structure their passage from work to home in such a way that they are able to leave behind their frustrations and conflicts to a degree that they do not set the agenda for one's life at home.

This chapter has explored the importance of stewardship of one's own life as a prerequisite for transforming ministry.[13] Only the minister who engages in vital spiritual practices and who honors complex boundaries is free to engage fully in the life-giving relationships with others that characterize transforming leadership. We continue our exploration of healthy relationships in the next chapter where we look at admiration, affection, and respect.

○ ○

Personal Reflections

1. How are you doing in the stewardship of your own life? What is going well and what needs to be changed?
2. Which spiritual disciplines most nourish your soul? How has this changed over the years?
3. Which of the classical spiritual disciplines that you have not yet tried appeals to you? How could you try this particular discipline?

Group Conversation

1. Have each member of the group share a favorite spiritual practice. Besides describing it, you might lead one another in that practice. What can you learn from one another?
2. Discussion in the church about boundaries usually begins with clarity about sexual boundaries. What are some of the other boundary issues that you consider important which might cause difficulties for ministerial leaders?

Spiritual Practice

Thank God for the people who are in your "Circle of Support" (pages 112–113). Find some tangible way of expressing thanks to them for what they mean to you.

Transforming Action

Are there roles on the "Circle of Support" list that are missing from your life that might help strengthen your spiritual well-being? What people could you ask to play that role for you? Initiate contact with them and explore what this might mean?

Relational Ethics: Admiration, Affection, and Respect

THE KEYNOTE SPEAKER AT OUR city's Martin Luther King, Jr. Day breakfast said, "All of us need four hugs a day in order to live, eight to be sustained, and sixteen to flourish." She was right. She went on, "We hear a lot about sexual harassment. That's very important. But we do not hear enough about love."[1]

Love has the power to transform. God intends us each day to be surrounded by our Creator's sustaining love, Christ's redemptive love, and Spirit-filled love that opens us to give and to receive ministry in transformed relationships. Church bodies are now giving attention to knowing, respecting, and keeping boundaries (see chapter 9). Doing something about sexual abuse was centuries overdue.[2] Having become more aware, where are we now? Abuse is an issue of power; it comes from a sense of entitlement. Even though much has been written, and many workshops given, people are still offending, people are still hurting, and we are still learning. We can love people only if we let go of our obsessions with power and domination.[3]

Both men and women are saying, "I have to be so careful. I try not to touch anyone—anywhere." How do we live in ways that respect boundaries and yet express affection? These are genuine concerns, particularly as we live together as women and men in a community—the church—where we are on the way toward (notice we did not say "have arrived") more transforming relationships?

We need to love and be loved.[4] We are sexual beings who relate to one another as sexual beings. We are created to be gift and joy to one another, not to treat each other as toys or as pawns in a power play. In our doubts, fears, and obsessions, we distort and betray. As people transformed through the cross, we are called to renewed relationships of responsibility and mutual accountability. Because we each need admiration, affection, and respect, we need to give these to others.

One can read this chapter on many levels. One could think about and reflect on relationships on a staff or in a team ministry or between leaders in different congregations. One could also reflect on relationships with members of the faith community one serves and on personal relationships with colleagues, intimate friends, and members of one's family, (including spouse, parents, and children). All of these people are gifts from God,[5] and also people whom we hurt and who hurt us. This book is about leadership in relationship. Ideas in this chapter may resonate with various relationships in different ways. The goal is joy not pain, life not death.

One could look for a lifetime for that perfect working relationship, that perfect friendship, or that perfect mate or companion.[6] The challenge is to figure out how to regard the people in our lives now, how to collaborate in current working relationships, and how to foster life-giving friendships and commitments. In this chapter we explore three dimensions of regarding one another: "admiration," "affection," and "respect." We realize, of course, that human relationships are complex, and they certainly cannot be discussed in those terms alone. However, by exploring the various combinations of these three words, we can begin to understand the complexity of our relationships and to work with realistic expectations. For example, we can respect a colleague but not necessarily admire him or her. Or, we can admire someone without necessarily having affection for him or her. To have affection for someone without respecting him or her causes particular problems. In thinking about each of these words and their combinations, role and relationship clarity are essential.

What do healthy ethical relationships look like? The issue is not just, "What am I allowed to do and prohibited from doing?" Nor is it simply a matter of "self-care" so that other people do not wear me out. The questions are about identity, role, relationship, and stewardship of self and others. God's will is to transform us from death-dealing to life-giving relationships.

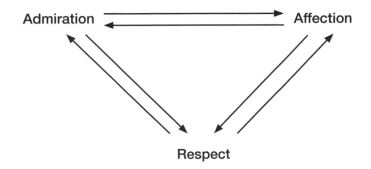

Admiration

What do you think of when you use the word *admiration*? Here we define *admiration* as "looking up to, having a high opinion of, perhaps even regarding with awe." We may admire a person's eloquence, wisdom, or appearance. We may admire their ability to relate with people easily, their quick wit, or their skill with words. What other characteristics do you admire? Whom do you admire?

Strangely, we may even admire, or at least regard with awe, negative characteristics: "I admire him for his audacity, his hubris, but I really would not want to be like that." We need to be clear whom we choose for role models, and why!

I can admire someone I know or someone I have never met, such as an historic figure. Throughout our lifetime there are many people whom we have admired. We look up to them. Short or tall they have a certain "stature" in our eyes. We appreciate them for who they are and what they represent. We may admire the courage of a person who lives in poverty as much if not more than a person who lives among wealth. Healthy admiration is a vehicle of God's grace to help us grow in virtues of the Christ-like life. Unhealthy admiration that negates our own self and gifts can be a form of idolatry.

We may be objects of people's admiration, perhaps without even knowing it. Having a need of such adulation for our own self-esteem or seeking it for egotistical power is unhealthy and fruitless. However, when we know Christ is the center of our being, people who look to us for wisdom and guidance present us with a holy calling. The light we reflect is Christ's light. Such ethical admiration can be life-giving.

One might say that "admiration" is primarily an attitude, although emotions and actions are involved. Someone I might have admired at first from a distance, I now see as pretty ordinary. Initially awestruck by someone's "self-confidence," I may now see that person's confidence as excessive to the point that it denigrates other people. We also consciously can change our attitude. A relationship can be transformed when I look at someone in a new way and try to see something about that person I can admire. The Creator God has provided admirable characteristics in abundance in diverse people. Blessed are we when we can learn from someone we admire. We are transformed. Blessed are we all when we can live, centered in Christ, in mutual admiration and thanksgiving to a gracious God.

Affection

What do you think of when you use the word *affection*? Here we define *affection* as "to have a fond or tender feeling toward another." When we feel affection for people, we enjoy working with them and simply appreciate being together. Affection can be one-way or reciprocal. It may involve attraction. Affection or attraction can become exclusive or obsessive. Affection is primarily an emotion, but it also involves attitudes and can lead to action or, when wisdom dictates, to refraining from certain actions. C. S. Lewis in his classic work, *The Four Loves,* distinguishes affection from friendship and from eros.[7] While that is helpful, for our purposes we use affection to include all three.

Because we are at all times sexual beings, affection may be or have the potential for becoming a sexual attraction. Eros is a wonderful gift in a monogamous relationship, but an inappropriate attraction can lead to endless problems and pain. We will develop feelings for certain people, but we can choose whether or not we act on those feelings. "It" does not just "happen" *to* us.

In the broader sense of the word, healthy mutual affection is life-giving. To live a life void of affection is not only lonely, but can actually make us ill. Affection can grow deeper through the years when properly nourished. However, when we believe we can find affirmation from only one certain person we are elevating that person to God's place. When I love or place my trust in that one alone, I set myself up for unrealistic expectations. I am cut off from the one God who alone is totally trustworthy and able to care for me with unconditional love.

Because affection is an emotion, we cannot decide whom we will "fall in like" with. But we can foster an attitude of openness to God's Spirit growing our affection even for a person whom we have previously disliked.[8] Affection "on purpose" can broaden our ability to appreciate—not just endure—the people who "happen to be there" in our lives of ministry and can open us to learn from people way beyond our small circle of friends.[9] We were created by God to hold each other in affection. We will experience loneliness and jealousies and misunderstandings, but God's love empowers our relationships to be guided by love. With Christ in the middle of any relationship (Christ is already there!), affection gives life and joy. When God's love transforms our neediness so that we might freely give and receive life-giving affection, the entire community is transformed.

Respect

What do you think of when you use the word *respect*? Here we define *respect* as "to regard with esteem." *Respect* is a willingness to show consideration or appreciation for someone. Genuine respect, which regards the other as one made in God's own image, is a solid basis for collaborative relationships. Respect begets respect. Respectful leadership can transform whole communities. Whom do you respect? Who do you think has respect for you? It is difficult to have respect for others when one does not have respect for oneself.

Respect is primarily an action, but it emanates from attitudes and emotions.

In the past one might have referred to respect as honoring or treating with civility. I can act honorably towards all kinds of people, respecting their person, their name, their gifts, their ideas, and their space. The call to an office of respect in the church may be accompanied by a subtle temptation—drifting into lack of respect for those whose work or status is "lower" than ours. Leaders need to exercise respect in all of their relationships. We can choose to act respectfully. We can respect people we do not like and have a good, if merely formal, relationship with them. Sometimes respect can grow into affection, even admiration.

We need love in order to thrive. Respect is also a very basic human need, perhaps even more basic. On the evening news we may hear those who have lashed out in anger say, "They didn't respect me." Some who have suffered a lack of respect may have so little self-esteem they have no voice to cry out. Respecting people helps them respect their own gifts, abilities, and roles in the community.

To be a Christian is not merely to pretend to "be respectable," of course. None of us can ever be respectable enough. Confession includes admitting our inability to earn God's respect. It is amazing that in the midst of our huge collective human disrespect for God, for God's created ones and the environment, that God not only steadfastly loves us, but respects us, entrusting us with responsibilities for mission, including care of the earth and care for the world's people.

By the power of the Spirit we can respect even those who do not respect us, without losing our own self-respect. That does not mean we should become doormats. Jesus Christ has already borne our humiliation through his birth in a less-than-respectable manger, through his ministry being dismissed, through being spit upon, and through his innocent death on a cross. Christ frees us from the domination of those who would "lord" it over us (see chapter 6); Christ frees us for powerful servanthood that begins with respect for those among whom we are called to minister.[10]

Rarely do relationships contain equal measures of admiration, affection, and respect. As we arrange these three words in different combinations, we illuminate both the problems and the possibilities of relationships in transformational leadership.

Admiration and Respect

Admiration without Respect. If we are merely admired, but not respected, as leaders we might not be acting with integrity. With the power that admiration can bring, taking advantage of people becomes a real temptation. To be admired without respect can also result in creating distance between us and others. We may be idolized rather than seen as a person with human needs. Admiration without respect hinders healthy leadership.

Coming at this combination from a different angle, we may be negatively impressed with someone's unbelievable ability to manipulate a group, to conceal the truth, to wield power, or even to dominate a whole congregation. We do not respect such behavior, but the problem is how to deal with such manipulation. People seem only too willing to be taken in by this kind of leadership. We may fear that no one will believe us if we say the emperor has no clothes. Our willingness to defy may lead to our own demise. Disrespectful, abusive, negatively "admired" power needs to be stopped. We need to seek good counsel and support and then use a clear, direct strategy to change the situation.

Respect without Admiration. On the other hand, respect without admiration can be stale. Congregations may sag in apathy when they and their leaders merely "respectfully" exist together. Some leadership manuals may suggest the need to encourage "change," or even, "shaking things up a little." But the stale congregation has deeper problems that *mere* change will not cure. What may be missing is a sense of mutual admiration, of really being able to see and appreciate one another, individually and as a community. As you think about your own congregation, do people really appreciate and admire each other in joy?

Respect without some level of admiration soon is no longer even respect. Congregation members may take for granted they are needed to warm the pew and give their money, but are they really needed? Even the most self-assured person needs to be verbally valued. "Am I of worth?" they ask themselves. That question is quickly coupled with, "Is it worth it?" We deteriorate into formalities, then into blame and self-negation. We human beings will do that to ourselves and to others if we do not intentionally foster admiration.

Admiration with Respect and Respect with Admiration. When we respect those whom we admire and respect ourselves as well, we will not unnecessarily defer to power. Nor will we allow ourselves to be admired for our office and disrespected as a person. People may want our time and our attention, our being a special person in their life, because we represent the holy. We represent a place where they can lay all their troubles and pain. They may not realize that they are not respecting our time or our person. We can set limits by saying, "These are the times and the ways you can reach me." In this way we help them discern what is and is not an emergency. We can help people learn how to respect us.

We minister, but we are not omniscient ("I need you to tell me when your father has gone to the hospital"), omnipotent ("I am very willing to help, but I can't solve all the problems in your marriage, church council, etc."), omni-present, ("I will be at the church picnic, but after I make a hospital visit."). What seems like bad news to some people ("I am not God") is really good news: *God* is God. Respectful admiration can lead to healthy shared leadership.

It is hard to work with someone we do not admire. But we can! Respect is the key. Admiration can follow. Perhaps our image of admiration is too idealized. Think of a person from your past whom you admired. What were some characteristics of this person? Did you want to claim some of those qualities for yourself? Have you? But we also have grown in our own formation, self-identity, and confidence. We have the opportunity to purposely broaden the range of people whom we respect and admire. We can appreciate people with all sorts of gifts, and that neither adds to nor detracts from our own identity. To admire someone, whoever they are, is a gift in itself.

A faith community can participate in its own transformation (see chapter 13 on asset-based ministry). There are many simple activities that up-build, support, and strengthen us for ministry (see "Transforming Action" at the end of the chapter). Seeking to intentionally increase the action of respect and the attitude of admiration is not just pretended piety or merely "being nice." In a society that frames nearly every encounter as a competition, is riddled with violence, and spikes the ratings of TV shows where people are not just rude, but mean, respect with admiration may seem strange, even counter-cultural. But grounded in God true respect and mutual admiration helps transform community.

Affection and Admiration

Admiration without Affection. Recall a relationship with a person whom you admired, but did not feel particularly close to. You were separated by role, status, or age. Yet they were role models. We learn simply by watching how people handle challenge, struggle, and success. Whether they like—or even know—us is not an issue. A danger is feeling somewhat insignificant compared to the admired one. Admiration for others can serve us well, especially if we appreciate ourselves and who we are becoming. We need to recognize this relationship for what it is and for what it is not, so we will not be disappointed. This person is not a close friend and does not need to be.

A warning: admiration without affection may mean competition rears its ugly head. I may admire someone's ability to the point of being envious of his or her gifts, or being jealous that they will take some attention away from me. In a competitive society, relationships are framed in terms of winners and losers.[11] Ministry is not a competitive sport.

Affection without Admiration. We may feel affection for someone we do not necessarily admire. This may happen when we see the needs of people and are moved to tenderly care about them. We need to be careful that such feelings are not mere pity, for none of us as leaders is in such a high position as to look down upon those who are poor or in suffering. Rather, real feelings of empathy help us identify with the thoughts and feelings of another. Even so, we need to guard against saying "I know," when we really do not, because that may be the highest form of arrogance.

A very different way of thinking about affection that does not necessarily involve the richness of admiration is a friendship that is light. Such a relationship can be healthy, fulfilling, and fun. People living in Christian community need to be able to have fun with one another. Affection has its own rewards.

Affection with Admiration and Admiration with Affection. Yet, in the examples in the two preceding paragraphs, are not *both* admiration and affection needed? When we are feeling affection for people and attempt to really understand them, we will begin to admire their courage or their steadfastness. This is different from mere pity, which, in the end, leaves people feeling neither loved nor admired. With admiration, the emotion of affection takes on flesh in real care, and in our being present, really present, with people, listening with all the energy we have. There is a gentle strength to our ministry, indeed to our leadership. Whatever the ministry setting, the primary advice to leaders is, "Love the people." Such deep caring affection can grow into admiration. Transformation!

Likewise, the mutual affection of friendship will not grow or deepen, or perhaps even last, without the ingredient of admiration. Transformed and transforming leaders will need the joy of sustainable friendships that up-build one another in love.

Blessed is the relationship with both.[12] Sometimes friends themselves describe their relationship as a "mutual admiration club." Such a relationship feels wonderful and it is indeed a gift. Such friends can lead each other through difficult times and share times of celebration. Such a relationship, if truly healthy, will lead not inward to exclusivity, but outward towards being able to love those we serve even more effectively.

Admiration with affection may be a description of a good mentoring relationship. Mentors are different from role models. At its best the mentoring relationship is chosen—mutually chosen. The mentor sees something in us, some promise, which may include genuine affection--with integrity. Likewise, we recognize in the mentor, not just knowledge, but wisdom. We know and are known. A good mentor can help us move through a transformative time in our lives.

There is a life span to mentoring relationships, based on the fact that both mentor and mentee are constantly changing. If the relationship is marked with integrity, the affect on a person's life is indelible. Care is necessary so that the relationship is not betrayed nor mistaken for something it is not, and so that the mentor does not try to shape the person in his or her own image (another form of idolatry). The mentoring relationship can grow and mature into a long-standing friendship, whether maintained weekly or yearly. Those in such a relationship can usually pick up the conversation right where they left off. The friendship is deeper and the admiration now more clearly mutual.

Respect and Affection

Respect without Affection. When we begin with respect we have the basis for collegial, collaborative relationships. But relationships that lack affection may be cold. Even the appearance of indifference hinders ministry. The faith community without the nurturance of affection will have a difficult time growing into a caring community.

Another facet to consider: A leader may say, "I have respect for the people whom I am serving, but because of their lack of affection toward me, I am not nurtured." We do not receive any literal or figurative hugs. Depleted, we may conclude we are neither loved nor respected. Depending upon our personality type, we may become more and more secluded, thereby cutting ourselves off from potential affection. Or, in need of someone—anyone—to talk to we may engage in unhelpful self-disclosure with a shut-in, youth, or counselee, forgetting the appropriate role we are to play in that ministerial relationship. People who are shut-in appreciate our visit and seemingly offer unambiguous affection. But beware. When we hear ourselves talking more about ourselves than listening, this should be a sign to us that we cannot use professional relationships as a substitute for intimacy, or as the only place to have our spirituality refueled. (Refer again to the "Circle of Support" in chapter 9). In a counseling situation we may empathize because we have had a similar problem, but we are not caring about that person when we spend the time revealing everything about ourselves. We could indicate we really *do* know what they are going through, but in a more opaque way.

Affection without Respect. This combination is the most dangerous. When a person feels attracted toward another but does not respect that person, one is objectifying him or her to gratify one's own needs. Churches need boundaries, and many have initiated and now enforce guidelines for maintaining such boundaries. The ELCA uses "Visions and Expectations" for its rostered leaders and for those preparing for public leadership in the church.[13] In Martin Luther's terms this is the "first use of the law," God's law as curb.

Boundaries are necessary because when seeking our own self-gratification we will be very capable of self-deception, such as:

- "This will not happen to me." (Truth: Inappropriate sexual behavior does not just passively "happen to us.")

we think we deserve admira...

- "I will not be the object of anyone's affection," e.g. I am too old, too young, too unattractive, too fat, too thin, etc. (Reality: Attraction is no respecter of body type or age, but is related to people's need for affection.)
- "I won't break any rules. I will not have sex with anyone." (Truth: Emotional exploitation itself is damaging. Leaders are in positions of power; therefore, they will be—and should be—held responsible.)

Congregations, seeing leaders as holy persons, also engage in self-deception:

- "The pastor is a holy person; therefore, nothing sexual will happen." (Reality: Clergy are sexual beings. Simply being a caring, listening "holy person" can contribute to attraction.)
- "Some people are more 'safe' than others, especially heterosexual married men." (Reality: Most sexual misconduct in the church is committed by heterosexual married men.)

When leaders have engaged in inappropriate acts of affection without respect, afterwards they may try to find ways to excuse or justify themselves:

- "It was inevitable; we are sexual beings." (Truth: We are sexual beings, but no action is inevitable.)
- "I was merely helping; sexuality was not the main issue." (Truth: "Helping" is not an excuse for using some one to meet our own needs. We lack showing respect when we know the rules but consider ourselves above the rules.)
- "This is my private business; my life is my own. I work hard. I have an important position, so I am entitled." (Truth: The call to public ministry means that our private actions have communal consequences—damage that can last for years.)

Churches may also try to avoid the problematic issue by saying:

- "This problem can be solved by the leader simply taking a new call elsewhere." (Reality: Passing on a problematic leader only invites repeat patterns in that new congregation.)
- "There are more important issues to think about, such as the global economy." (Truth: The global economy includes sex trafficking, widespread abuse of women and children. Locally and globally sexual abuse is an important issue we all need to address.)

Respect with Affection and Affection with Respect. Respect is an excellent beginning, a firm foundation. When we regard each other with respect, we honor people whom the Creating, Redeeming, Spirit-filling God honors. Remembering this sustains us to be able to act consistently with respect in our words, our actions, and our decisions, even when going through difficult, murky conflict. Respect that prevails in the hard times when people cannot stand each other can bear fruits of affection beyond our negative views of each other. We can act ourselves into a new way of being. No, we are not called to pretend, but through respectfully extending consistent ministry, the community can grow to appreciate, to reciprocate, and eventually even to grow in mutual care for one another with genuine affection, in spite of differences.

When considering our personal need for affection while being consistently respectful, it is helpful to remember that we need to tend our own needs for affection through close friends, spouse, and companions in appropriate ways. Thereby we need to respect those with whom we share intimacy by not laying on them the burden of our professional responsibilities. Role clarity is essential. The pastor's spouse is not the pastor. One can make clear by establishing up front, and re-establishing, as needed, the identity and role of the spouse. He or she can express affection for the congregation, and yet clearly and consistently say, "I am not the pastor," "I don't know," (this *can* be said genuinely when they really do not know) and respectfully, "I will tell her/him you called." Spouses need to be free to establish their own relationships within and outside the faith community. (See more about this in chapter 11.)

It is important for leaders to know how to express affection to those whom they lead. "Safe touch" is not just knowing where *not* to put one's hand, but replacing presumption with request[14]: "*May* I give you a hug?" or "As you are comfortable, let's join hands to pray." We may need to make clear that a person's fantasy will not materialize, by saying, "This is not going to happen" or "That is not going to be." To respectfully reframe the relationship when someone wants more of us than is appropriate to give, we can say, "I cannot be that for you, but I can be this"—your "pastor," your "teacher."

Affection without respect can damage, even kill. Affection *with* respect, appropriate loving care for others, is life-giving for the individual and for the community. Ministry needs to be cruciform shaped. That means that all of us are capable of betrayal and deceit.

According to Luther's second use of the Law: God shows us our sin and drives us to the good news of Jesus Christ who died for us on the cross. Even our very "best" ministry may have exploitative motivation. Daily we need to be called to repentance so that our ministry can be rooted in the forgiveness of sins. Centered in God's love that brings life and not death, we are no longer in bondage to our own self-seeking. Through the power of the Spirit we can refrain from the exploitation of boundary crossing, reframe relationships, and reclaim new possibilities for healthy co-labor. In order for such transformed leadership we will need spiritual guidance so that we respect ourselves, tend close friendships, honor marriage, and fully respect those among whom we serve. Affection, including attraction itself, can be transformed.

Of the three attitudes discussed in this chapter, all are important, though "respect" may be paramount. Blessed is the relationship where admiration, respect, and affection are all present in full measure. This may be rare, but perhaps it need not be. Where God's grace and unconditional love in Jesus the Christ is at work transforming us by the power of the Spirit, we can admire, respect, and have affection for one another.

○ ○

Reader Reflection

1. Reflect on one important relationship in your life right now. What aspects of respect, admiration, and affection are present? Are they mutual?
2. What difficulties do you experience? What are some possibilities for transformation?

Group Conversation

1. Take one pairing of the three words that have been explored in the chapter. What are challenges that you are experiencing in that regard? Listen carefully to one another. What are some deliberate changes that you might make?
2. With regard to respect, affection, and admiration, how would you assess your congregation as a whole? What in particular needs to be addressed?

Spiritual Practice

1. In a time of reflective prayer, consider your own need for affirmation, respect, and affection. How and through whom might God be caring for you?
2. Are there some unrealistic or unhealthy expectations you have of those with whom you live and work? In what ways might you look to God for mercy, love, and courage?

Transforming Action

1. At a group gathering, go around and share one specific suggestion about how you can respect each other as members in this faith community.
2. Take time in that same group to pair-up. Name one trait or gift you admire in the other person. Share these in the larger group.

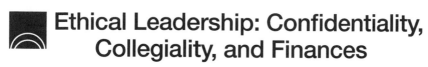
Ethical Leadership: Confidentiality, Collegiality, and Finances

BY WHAT ETHICAL STANDARDS DO leaders in the church operate? Transforming leadership requires a high level of *integrity* in order that the people have utmost confidence in those who lead. To live an ethical life is not merely about keeping rules or keeping up appearances (and certainly not about "doing my thing" until I get caught). However, any of those might be what people think of as ethics.

Ethical leadership relates deeply to ministerial integrity. The word integrity means "wholeness" or "soundness."[1] The word *ethics* can relate both to one's character and to a system or code of conduct, principles of right and wrong. To think about ethical leadership is not merely a negative (what not to do), but a very positive endeavor. We seek to discover both who we are—our inmost selves—and who we are in relationship to others, so that both can be constantly transformed by the power of God's love.

For those serving in called ministry, ministerial integrity has three parts, summarized by the following outline:

TRADITION — Theological Integrity — Faithfulness, Coherence, Consistency

EXPERIENCE — Personal Integrity — Honoring Self and Others
Establishing and Respecting Boundaries
Sincerity (Genuineness)

CULTURE — Professional Integrity — Competence
Fairness/Equality
Confidentiality

All three aspects of integrity are indispensable to a full under-standing of the term. Transforming leaders are rooted in a tradition that provides the standards for theological integrity. They are called upon to demonstrate personal integrity, and they are expected by the culture to live up to the standards of professional integrity.

While most professions have ethical standards that apply to all practitioners, this is stunningly not the case with clergy. Individual denominations may have guidelines for ethical practice and dis-cipline policies for their own membership, but there is no unified ethical code for all church workers, including pastors and diaconal ministers.[2] In the fields of medicine, law, counseling, social work, realty, financial planning, and hair styling there exist formal ethical standards of behavior that regulate practitioners. It is a scandal that the clergy profession has never developed and adopted its own ethi-cal code.

Some individual Christian ethicists have done creative work toward addressing this gap. W.D. Ross has articulated seven *prima facie* duties to guide ethical practice.[3] Karen Lebacqz, in a recent appropriation of Ross's work adds two additional duties to his list:

> Those [duties] based on prior acts of my own include (1) making reparation for wrongs done, and (2) keeping promises. Those based on the prior act of another are (3) duties of gratitude. (4) Doing good (beneficence) and (5) avoiding evil (non-malfeasance) are gen-eral duties, as is (6) the duty of justice or equitable distribution of goods and evils. Finally, there is (7) a duty of self-improvement (in virtue and intelligence). To this list, we might add (8) respect for the liberty and self-determination of the other (sometimes called the duty of autonomy, sometimes the principle of respect for persons), and (9) truth telling.[4]

These can be considered as fundamental ethical principles for ministe-rial practice.

Richard M. Gula has masterfully crafted a proposed code of eth-ics for pastoral ministry. After providing a clear statement of purpose and theological framework, Gula develops his proposal to include the following categories: ideal characteristics of pastoral ministers (holiness, love, trustworthiness, altruism, and prudence), professional obligations (theological competence, service of people's need for sal-vation, commitment to the other's best interest, care of ourselves, and use of power), sexual conduct, and confidentiality.[5] Transforming leaders would do well to adopt their own ethical code, employing resources like these for local use in partnership with congregational leaders or to become involved in a general movement to develop an ethical code for use in the entire profession.

Ethics can be defined as "intentional and disciplined reflection, together with a community, on the decisions we must make in the living of our lives."[6] Theological ethics operates with the vivid awareness that the decisions we face and the reflection process leading to them are carried out in the presence of the living God, who is ultimately the one who will judge the living and the dead. Transforming leaders are expected to behave in a way consistent with the moral tradition in which they stand. While none are without sin, including ordained and consecrated ministers of the church, it is nonetheless the case that those involved in public ministry are expected to adhere to high standards of ethical behavior. The perceived hypocrisy of those who are leaders in the church is a major stumbling block not only to faithful members but also to those standing at the threshold of the church, looking in and contemplating the possibility of the Christian faith for their own lives.

Chapters 9 and 10 have already explored a variety of important matters pertinent to the practice of sexual ethics in the church. This chapter will concentrate on three further areas of vital importance: confidentiality, collegiality, and finances. Those who engage in transforming leadership need to demonstrate standards of behavior in all these areas that lend integrity to the practice of ministry in the communities they serve and thereby avoid undue charges of hypocrisy.

Confidentiality

This book began with a strong focus on building a climate of trust as the foundation for transforming leadership. The ethical value that provides foundation for people's trust is confidentiality. People have a fundamental expectation that their leaders will be trustworthy. Even when there is no explicit agreement that a conversation is confidential, people will rightly assume that their pastor or diaconal leader will hold the information shared in confidence. The number of situations in which transforming leaders need to be mindful of confidentiality is endless: in consultations with counselors about church members; when informing new staff about people's lives; in making sermon or teaching illustrations; when preparing members to visit inactive members; on nominating committees; when writing for the church newsletter or webpage; in talking to colleagues; and in sharing with members of one's own family.[7] It is important to make clear to the faith community as a matter of policy that members of one's family, especially the spouse in the case of a married minister, does not hear the confidential communications made to the minister. While this covenant will be tested in countless ways, it is crucial to the practice of transforming ministry. For example, church members may assume a spouse *does* know such information, so it will be important to have both minister and spouse clearly say and demonstrate they do not.

The right to hold matters confidential developed first in the Roman Catholic tradition in relationship to the sacrament of private confession, especially in the medieval period.[8] Western law has acknowledged confidentiality as a core value of ministry and has extended this legal protection to other professions as well, notably medicine and law. Those who confided to the priest their sins in the confessional, seeking absolution, and those who heard these confessions were granted the privilege of maintaining confidentiality under the "seal" of the confessional. According to Canon Law, the sacramental seal is inviolable. Confidentiality is foundational for pastoral ministry. One should never underestimate the degree to which trust, based on confidentiality, is indispensable to the practice of ministry.

In considering the ethics of confidentiality, it is important to distinguish between four basic terms: secrecy, confidentiality, privileged communication, and mandatory reporting. *Secrecy* refers to information absolutely concealed from others. "A secret is some hidden knowledge pertaining to a person by strict right, which another may not lawfully seek to possess, use, or dispose of (*i.e.*, reveal), contrary to the reasonable will of the owner."[9] Certain secrets people may choose to disclose to their pastors.

Confidentiality refers to "the act of protecting from disclosure that which has been told under the assumption that it will not be revealed without permission."[10] By being protected recipients of such disclosures, ministers can thereby contribute to the spiritual well-being of those who confide in them. *Privileged information* is a legal term that refers to "disclosures from clients to clergy, by word or writing, that are exempted from being offered as evidence in court."[11] Laws regarding privileged information govern not only clergy-parishioner but also husband-wife, attorney-client, and physician-patient relationships. Insofar as each state has its own unique laws governing what is allowed as privileged information, it is crucial that the minister know the laws of the state in which he or she is practicing. For example, there are frequently requirements for *mandatory reporting* of instances of spouse abuse, child abuse, and elder abuse. Pastors may (and increasingly may not) be exempted from such laws, so it is vital to know the law of the particular state. In interpreting specific statutes, it is important to distinguish between *permissive* language that allows clergy to report without fear of legal reprisal and *mandatory* language that requires clergy to report. Also the term, *privileges abrogated*, indicates that clergy are not granted the immunity of privileged information.

The legal limits of confidentiality may have ethical implications for how one frames private conversations with parishioners. It may be very useful to develop a policy in consultation with the congregation about the practice and possible limits of confidentiality. Some pastors have developed a statement that can be signed by those who enter into a counseling relationship that discloses the legal requirements of the state about privileged information and mandatory reporting. Wherever possible, it is wise to clarify the expectations about confidentiality in advance by direct conversation. The burden of proof for making explicit people's expectations about and establishing possible limits regarding confidentiality belongs to the minister.

Particular cases provide especially vexing dilemmas for ministers. While Article 1 of the Bill of Rights protects the free exercise of religion, much depends on whether a certain instance of the sharing of information is understood to be a matter of expressing one's religion. A number of celebrated court cases have helped to delineate the meaning of separation of church and state in relationship to privileged information and clergy confidentiality. But the boundaries continue to be tested. In the past, U.S. courts have generally upheld clergy privilege, although constant vigilance is needed to defend confidentiality as being integral to the practice of ministry.

Apart from the requirements of the law, are there any exceptions to the expectation that ministers hold disclosures in confidence? Interestingly, even in the Roman Catholic tradition there are a few circumstances that mitigate the keeping of confidence. All of these pertain to instances when life-threatening harm may be enacted, were a confidence to be maintained. Such confidences include statements about committing acts of physical harm to the self (e.g., suicide), to others, or to the confessor. In such cases the moral tradition has allowed for disclosure of intended harm in order to protect the security and lives of those threatened. In cases where harm has been threatened and also in cases where the law requires mandatory reporting, one ethical approach might be to encourage (and even offer to accompany) the person in making a *self-disclosure* of his/her intentions or past actions to the appropriate authorities. In this way the minister would negotiate the narrow path between the expectations of the tradition/law regarding disclosure and the value of maintaining confidentiality.

Other difficult ethical dilemmas confront ministers in situations that raise questions about the obligation to divulge confidential information: to parents about their minor children; the instance of a crime not yet committed; or in cases of the defamation of the minister's character. One of the ethical dangers ministers face is that of rationalizing the disclosure of a confidence out of one's own need to exercise power over others or just out of the need to tell someone. Therefore, we recall the crucial importance of having our own spiritual counselor or confessor to help relieve our own anxiety so we avoid the "need" to tell someone, thus protecting the well-being of the confidant and all those who are affected by guarding the confidence.

In reflecting on the complexity of the issues involving the value of confidentiality, it may be helpful to distinguish between "levels" of confidentiality, placing at highest levels those disclosures that are most guarded and at the lowest levels those instances where the meaning of confidentiality becomes ambiguous. The following ninefold scheme is offered as a guide for reflecting on the ethical obligation of ministers in relation to confidentiality.[12]

Levels of Confidentiality

The following levels of confidentiality express a kind of hierarchy of forms of confidentiality. These levels primarily differ in the sphere of control. A confession made in private assumes a higher level of confidentiality than a request of an entire congregation to keep a particular bit of news in confidence—at least for a brief time.

1. *Confessional seal:* Information is shared in the formal context of private confession.
2. *An entrusted confidence:* Agreement is verbalized prior to a conversation that the information is to be held in confidence.

3. *A promised confidence:* Subsequent to the conversation, a promise is made to hold the material in confidence.
4. *An implicit confidence:* Information is shared based on an implicit understanding of the pastoral relationship without an explicit verbal agreement regarding confidentiality.
5. *Staff-only confidence:* Information is shared among a select group of colleagues for the well-being of mutual ministry. Permission to share sensitive information should be obtained from the person in advance.
6. *Consultation:* There can be two types of consultation: a) sharing of non-identifying information in obtaining a second opinion or guidance for ministry; or b) direct communication about the specifics of a particular person. In the latter instance, permission to consult should be obtained in advance.
7. *Collegial sharing:* General information is shared for consultative purposes. One needs here to beware of violations of confidentiality.
8. *Church council/church committee confidence:* The importance of confidentiality is discussed in advance of the sharing of information.
9. *Congregation confidence:* Information is shared with the congregation under the expectation that it will be held in confidence.

For purposes of staff-only and consultation (levels 5 and 6), permission to share information received at higher levels (1, 2, and 3) should be obtained. In collegial sharing (level 7), the minister should carefully examine the purpose served. Too often clergy gatherings can be occasions for the needless sharing of information that should be held in confidence. In council/committee meetings or at congregational meetings (levels 8 and 9), policies need to be considered that regulate the discussion of sensitive information about members. Confidentiality becomes extremely difficult to maintain as the circle of those who know the information grows in size. It may be meaningless to seriously consider that an entire congregation will be able to maintain a confidence (level 9).

While this chapter has looked at several instances where it may be necessary to disclose information shared in confidence, it would be dangerous to allow these exceptional cases to undermine the value of confidentiality in pastoral ministry. Maintaining a clear ethic of confidentiality helps to establish the trustful climate in which transforming leadership may flourish. "Confidentiality means that the information the minister has received is confidential and will not be used in any way except to enhance or benefit the giver of that information."[13] Under normal circumstances the minister is to hold pastoral conversations in utmost confidence. Where this happens, trust grows.

Collegiality

Ministerial ethics requires that one uphold and respect the rightful ministry of others in the profession. This ethical standard applies to other ministers on staff, predecessors/successors, judicatory staff, and ministers of other congregations, both those of one's own denomination and ecumenically. Maintaining this standard is challenging, especially when either one's own ego or the finitude (sinfulness) of other people intrudes. We can only begin to address the variety of dilemmas that challenge an ethic of collegiality. We do so by addressing some of the most common situations that threaten the practice of collegiality.

1. *Staff ministry.* In order for staff ministry to be transforming, there must be a covenant of mutual respect among all those involved.[14] The establishment of such a covenant of respect begins with the call process, in which direct, honest, and serious discussion needs to take place about mutual expectations and commitments. This discussion must especially make possible the genuine engagement of the most vulnerable participants. Clearly demarcated job descriptions help to establish portfolios of responsibility and to assure clear boundaries in the sharing of common work. Lines of accountability need to be clear. Both disciplinary and grievance procedures need to be in place.

Once a covenant is entered, members of a staff need to spend regular and intentional time together in Bible study and prayer, praying for one another, for the needs of the people, and focusing on the missional purposes of the church. Staff meetings need to include time set aside both for building mutual relationships as well as for the business of planning for ministry tasks. The art of discussing sensitive issues needs to be developed and nurtured, especially allowing the voices of the least powerful members of the staff to be expressed. Staff retreats need to be held on a regular basis, at which (at least occasionally) outside consultants can provide useful insight into matters of common interest.

On numerous occasions, the demands of ministry will reveal the shortcomings of the various members of a staff. One of the most important of all practices in staff ministry is the commitment to uphold one another with integrity in public settings, where the situation might tempt one to critique one's colleagues. Differences of opinion and performance evaluations need to be discussed in appropriate settings with the appropriate people present and by following established procedures.

Because staff ministry is complex, the temptation is to take short cuts and not devote the necessary time and effort to the care of staff relationships. For this reason, many staff ministries have failed to flourish. However, where a covenant of mutual respect has been established and the members of the staff carefully steward one another's gifts, staff ministry can be one of the most eloquent witnesses to the power of transforming leadership. While admiration and affection are good gifts, in staff ministry respect is the most important gift of all (see chapter 10).

2. Predecessors and successors. Judicatory officials know how difficult it can be for ministers to negotiate the boundary between one ministry setting and another. They are often consulted when this boundary has been violated. One particularly complicated boundary is occasioned by the retirement of a colleague who continues to live in the same area and, in some instances, remains a member of the parish. Congregational members themselves are often unclear about professional boundaries with former pastors, and they may continue to seek pastoral services from predecessors. Moreover, every minister has at some level the "need to be needed." Out of this particular need the minister may respond inappropriately to a given request.

It is vital that the ministry profession develop very clear expectations that predecessors maintain a vigilant boundary with respect to the ministry of one's successors. This includes praying for and publicly affirming the gifts and abilities of one's successor. There are virtually no occasions where it is appropriate for a minister to continue to offer pastoral services after having left a particular call. One must abide by an ethic that entrusts all future ministry to those who come after. For example, it is always inappropriate to put one's successor in the position of having to decide in a given case whether or not a predecessor may perform a wedding, baptism, or funeral. The successor is thereby put in a position where there is no constructive reply. The ministry of the successor is undermined in every case, whether the answer is "no" (the people making the request for service are upset) or "yes" (one's own proper authority is diminished). The only exception to this rule would be an official occasion, like celebrating a church anniversary or other special event, to which former ministers might be formally invited. Otherwise, predecessors need to learn to relate in ways that put into the background the pastoral dimension and genuinely respect the ministry of one's successor(s).

Although there are some instances where a predecessor minister has continued to remain as the member of the congregation after retirement, in general this is not a successful practice. There are too many occasions where boundaries can be crossed so that the ministry of one's successor is undermined, even without intent. No matter how difficult and challenging, the best practice for a retiring minister is to join and develop relationships in a new congregational home, even if that might mean attending a church of a different denomination.

3. *Judicatory officials.* Regional (synod or district) staff and denominational (national or churchwide) staff are to be counted among the colleagues with whom we have significant ethical obligations. Those elected or appointed to such positions as bishop, assistants to the bishop, directors of denominational units, or assistants in the denomination have major responsibilities for the well being of the whole church. They are stewards of our ecclesial connections with one another and stewards of major missional foci of the church. These officials are crucial partners with local communities of faith in carrying out God's missional purposes. Many vital ministries, such as starting new congregations, theological education, world hunger programs, or global mission, could not be organized effectively or on a sufficient scale without the partnership of the whole church.

Tragically, we live in a time of serious alienation between the local expression of the church and the larger denominational institution. People have begun to distrust institutions over which they feel they have little control. Regional or national church offices have frequently fallen under serious criticism for their failures. We would do well to question how much of this phenomenon is really a failure of regional or national church programs and staff or a consequence of local communities needing to identify a scapegoat to blame for anxieties, pressures, and negative changes that are beyond their control. Many local congregations have experienced dramatic changes to their economy that lead to loss of population, the closure of businesses and schools, loss of employment, and new social problems. These kinds of challenges place new expectations on the regional and national church. Many of these problems exceed the capacity of the regional or national church to "solve," although they are important partners in the attempt. The result can be increasing alienation and even scapegoating of the larger church by people on the local level.

Transforming leadership entails synergetic partnership with colleagues who serve on regional and national church staff. This means building personal relationships with them. It involves proactively representing the programs of the larger church, looking for occasions to invite representatives of the larger church to visit one's congregation, and advocating significant financial support for the whole church in the congregational budget. This requires ongoing attention to interpreting the ministries and mission of the denomination in the life of the congregation. By developing constructive partnerships with judicatory staff, one increases the transformative impact of the congregation beyond itself. Encouraging members to attend local cluster/ conference events begins to build up a sense of the whole catholic church (see chapter 3). Synod sponsored youth gatherings, choir festivals, or mission events are wonderful occasions to expand the congregation's sense of God's mission. Representational participation at regional/synod assemblies educates members about the responsibilities and opportunities of being part of the denomination. Leaders can even organize a visit to the churchwide office or attend a global mission festival. When people build relationships and experience collegiality (being part of the whole church), it is much less likely the talk will be about "them." Instead people will feel like they are part of the church in the widest sense of the word.

One of the lost arts in church politics seems to be the art of "loyal dissent." This means that even when a leader disagrees with a position taken by the denomination, this is not allowed to become an occasion for sowing seeds of discontent with everything the denomination stands for. Too often we have witnessed local leaders promoting a schismatic spirit that in the long run does not serve the interests of a local church. Rather, it is important that local leaders engage ministry in partnership with regional and national officials, in spite of particular differences of opinion. Transforming leadership focuses on the assets of the church, whether on the local, regional, or national level, and builds ministry on that basis (see chapter 13).

4. *Ministers of other congregations.* As a local minister builds a circle of support to help sustain ministry (see chapter 9), colleagues serving as ministers in other congregations are some of the most important persons to consider for that group. Deep friendships that help sustain life in the face of death are to be discovered in relationships with such colleagues. Depending on the locale, these colleagues may be from denominational traditions other than one's own. This is a great ecumenical gift!

Living in relationship to colleagues also can become an occasion for ethical deliberation, especially in an age where there can be intense desire for congregational growth. How does one relate to the disgruntled members of another congregation who come to visit your worship service on a Sunday morning? How does one respond to the couple which belongs to another church and comes to see you about holding their wedding in your sanctuary? Because we exist in a time in which success in ministry is very often measured by numbers, this can lead to competition for members.

Transforming leadership involves affirming the ministry of others, including the ministry of other churches and pastors of other traditions. This means encouraging discontented people from other congregations to seek reconciliation at home. It means calling a colleague on the telephone to seek advice about how to best minister in the cases noted above. It means placing a priority on honoring the ministry of others, rather than using conflict in other places as an occasion to increase one's membership. While there may be cases where a transfer of membership is the best option, this should only be done in full disclosure and partnership with other colleagues in ministry. One of the most painful experiences in ecumenical ministry is to discover that a colleague from another church does not abide by this same ethic in relationship to members of your church. Here is another obvious reason for the adoption of a profession-wide ethical code for those who practice ministry.

Finances

Great ambiguity surrounds a discussion of a "paid" ministerium. From the very outset, many questions are raised about who "owns" the vocation and voice of the paid minister. Is the paid minister thereby obligated never to say or do things that might offend one's employers? In the everyday work world, that is commonly the case. There are also many issues surrounding just and fair compensation for one's labors. In many cases, ministers' salaries are very low in comparison to other professions. Who advocates for ministers in the salary negotiation process? What is a just wage? What if the minister's salary is greatly out of proportion to the average salary of congregation members (either much lower or higher)? Why are there such discrepancies in ministerial compensation depending on where one serves? Many such questions can lead to the conclusion that a better way must be devised to handle clergy compensation. Some have even raised the question of a church-wide salary equalization policy.[15]

More ambiguity surrounds ministerial finances. Ministers, in one study, were noted as the second worst financial risk to lending institutions (e.g., defaulting on loans or bankruptcy), trailing only lawyers. In a society that measures worth in terms of income level and buying power, ministry can seem like a lesser-valued occupation. Low salaries can lead to a diminished sense of worth, resulting in significant discontent among ministers and leading to an undermining of transforming leadership. This situation has been complicated all the more by the level of indebtedness faced by many ministers upon graduation from seminary. Managing finances ethically can be a major challenge to many ministers.

There are few professions whose salaries are as public as those of ministers. Every year at a congregational meeting, one's salary is up for public discussion. Every month in the financial report members have access to the expenses related to the employment of the minister, including salary, housing, pension, health insurance, transportation allowance, etc. It is very easy for this public scrutiny to become an occasion for performance critique by people who may have an axe to grind on a particular issue. This can be amplified in smaller congregations where the portion of the congregational budget related to the cost of supporting a resident pastor may well exceed fifty or even sevety-five percent of the budget total!

Transforming leadership in relation to ministerial finances involves intentional and structured partnership between the minister and trusted congregational leaders. The congregation needs to develop a support system, such as a mutual ministry committee, where the financial needs of the minister and all members of the congregation's staff can be reviewed in a safe environment. Here, synodical or other judicatory compensation guidelines can be reviewed on an annual basis, and the committee can make recommendations accordingly to those formulating the budget. In the best scenarios, the minister him/

herself can be directly involved in the conversation with the committee members. This is also a forum where the minister should serve as an advocate for equitable salary considerations for other members of the church staff, one of the ethical obligations for ministers in the budgeting process.

The dangers of self-deception in relation to finances are great. One can be tempted to use one's position as a minister to solicit financial favors from parishioners or from those outside the congregation. Indeed, sometimes such favors are readily offered by others without solicitation. But one must ask what implicit obligations one incurs by accepting such favors. Is one's integrity violated thereby? This even has implications for the honorariums one might be offered as a minister for services rendered, for example, at a wedding or funeral. Such honoraria might be handled in a variety of ways, ranging from refusing to accept these (especially from church members), to receiving these at a set amount as an understood part of one's compensation, or to placing them in a special fund to support the poor or others in need. What is most crucial is that the minister and congregation establish a mutually understood policy concerning such matters that can be made available in such circumstances. A policy protects the integrity of the minister and promotes transforming leadership.

Another financial question that confounds many ministers is whether to know what members of the congregation are contributing. Strong arguments can be raised pro and con. A useful rule of thumb is that it would at least be useful for the minister to know when there are significant changes in someone's giving pattern, both notable increases and decreases. Insofar as congregational giving is one barometer of spiritual well-being, such knowledge can be useful.

Finally, there is generally a direct correlation between the level of financial commitment on the part of the minister and the overall stewardship of people in the congregation. Where ministers are generous, people tend to become generous. For this reason, transforming leaders need to model generous financial giving, beginning with growth toward and beyond the tithe.[16] Where such giving seems unimaginable, or where financial circumstances are blocking the thriving of ministerial service, this may be an indicator that outside help is needed in learning how to budget and how to live according to one's means.

This chapter has examined three key areas of ethical practice—confidentiality, collegiality, and finances—that can contribute to transforming leadership, or that can detract from such leadership by their absence.[17] In the next chapter, we turn to another core dimension of ministerial practice, the stewardship of time.

o o o o o o o o o o o o o o o o o o o o o o

Personal Reflection

1. What are the most difficult issues you face in maintaining confidentiality in your congregation?
2. Who have been your predecessor leaders in ministry in this congregation? How well have they maintained an appropriate boundary? For whom have you been a predecessor? How well have you done? This question applies to lay leaders also.
3. In regard to finances as presented in this chapter, what are the most challenging ethical issues that you face?

Group Conversation

1. What are the most difficult issues you face in maintaining confidentiality in your congregation? (How do you think about this similarly or differently from the answer you may have given to the same question in the Personal Reflection above?)
2. What are some of the qualities you value in a colleague with whom you work? (Colleagues from your work setting may or may not be *in* this group conversation now, e.g., this may be a staff meeting or it may be an ecumenical group of leaders from various congregations.) Which of these qualities do you recognize in various members of this group here? How do others in this group see in you the very same qualities that you indicated you value?
3. Does your church have a policy on honorariums received by ministerial services? What competing values are at stake in developing or revising such a policy?

Spiritual Practice

Invite your spiritual director or a trusted pastor to act as your confessor using an order for private confession and absolution.

Confess your sins, including the problematic parts of your successes, as well as your failures and shortcomings. Hear and trust God's word of pardon.

Transforming Action

Discuss with colleagues in ministry the need for a ministerial code of ethics. How might you move this discussion forward into action?

Leaders under Stress:
The Transformation of Time

WHEN WORK BECOMES A RACE and rest a mirage, we wonder—anxiously—about the tyranny of time. Working more hours in more places then ever, we are stressed out. We are too tired to welcome the Sabbath. Our society has adopted 24/7 time and we suffer the epidemic of access to non-stop information. So, what is our relationship with time and how can we experience the healthy rhythm of holy work and Sabbath rest? How can the very concept of time be transformed for transformational leadership?[1]

We seem to live in a "timelock" (not unlike traffic gridlock). Timelock occurs when demands on our time become so overwhelming that it feels impossible to wring one more second out of our crowded schedules. We are committed to God's mission, yet we wonder if simply "running around" *is* mission? Why in an age of unprecedented labor-saving devises and opportunities for recreation, do we find ourselves working longer hours and seemingly enjoying less the luxury of leisure? Any number of factors may contribute to our dilemma.

Living in a Timelock

The Vanishing Pause. Instant communication brings the expectation of instant response (in an already instant-gratification society). Formerly, we may have had to wait a few days for a reply to an inquiry, but we have stepped up the pace—responding to an e-mail, text-message, or cell-phone call during any pause in time, whether in our study, at the airport, in a restaurant, or even in the midst of a personal conversation. We schedule ourselves to the minute and have little time to catch our breath, much less ponder.[2] By eliminating "unnecessary" delays we have become uncomfortable with even a few minutes of solitude. Have we come to think of transformational leadership as filling every second rather than waiting for the Spirit to work in and among us in transformational ways?

Multitasking. Most of us have learned to do two, three, or five things at once. While we "wait" for the computer to boot-up, we can return a voice mail message, page through a stack of magazines, and perhaps schedule a meeting with someone standing at the office door. We seem not to know how to stop. A solo pastor moving into a team ministry anticipated sharing multiple tasks. He discovered, "We feel so overwhelmed by the complexity of schedules, we are hurrying each other into more and more stress."

The Bondage of Choice. Freedom of choice for many has become a bondage of choice. We have so many TV channels to surf, so many websites to explore, so many iPod videos to download, so many stores to shop, so many time-consuming timesavers, and a multitude of leisure-time activities, selecting from among them can become overwhelming. Choosing from the "personal options" on a recorded message irritates. We seem overwhelmed by the multitude of ministry possibilities that surround us. In the midst of so many demands, we experience the tyranny of time. But nostalgia for a simpler time is not the answer. We cannot go back and probably would not want to. Those "simpler times" carried their own burdens and complexity.

Who or What Is Time to You?

The issue may be a deeper one. What is our relationship with time? Who or what is time anyway? The answer may be unique to each of us.[3] Some would say:

- Time is like a train I cannot catch. The faster I run, the faster it speeds away from me.
- Time is an airport moving walkway. I can move faster than it does.
- Time is a taskmaster, standing over me in judgment.
- Time is a healer and patiently waits for me.
- Time is money. I budget the time I spend on a project or with certain people.
- Time is a shadow, always near, but ever changing, seemingly playing games with me.
- Time is a set of chains keeping me in bondage.
- Time is a bargaining chip. I use it to negotiate.
- Time is a dull friend who hangs around. I have too much time on my hands.

- Time is power. I use it to compete and I like to win.
- Time is elastic, stretching, expanding, but sometimes it snaps back in my face.

Is time for you a thief or a tool? A dictator or a guest? An event? A commodity? A gift? What is your image of time? What is your relationship with it? And how does that image differ from the image of others with whom you interrelate daily? How might our concept and use of time be transformed so that we are freed from stress for healthy leadership?

Time Unveils Our Goals and Gods

The balance of holy work and Sabbath rest is a deep spiritual issue that relates to the decisions we make each day. Our use of time shows us and others the values we hold, our goals, and, at core, our gods. Time is a gift to be cherished, not hoarded nor squandered. Martin Luther begins his catechetical explanation to each of the Ten Commandments with the phrase, "We are to fear and love God, so that. . . . "[4] Today our idolatry takes shape in our addictions and obsessions. It is easy to blame our bondage on too many responsibilities, but the real question is, "How do I live in relation to God so as to be a good steward of God's good gift of time?"

As leaders, we do not have all the time in the world, but each day we do receive the gift of time. Each breath and each heartbeat is a gift. The rhythm is work and rest. Even the heart beats and rests, beats and rests. We inhale and then we exhale. We work and we rest. When we move away from trust in God as the giver of time, we are tempted in our anxiety or our greed to gobble up time—our own and others—becoming more and more satiated, stressed, and yet unsatisfied. God can transform our idolatrous relationships with time and free us from our bondages so that time itself is blessed.

Time can be described as *chronos* (the actual, specific time) and *kairos* (the "right" time or the timely moment). Both kinds of time are gifts of our Triune God. We have a Creator God who sets the days and seasons in motion. Imagine our confusion if a capricious God, on a whim, provided one day with eight hours and the next day with forty-three? We have a God of encounter. At the right time, Christ was born in the fullness of time. One could say that "time" itself is transformed because we are set free so that obsessive and addictive relationships with time can no longer hold us hostage. The Holy Spirit through Christ shapes us for new opportunities for holy work and Sabbath rest. We will not quantitatively have more time, but we will see work in a new way and receive occasions for rest as genuine gifts.

Rest, God declares, is important. Sleep is not wasted time; relaxation is not sinful. In our race with time, we have become a sleep-deprived society, causing accidents on the road and on the job, and stress in human relationships. We do well to remember that God rested and invites us—commands us—to rest (Exod. 20:8-11). Jesus, the Human One, slept.[5] The Spirit refreshes, inspiring and breathing into us faith-filled new life for love and service.

Each of us may have different problems with time. Therefore, articles on "Ten Things to Do to Save Time" may not be a one-size-fits-all solution. The very proliferation of such articles shows both the pervasiveness of the problem and the elusiveness of the solution. The answer may not be to "save time" but to believe that God in Christ has already saved us and transformed us for a new relationship with the timeless God.

Sabbath Centers on the Word

Remember the Sabbath Day to keep it Holy! In the Large Catechism, Martin Luther wrote, "'Sabbath' which properly means to rest, that is, to cease from labor; hence our common expression for 'stopping work' literally means 'taking a holiday.'"[6] Luther observed that "Nature teaches and demands that the common people . . . should also retire for a day to rest and be refreshed."[7] He adds the element, "Second and most important, we observe them [holy days] so that people will have time and opportunity on such days of rest, which otherwise would not be available, to attend worship services, that is, so that they may assemble to hear and discuss God's Word and then to offer praise, song, and prayer to God."[8]

Later, Luther questions and answers: "What is meant by 'keeping it holy'? Nothing else than devoting it to holy words, holy works, holy living."[9] Luther makes clear that it is not our work that makes the Sabbath holy. "The day itself does not need to be made holy, for it was created holy. But God wants it to be holy for you."[10] This is more than simply refraining from work, or working hard at our play. Vacations often exhaust rather than refresh.

Luther says, "Truly, we Christians ought to make every day such a holy day. . . . However, as we have said, because we do not have the time and leisure, we must set aside . . . at least a day for the whole community, . . . and thus regulate our whole life and being in accordance to God's Word."[11]

Leisure in and of itself is not the chief aim. Rather, "the Word of God is the true holy object above all holy objects."[12] Sabbath is not just a day off. Such a view leads us to conclude attending church is merely another obligation from which we deserve a break, rather than a gift for the communal refreshment of worship.

Tilden Edwards in his classic book, *Sabbath Time*, says that Sabbath is an intentional halt to work. The focus of Sabbath time is on appreciating rather than manipulating. Sabbath rest checks the greed of our mind having to control things and people. It is time to praise God as an end in itself. Love of the Triune God is open and freeing, painful and playful, connecting and transforming.[13]

Martin Luther links work and rest, by saying, "Conversely, any conduct or work done apart from God's Word is unholy in the sight of God, no matter how splendid and brilliant it may appear."[14] Sabbath, for Luther, centered on the Word. In the Small Catechism he wrote, "We are to fear and love God, so that we do not despise preaching or God's Word, but instead keep that Word holy and gladly hear and learn it."[15] The Word truly refreshes, for "such is its power that it never departs without fruit. It always awakens new understanding, pleasure, and devotion, and it constantly creates clean hearts and minds. [Even when we feel dead, God's] "Word is not idle or dead, but effective and living."[16]

Centered on the Word, we are once again forgiven for our obsessions with time to be engaged in the mission to which God calls us. We do not just "keep" the Sabbath holy, but it keeps us. Rested in God's freeing love, we can return to our vocations, to the places and relationships of our daily work. None of us has a calling, vocation, or "work" that is more important than another's ministry in daily life (see chapter 16). Whatever our tasks and responsibilities, however exciting or mundane, our work is made holy by the God who is present with us each moment of the day.

Some people say that "Time is a great healer," or that "Time is the wisest of counselors." Even though at the beginning of this chapter we personified time in order to reflect on our relationship with it, it is not "Time" that heals or guides, but the God who gives us the gift of time. The same amount of time in the course of a day comes to all of us. God's gift of time provides us transformative possibilities. "What we do with it can change the whole course of life. It can be the time when health is restored or a wealth of ideas is discovered. Or it may be the opportunity to tell someone we love them."[17]

Ralph F. Smith, when he served as Professor of Liturgics and Dean of the Chapel at Wartburg Theological Seminary, preached about the fragility and the possibility of time:

> We do not have, you or I, all the time in the world. We know that. . . . Yet no matter how much our head and our heart tell us that we do not have all the time in the world . . .
>
>> to write that letter of thanks,
>>
>> to take that meal to an ill friend,
>>
>> to clean up the environment,
>>
>> to finish those few important projects,
>>
>> to tell a husband, wife, children, parents that we love them, and
>>
>> to show it.
>
> No matter how much our head and our heart tell us that we do not have all the time in the world . . .
>
>> to spend a quiet moment with someone dear to us,
>>
>> to sing a song,
>>
>> to pray a prayer,
>>
>> to gaze at the glowing embers of a fire,
>>
>> to see the sun rise and set,
>>
>> to listen to the cry of someone in need,
>>
>> to ask for strength and courage to face an uncertain future.
>
> No matter how much our head and our heart tell us that we do not have all the time in the world . . . we so often live as though we do. Now saying that could be the most oppressive and debilitating word I could possibly say to you today. . . Ah, but you see, in our post-resurrection perspective, it is already too late . . . and it is never too late. We do not have all the time in the world, but we do have time.[18]

Healthy Rhythms Lessen Stress

We do get tangled up in time. We tangle each other up when we have a difficulty keeping time commitments. Stress describes our era. God gives us time, God's time, for both holy work and Sabbath rest. This rhythm—and the knowledge that the Creator God holds our busy lives in God's hands—helps us untangle our time.[19] Here are some suggestions for leaders to aid in developing healthy rhythms:

Alleviate the sense of time urgency. We feel overwhelmed, and we fear that we will be unable to cope with tasks to do and commitments to keep. Our self-worth is based not on our winning an urgent race with time, but on God's gift in baptism. Sometimes the less essential imposes itself as urgent. We need to discern what is important. Is it urgent but really not important? Is it important but not urgent? Making plans and keeping lists helps, but only when we can clarify what is urgent and what might be scheduled for another time.

Understand differences in body time. Some people are fresh and ready to think creatively at a very early hour; others experience their most productive time late at night.[20] Transformed by God's grace, we are freed of judgmental comparisons. When we work together, whether that be in a staff setting, or in any partnership, including marriage, we need to determine what needs to be done at the same time and be flexible with work that can be done separately. Each of us can work and rest according to our own body rhythms.

Be specific about appointments. "Let's meet sometime . . ." can be heard as a brush off. Merely intended ministry is not ministry. Miscommunication or missing appointments can exacerbate conflict. Whatever their status, people are important, and so is their time. Mutually setting and collaboratively keeping appointments honors one another, as does really being present with one another, free of interruptions and distractions. Wise leaders will have learned that.

Respect each person's time and gifts. People work at different paces. People can accept that fact. Leaving work undone for another to finish is more difficult. Respect for coworkers and volunteers is crucial. We share leadership well when we include all, honor different gifts and different time patterns, *and* expect all to fully use their gifts. Shared leadership encourages us to be interdependent rather than merely dependent, to keep commitments, and complete work when it was promised. Transformation does not need to be merely a theoretical ideal; it can be an attainable reality when leaders employ specific skills in mutually accountable ways.

Refrain from engaging time as a power play. Keeping people waiting may appear to increase our prestige, but that practice actually diminishes our image. There is no room for such power plays in the shared mission of Christ. As part of the ongoing tending of relationships we need to be aware of such power plays and deal with them. Respecting another's time is a matter of justice. Using another to be our alarm clock prolongs unhealthy dependence. Likewise, we cannot manage other people's time for them. We need to be able to expect our co-laborers to be able to manage their own time, while being aware of the differences and possible challenges presented as coworkers and volunteers approach time differently.

Realize that each person has specific trouble with time. Just as we each have a different image of and relationship to time, each of us has our own particular challenges. Some of us are burdened with procrastination, others with being a perfectionist, and still others with apathy or irresponsibility. It is important to probe the root of each specific issue. (Chapter 14 on family and congregation systems provides guidance for some of these issues.) Rather than relying on excuses, knowing that God loves us unconditionally can empower us to deal with our unhealthy obsessions, compulsions, and shortcomings. With renewed self-esteem, transformational change is possible.

Be able to appreciate "local time." Cultural patterns create different "time zones" not only geographically, but also socially. We need to understand and enter into the rhythms of the lives of the people among whom we serve. How early or how late may one call? How much time do people need for informal conversation before discussing "business"? How long does it take for people to make decisions? Recognizing the cultural and social patterns of local time will help the transforming leader gain acceptance and more effectively develop a sense of shared mission.

The tyranny of time can disable and divide people. When we understand and honor each other, we can work toward a new relationship with time. We can "spend" time together. We can appreciate the simple joy of sharing time in work, in prayer, in simply being together.

Different People Need Different Strategies

So, how does each of us deal with bondage to our own specific time-binds? Here are a few examples of various challenges and a strategy to address each.

If I have trouble managing time, having no idea where it goes, often missing appointments, I may need to keep a time log for a week so that I can live with the constancy of God's *chronos* time more comfortably and accountably.

If I watch my time too closely, needing to control each moment of my time, I may need to set aside my watch for a day and experience some of God's surprises.

If I let time be my motivator, telling myself, "I work better under last-minute pressure," I may need to approach my daily vocation in a new way, as holy work, fully appreciating and utilizing each hour of each day, not just the last hour. This can lead also to more healthy relationships with those whose own work depends on my timely completion.

If I rush from one appointment to the next, trying to be in three places at the same time, I may need to realize that I am not God and cannot be omnipresent. I am not responsible for keeping the whole world running, but I am loved by God to be in loving relationships.

If I let others take advantage of my time, I may need to remember how valuable and precious I am to God and set clear boundaries so that others learn to respect me and my time.

If I use time as a power tool, keeping others waiting to enhance personal advantage, I may need to remember God's power over all and to see others as people whose time is just as valuable as my own.

If I am lonely, with "time on my hands," I may be searching for clarity in God's call. I may need the guidance of Christian community so that I can discover the gifts God has given me to serve in God's world.

If I long to spend time with family and friends, but feel too tired to really enjoy either, I may need some time alone. Solitude can provide perspective for thanksgiving. Freed from the stress of worrying if I'm "spending" enough time on them, I will then be able to see people not as burdens but as gifts so that we might enjoy our time together.

o o o o o o o o o o o o o o o o o o o

Personal Reflection

1. What is your image of "time"? Describe "time" in one word, image, or phrase. (Sketch if you like.)
2. Have a "conversation" with time. What do you want to say to it? What might it say back?

Group Conversation

1. Share with each other:
   - Your image of time
   - One problem you have with time
   - One helpful idea you have discovered for dealing with your specific time-bind
2. Share how each other's struggle with time impacts you and one way you can support each other in befriending time.

Spiritual Practice

1. Identify a holy time and a holy place for daily Sabbath, in addition to Sunday.[21] Maybe for you it would be a brief period first thing in the morning, or a pause in late afternoon. Create a quiet place that is not used for work. Make it your own and give yourself the freedom to simply look around, breathe deeply, and rest.
2. Do not burden yourself with expectations of devotions "accomplished," but add prayer, Scripture, or journaling as you are ready.

Transforming Action

Depending upon which type of person you are, actually do one of the following:

- If you tend to want to control time too closely, take off your watch for a day and see how it feels and how much you are able to accomplish anyway.
- If you have little concept of time, keep a time log for a week and see how it helps you see where time goes and how you might organize your time more effectively.

Opportunities Unleashed

section four

FAITH COMMUNITIES ABOUND WITH ALL kinds of people and all sorts of gifts. How can transforming leaders focus their energies not on perceived deficiencies but on the gifts God has already provided? Congregational systems may appear to be intransient. By the power of God's Spirit working through insightful leadership, transformation is possible. People are always in motion. The evangelizing community has people "on the edge"—some on the verge of leaving but also others on the verge of entering. Opportunities abound for the challenge of people learning the faith: learning to speak it and to live it. Transforming leadership is finally measured by the gospel becoming manifest in all of our ministries in daily life in the world.

Transforming Gifts:
Assets-Based Congregations

"WHAT IS WRONG WITH THIS church?" "We can't find anyone to lead vacation Bible school." "We put announcements in the bulletin, but no one ever volunteers." "The same three people have been on the stewardship committee for the last six years." "How are we going to pay for the new roof?" The language of *scarcity* often pervades congregational life. According to this view, resources are in short supply. There are never enough people willing to do all the jobs that need to be done. There is never enough money to pay for all the things that need to be bought. Leadership in the church is constantly about plugging holes. Committee structure requires that you find enough people to attend the scheduled meetings. Monthly church council meetings discuss budget shortfalls and how to do fundraisers to make ends meet.

According to the logic of scarcity, the life of the church is about addressing shortfalls and the problems they cause. One might even say that leadership primarily deals with problem solving. Leaders operate with a preconceived idea of what needs to happen and proceed with an agenda to accomplish their perceived goals. People and resources are the means toward this end. When issues or people get in the way of their agenda, they become problems that have to be resolved.

Now, while it is true that leadership involves mobilizing people to deal with the most difficult challenges, this does not necessitate turning ministry into a set of problems with accompanying solutions. Instead, transforming leadership looks at the church as God's gifted people. In the spirit of 1 Corinthians 12, there are many members in the body of Christ, each with unique *charisms* (gifts). Each member of the body has something vital to contribute to the functioning of the whole.

Appreciative Inquiry and Assets-Based Ministry

An ancient practice of the church has in recent decades been given a new name, "appreciative inquiry." Appreciative inquiry is the method that underlies an alternative approach to leadership called "assets-based congregational development." Appreciative inquiry is really an ancient practice that begins with the premise that God has richly blessed the church with gifts. The gifts of God are bountiful, and we build transforming ministry out of this abundance. Instead of beginning with deficiencies and lacks, appreciative inquiry operates with the assumption that congregations—each and every one of them—have all the gifts that are needed for creative and vital ministry! In part, this premise is similar to the proverbial wisdom of affirming that the glass is half full, rather than half empty. Such an assertion is not merely wishful thinking but has a powerful effect on how a leader and a people understand themselves.

The conviction is widespread in the church that congregations do not have enough people, money, participation, expertise, talent, skill, etc. Rather than focusing on the good gifts God has provided, primary—if not exclusive—attention is frequently directed at who and what is absent. Gary Goreham summarizes eight central assumptions of appreciative inquiry[1]:

1. In every society, organization, or group, something works.
2. What we focus on becomes our reality.
3. Reality is created in the moment, and there are multiple realities.
4. The act of asking questions of an organization or group influences the group in some way.
5. People have more confidence and comfort to journey to the future (the unknown) when they carry forward parts of the past (the known).
6. If we carry parts of the past forward, they should be what is best about the past.
7. It is important to value differences.
8. The language we use creates reality.

At the heart of appreciative inquiry is the matter of how one frames the discussion. How do we construct ministry and mission? Do we begin with preconceived ideas about the way things must and ought to be and then proceed to fill in the gaps? Or, do we allow mission and ministry to unfold, starting with the people and gifts that God has actually provided, moving into the future as an adventure that God promises to create, taking seriously who we really are? Transforming leadership frames ministry in terms of people's gifts, valuing and appreciating each one as having something precious to contribute to the life of the whole.

Appreciative inquiry as a method invites people into a discovery process of identifying and naming their gifts and assets. The fundamentals of appreciative inquiry are not complex, but they are very consequential for the well-being of the church. The process of assets mapping can be implemented in a variety of settings with salutary effect: council or committee meetings, congregational gatherings, youth groups, women's or men's organizations, or a visioning process. An initial exercise in assets mapping can be undertaken in a group in a time span of 60 to 90 minutes.

Luther Snow names and describes five basic types of assets that can be surfaced: physical assets, individual assets, associational assets, institutional assets, and economic assets.[2] Physical assets include physical objects that one possesses or to which one has access. Individual assets include the talents and abilities of people. Associational assets include the more informal connections or networks that exist between people. Institutional assets include the formally established structures (organizations) that are available as resources. Economic assets include financial resources, investments, borrowing capacity, and the potential productivity of the group.[3] Within the process of assets mapping, the convener asks key questions to discover assets that may be less obvious or hidden from view. Resources for identifying individual gifts and congregational assets include Bible studies, interview guides, planning processes, gift inventories, self-discovery tools, and leadership retreats.[4]

The basic process of assets mapping includes three elements: recognizing the presence of assets, creatively connecting the various assets with one another, and inviting people to employ their assets together in ministry. Assets mapping is a participatory process in which people brainstorm together about what their assets are, creatively link together these assets, and generate ministries from the synergy of working together at what they enjoy doing. In this process, groups first identify as many assets of the congregation as possible, including assets that might initially be disguised as liabilities. Second, the varied assets are brought into affinity with one another as similarities are acknowledged, patterns emerge, and synergies between particular assets are affirmed. Finally, people invest in sharing their assets for the sake of the common good. Instead of operating according to a pre-established agenda for the ministries of the congregation, assets mapping invites originality and spontaneity in addressing perennial challenges in new ways, as well as drawing upon those gifts that most energize people's involvement.

Employing the approach of appreciative inquiry and the method of assets mapping brings forth amazing energy and excitement among the people involved. It can be transformational. For example, in one congregation the annual stewardship campaign had become drudgery, something the members of the stewardship committee viewed as a necessary evil and the rest of the congregation dreaded. In lieu of organizing a fall stewardship drive, this congregation made the decision to engage in a year-long process of assets mapping, breathing new life into established ministries by creatively incorporating the assets that surfaced from the inventory of people's gifts and, even more importantly, generating several new ministries that had previously never been imagined (for example, making prayer shawls for the sick and baking bread to be delivered to worship visitors). It is advisable that the method of assets mapping be introduced over an extended period of time in order to catalyze a paradigm shift toward appreciative inquiry in the entire life of the congregation.[5]

Assets mapping shifts the very ministry paradigm from one of "fixed-sum" thinking to an "open-sum" approach.[6] Fixed-sum (or zero-sum) thinking refers to the conviction that there is only so much to go around—so much power, so much money, so much volunteering, so much everything. In this paradigm, resources are scarce and can be used up. In fixed-sum thinking, if one member of the group gains something, this automatically means everyone else loses to the same degree. Open-sum thinking lives, by comparison, with the presupposition of abundance. There are many more assets available than we can ever possibly exhaust, although we may need to draw upon different assets than those that are presently recognized. According to the logic of the open-sum paradigm, when you gain something, then I also am the beneficiary. (Note the similarity to the concept of shared power in chapter 8.) Even more, when you gain something, the whole group benefits through you. In the ancient words of Paul, "If one member is honored, all rejoice together with it" (1 Cor. 12:26b).

Assets-based congregational development is a powerful resource for transforming leadership. Through the implementation of this method, the focus begins to shift dramatically from the role of particular leaders to the leadership of the whole community. In this approach, the gifts of the people are recognized, appreciated, and fostered. We thank God in our public prayers and express gratitude to people in personal correspondence (thank-you notes) for gifts shared. We train new leaders for the church by building from both their inherent and their cultivated strengths. We become a "permission-giving" church, a church that radiates excitement about the creativity of what is emerging (rather than a church that narrowly controls who makes the decisions and which ministries are allowed).[7] We begin to see one another with new eyes. This does not mean that all problems evaporate. But it does mean that the church has the resources and gifts to face the future in confidence. For God does not leave us bereft of all we need.

Developing Leaders

A great temptation in leadership involves letting certain people's negativity take control of one's ministry. Our expectation for the church is that people should behave respectfully and maturely, cooperating for the good of the whole. Yet, in virtually every group there are certain members who are unrestrained in their ability to sabotage, undermine, and generate unproductive conflicts. The natural reaction of leaders to such persons and situations is to try and "fix" them. Leaders focus their energies inordinately on the people who behave inappropriately. Leaders may even become preoccupied with certain individuals and groups, unnecessarily granting them extraordinary power and control over how the leader engages in ministry. In the midst of intense inward and outward struggle, leaders tend to lose their equilibrium.

If one is able—with the help of one's circle of support—to maintain one's center and keep the larger picture in view, however, there is another counter-intuitive approach that characterizes transforming leadership. Instead of directing one's energies primarily toward those who upset the system with their antics, one invests in building up the positive leadership of others. The role of the called leader—pastor or diaconal minister—in the leadership development of other people is often underdeveloped in the many leadership models. Transforming leadership, however, is not about the heroic leadership of the individual but the growing capacity for leadership within the entire faith community. Transforming leadership is shared leadership, as the gifts of other people are nurtured and celebrated.

Most congregations at one time or another ask people to fill out Time and Talent surveys. The items that appear on such inventories normally refer to established tasks that someone "needs" to do. All too often, these forms, once filled out, are tucked neatly in a file, seldom ever again to see the light of day. Occasionally, a committee may refer to them when they have a hole to fill. But for the most part, the Time and Talent sheets focus on getting people to do things that someone else in authority sees as necessary to keep the church functioning. Contrast this understanding of employing talents to the assets-based approach explored in this chapter!

Transforming leadership involves serious attention on the part of diaconal ministers and pastors to the intentional development of the leadership of others. Transforming ministry multiplies as new leaders are prepared to undertake key leadership roles, once reserved for a select few. One of the central convictions of the Reformation involved the priesthood of all believers. Yet, of all the theological commitments of Luther and the Reformers, this may be the one that has been least implemented (see chapter 16). Instead of celebrating the ministries and leadership of many, in several church traditions a sclerotic and deadening clericalism has taken root.[8] In many congregations, an unhealthy dependency of the people upon the pastor dis-empowers the laity. Both the laity and the clergy can contribute to this dilemma. The laity may fail to claim their proper voice and grow content in being the recipients of pastoral services. Some pastors may enjoy their prominence as the uncontested leader, although many more are very frustrated by their inability to motivate members into engaging in congregational mission.

Transforming talents into developing leaders begins with intentionality about the importance of the undertaking. As one listens to the stories of the people (see chapter 1), one can point out and affirm the talents that are noticeable in what the people are already doing. One can engage in conversation that points out the leadership qualities that one observes. One can take the time to thank people for the informal leadership they take in the everyday course of church business, such as an insightful comment at a church meeting, the initiative to do a task others had neglected, or an idea that could potentially improve outreach. Such cultivation of leadership is important not only in working with adults in the congregation but also with youth and children.

The capacity to encourage the leadership abilities of others is predicated upon the centeredness of the pastor or diaconal minister in her/his own call. Growth in the leadership of others is not a fixed-sum game that diminishes the leadership of pastors or diaconal ministers.

Ministry of Word and Sacrament or of Word and Service remains an essential contribution to the life of the community, especially when the leadership gifts of other people begin to flourish. These new leaders will all the more need the ministry of the gospel and the orientation of the Word to ground and guide them in their service. Transforming leadership entails partnership and shared power (see chapter 8). Transforming leaders are not threatened by the growth and competence of others; rather they celebrate the way their gifts contribute to the welfare of the whole.

Intentional leadership development can happen in numerous ways. *Training events*, either organized by the regional church or by the local congregation, can contribute to the leadership development of those involved on church councils, specific ministry teams (committees), or Sunday school teachers. Key people such as musicians or youth ministers can be encouraged to attend workshops or certification schools to enhance their leadership. It belongs to the very core of the calling of diaconal ministers to equip the baptized for service in the world. Depending on the diaconal minister's area of specialization, they are called to prepare people to give public leadership in the church's mission for the life of the world. Pastors, too, have a special responsibility to nurture those who are emerging as the future leaders of the church. In one model, a pastor invites those currently in leadership positions in the church along with other potential leaders to a gathering each week to talk about the vision and leadership challenges facing the congregation. In this way, leadership increases as a function of the whole body and new leaders are constantly being cultivated. Transforming leadership is strategic in setting aside the time and taking initiative in developing the leadership of others.

One of the richest arenas for developing new leaders takes place in *small group ministry*. On the one hand, small group ministry is nothing new to the church. Small groups in the form of committees, Bible studies, women's circles, men's organizations, youth groups, etc. have long been part of the normal business of the church. On the other hand, intentionality about the formation and functioning of small group ministries, including the nurturance of leaders, has become a burgeoning field only in the recent decades.[9] Small groups can gather around a virtually infinite number of concerns and topics. For example, small groups can be excellent venues for Christian people to pray together, study God's Word, provide mutual support, talk about the meaning of faith for their daily lives, and learn to speak the faith to one another. All of these contribute mightily to the development of responsible faith and the building of missional outreach.

In some instances, small groups may have the energy and flexibility to undertake prophetic ministries in the community that the entire congregation as a whole could not do.

One fundamental principle of small group ministry explicitly contributes to leadership formation: the principle of cell division. In small group theory, groups are designed to subdivide on a regular basis. This means that the leader of a small group should be responsible for the mentoring of a new small group leader as part of a group's functioning. In this way when the cell divides, a new person has been prepared to take over the leadership, and so the number of leaders multiplies. Among the leadership skills fostered in those who lead small groups are the following: public prayer, group facilitation, insight into group dynamics, problem solving, and pastoral care.

Those called as diaconal ministers and pastors have an important oversight function in making sure that small group leaders are adequately prepared for their responsibilities. Through small group ministry the number of those prepared for and entrusted with significant leadership skills increases exponentially in the congregation.[10] It may prove helpful to have the various small groups keep connected to the whole faith community, sharing what they are doing, and inviting insights, perhaps through a page on the congregation's website. This contributes all the more to increased partnership in transforming leadership in the church.

Transforming Money

Money is another asset that almost always seems in short supply in the church. Stewardship programs typically commence at the end of the calendar year and have a direct connection to annual budget planning. In much of our thinking about money, it is viewed as a means to an end. Without sufficient funding, the church cannot afford to have a building, pay the utilities, or compensate church staff. Therefore, schemes must be developed to "separate people from their wallets." At least this is how many church members react to stewardship campaigns. Many are convinced that it would be much better if the church would stick to "spiritual" matters and not get involved with unrighteous mammon.

One of the most revolutionary insights about stewardship occurs in discovering how much Jesus talks about money in the Gospels.

Eugene Grimm writes:

> If we were to strike the comments of Jesus about money, we would reduce his teachings by more than one-third. Sixteen of Jesus' approximately thirty-eight parables dealt with money. One of every seven verses in the first three Gospels in some way deals with money. In fact, Jesus spoke about money more than about any other single subject, except the kingdom of God itself.[11]

Jesus talks in the New Testament seven times more often about money than he does about prayer. If pastors or diaconal ministers were to talk about money like this, people would run for cover. Why does Jesus focus so intently on the relationship between faith and money?

Jesus teaches and preaches so vigorously about money, because it is the central idol in human life with which God must compete! The reason people resist stewardship and talking about money in the church is because when the conversation turns to money, one is naming the real idol that vies with God for our ultimate loyalty. Transforming money in the life of the church involves recognizing that *money is foremost a spiritual matter*, not just a means to an end. How one relates to and spends one's money is a key indicator of spiritual well-being or spiritual malaise.

We live in a society that measures itself by financial success. Accordingly, the debt load not only of individual consumers but the nation itself is dangerously high. We are summoned by God to be stewards of our resources in order to bring life to the world, not to try and secure our own happiness. God calls transforming leaders to model and teach that God is the Creator of life itself, that every good gift comes from God, and that we are stewards (not owners) of what God has entrusted to our care.[12] To live as stewards in a world that measures itself according to levels of consumption is extremely countercultural.[13] To abide by the logic of stewardship sets transforming leaders at odds with the values of church members and even their own socialization.

Transforming leadership entails clarity about the ministry of money. This begins with one's own life. Those working professionally in the area of stewardship note time and again the direct correlation between a leader's generosity and the overall generosity of the congregation. The spirit of generosity is contagious, even if no one else knows exactly how much the leader gives. Developing one's own "stewardship testimony" as a leader, to be shared publicly at worship or in teaching, is an important way of setting the tone for transforming how people steward their money. In preparing such a testimony, the leader must navigate between the two extremes of, on the one hand, saying nothing and, on the other hand, speaking in a prideful way. Here is an example of what a leader's stewardship testimony might be:

> I understand God to be the owner and giver of all that I have. However, in our society we are taught to believe that I have earned the things that belong to me. Even more, we are tempted to measure our worth by how much money we make and how many things we own. This is a struggle for all of us, including me as your pastor. As one way to counteract my temptation to trust in my dollars more than God, I have chosen to tithe one-tenth of my income to the ministry and mission of the church. I do this not in order to earn favor with God. God's grace and forgiveness in Jesus Christ are free gifts. I do so, instead, as a sign and symbol of my intention to love and serve God above all things. Tithing has become one of the spiritual disciplines that I practice as an attempt to always remember that God is God and that I am to love, trust, and serve God above all things. I invite you to consider your financial giving also as a spiritual discipline, a way you live out your relationship with God.

Transforming money into a form of spiritual worship is one of the most urgent leadership challenges in our acquisitive culture. Stewardship is less about the worthiness of the causes to which we are summoned to contribute and more the need of the giver to give. Made in the image of God, we were created to be generous people. Re-created in the image of Christ who gave even his life on the cross, we are to be a people of great thanksgiving. The primary posture for the Christian life is the posture of praise and thanksgiving for all God has done. "I appeal to you therefore, brothers and sisters, by the mercies of God, to present your bodies as a living sacrifice, holy and acceptable to God, which is your spiritual worship" (Rom. 12:1). Transforming leadership involves not only partnership in leading stewardship campaigns, but transforming our own relationship to money itself for the sake of spiritual wholeness. This is why Jesus talked so much about money. It remains our calling.

An assets-based approach to transforming leadership involves appreciative inquiry, developing the leadership abilities of others, and reframing our relationship to money as a matter of urgent spiritual importance. We are called to bring these assets into the service of others as we pay attention to the longings of the world around us.[14] The mission of the church is curtailed when "I" do not believe I have any assets, or that others do not, or that we as a community do not have enough. Finally, assets-based leadership comes down to trust: Do we trust in the mercies of a bountiful God or the myth of scarcity that leads us into fear?

○ ○

Personal Reflection

1. What do you really enjoy doing? In addition to the sheer joy of doing it, how might this become part of your ministry (if it is not already)?

2. Who are the people whom you have nurtured into leadership roles in the church? Think of some people whom you could be nourishing but are not yet. How could you begin?

3. What is your spiritual relationship to money? How can you be released from bondage to money as an idol?

Group Conversation

1. What are some of the hidden assets of your congregation? What are some of the ways these assets can be claimed and employed in the life of your church and beyond?

2. How does your congregation intentionally foster leadership development? How might you sustain good practices in this regard? What new initiatives might be taken?

3. How can the stewardship of money be addressed as a barometer of spiritual well-being in the life of your congregation? How can this take place throughout the year and not only in the fall?

Spiritual Practice

1. Write in your journal or on a piece of paper a list of all the assets and gifts that you appreciate about your community of faith. Count your blessings one by one, thanking God in prayer.

Transforming Action

1. At a church council meeting (or other appropriate meeting) divide the group into triads and do the following:
   a) Ask each person to write down one of his or her own personal gifts.
   b) Then have each of the triad members write down at least one gift they see exhibited by each of their two partners.
   c) Have the triad members share with each other what they wrote regarding their own gifts and the gifts of their partners.

Transforming Congregational Systems

"WHY DON'T THEY ACCEPT CHANGE?" This is a common cry of lament for those engaged in ministry. Too often we underestimate the power of homeostasis in the life of local communities of faith. Having examined in the previous chapter the value of an asset-based approach as an essential perspective for undertaking transforming leadership, this chapter will examine the complexities of change in intransient and resistant systems. One of the fundamental realities we face in ministry is that congregations do not desire change. Because we live in a world of constant and dramatic changes, people desire their congregations to be places of stability in their lives. Transforming leaders need to recognize and even honor the reasons for this resistance. Indeed, there may be excellent reasons why a congregational system has evolved into the way it is. One should not prematurely dismiss the values defended by those who oppose doing things another way. One begins the transformation process through careful listening to the reasons people are reluctant to embrace change, even changes that the transforming leader is convinced are necessary.

Understanding the Congregation as System

Transforming leadership needs to understand deeply that congregations consist not merely of the individuals that make them up. Rather, congregations have developed over time into configurations based on the sum total of the emotional interactions that constitute their history. This means that the constructs from family systems theory (which have proven immeasurably valuable for understanding the dynamics of family interactions) also have tremendous explanatory power for comprehending what is taking place in a congregation as system. A wealth of valuable literature has emerged in recent years that can assist the transforming leader to begin to interpret both one's own life and the life of the congregation through a systems perspective.[1] Operating out of a systems perspective can be a matter of survival for the transforming leader in particularly resistant systems, lest the called leader begin to take personally the reluctance of people in following the direction one would choose to lead them.[2] This chapter provides an overview of family systems with specific relationship to transforming leadership.

The primary conviction of systems theory is that congregations consist of a complex set of emotional processes that determine why things are the way they are. Within such a system, the influential members are not only the persons that one encounters daily in ministry but also all those people who have affected the congregation in previous generations. This means that numerous "ghosts" continue to occupy every congregation, wielding considerable impact on the present. The will of those who died, the anger of those who have left the congregation in conflict, and the frustration of alienated members over previous failed initiatives each contribute to the homeostasis of the congregation still today. Fortunately, the strengths, assets, and faith of the ancestors are also latent realities that shape the life of the congregation long into the future.

Systems theory encourages us to pay more attention to the *who* (persons-in-relationship) involved in the interaction than to the *what* (content) of a current issue. Very often conflict emerges less over the substance of what is being considered than over what is at stake emotionally for those who are engaged in the decision-making process. This is not to deny that issues of substance may be involved. But it does mean that one always considers seriously how the people in the system are emotionally caught up in the discussion. For example, the reaction of a certain member against a new idea may have more to do with a series of losses experienced in family life than about the merits of the idea itself.

Wherever differences of opinion emerge, one should anticipate the phenomenon of *triangulation*. This refers to the fact that wherever two persons experience tension between them, one can expect that they will draw into the fray a third person to attempt to address the anxiety. Regularly, this third person will be the called leader. If the called leader is one of the persons in the initial conflict, then one can rest assured that other members will be drawn in as third parties. Often in systems theory, the initial impulse is to see triangulation as a problem. And it can be when it results in alliances that make the differences all the more intractable. The transforming leader, however, can take a strategic stance by seeking to mediate triangles with reference to God's mission and Christ's cross as the third party we are called to consider. Enveloping the process of change in a spirit of prayerfulness, in which all parties are opened to seeking God's will, is a key role for a transforming leader.

The ideal stance of the transforming leader is that of a *non-anxious presence* based on remaining *self-differentiated*. Self-differentiation occurs where the leader is able to negotiate two essential leadership moves in tandem with each other. *First*, the leader remains "connected" with the people, especially with those who are at disease. This requires intentionality about staying in communication with those who are distant, and not letting the disagreement rupture the relationships. Staying connected often requires great humility and persistence on the part of the leader. It may mean going out of one's way to demonstrate that one cares for the other, that the leader values the relationship beyond any differences of opinion. *Second*, the leader remains free to state one's perspective, not imposing it on others but clearly articulating why one sees things in a certain way. The transforming leader does not shy away from offering a vision for the future and proposing ideas for how to arrive at that destination. In fact, people need to know what the leader is thinking. Holding back one's vision can seriously frustrate the transformation process. At the same time, one's viewpoint needs to be expressed with humility, not claiming divine sanction, but explaining how "I" see things, thereby inviting others also to respond freely as to how they (also as an "I") see it (see chapter 7).

This twofold stance of a self-differentiated, transforming leader sounds very simple: *"Stay in relationship with people,"* and *"Let them know what you think."* Yet so often, especially where the resistance is the most strenuous, one is tempted to defer on one or both counts. Particularly unhelpful are those tactics that begin to label one's opponents as antagonists or even as "clergy killers."[3] While the literature that employs such terms may have some valuable insights into how one should deal with conflict, the labeling itself is a step toward demonizing and dehumanizing others. This never contributes constructively to staying in relationship; instead, it creates deep barriers. While it may be healthy on occasion for members to transfer to another congregation, at its best the wounded relationship will be addressed even as one leaves. Otherwise, all too often the same pattern is repeated elsewhere. Even the most troubled and troubling people remain children of God and deserve being treated with basic respect and decency.

Exploring One's Own Family of Origin

What one discovers in times of conflict is the measure of one's own emotional reactivity. One of the keen insights of family systems theory is to discover how the emotional reactivity from one's own family of origin continues to influence one's relationships in ministry. Doing serious work with one's own family of origin by mapping out the genogram of one's own family[4] is of great value to the transforming leader. What one almost always discovers is a striking parallel between the emotionally loaded relationships in one's own family of origin—e.g., with a father, mother, or sibling—and particular persons in the congregation where one serves. For example, one may discover that the conflicted relationship with the congregational treasurer parallels emotionally the tensions experienced in relationship with one's own father. Or, the sense of being judged by a member of the congregation's council parallels in uncanny ways the sense of shame instilled in childhood by one's own mother. Such family systems work can help unveil the depth of what one brings as leader to the difficult relationships one experiences in ministry. Furthermore, it helps one also to think about the family system of others so as to discover why they may be reacting to the leader in such intense ways. This perspective can help defuse conflict and offers fascinating perspectives on one's entire ministry.

The goal of self-differentiation derives from the ideal of becoming a "non-anxious" presence (or perhaps better, "less" anxious). In family systems theory, one becomes non-anxious almost exclusively by gaining insight into one's family of origin and thereby understanding what makes one tick. While getting further training in family systems and doing one's own genogram are extremely useful and should not be neglected, the central claim of the Christian faith needs to complement and correct how one becomes non-anxious. How often in his ministry, Jesus told his frightened disciples, "Do not be afraid!" (see Mark 6:50).

Ultimately, there is only one source for becoming a non-anxious presence, that is, by trusting that one is saved by grace through faith in Jesus Christ alone. Only by believing that one is a child of God, precious to God for Jesus' sake, can one begin to ground one's ministry in the final source of non-anxiety. The promise of God's unfailing love and presence is the reason we dare not to be afraid. We are not justified by what other people think of us or by how well we engage in transforming leadership. Our worth and value derives completely and always from God's unmerited favor and grace. On any given day, anxieties, worries, and fears will threaten to overwhelm, but in the midst of it we hear the strong word, "You need not fear." This conviction again underscores the imperative that transforming ministry be grounded in a vital spiritual life, where one is time and again enveloped in God's unconditional regard (see chapter 9).

Games Congregations Play

Starting from our biblical and theological convictions, we are predisposed to expect that congregations will operate according to their identity and purpose as expressed in a classic text like Romans 12:4-8:

> For as in one body we have many members, and not all the members have the same function, so we, who are many, are one body in Christ, and individually we are members one of another. We have gifts that differ according to the grace given to us: prophecy, in proportion to faith; ministry, in ministering; the teacher, in teaching; the exhorter, in exhortation; the giver, in generosity; the leader, in diligence; the compassionate, in cheerfulness.

Clearly, this is the missional goal toward which transforming leadership aims.

What we fail to grasp, however, is that congregations, like all human groups, are plagued by the reality of sin that alienates them from their created identity and mission. Congregations are dynamic systems that have arrived at a certain way of being through a complex interactive process over time. Each congregation has its own collective personality based on the unique membership and set of historic interactions that led it to the present moment. This congregational story, for better or worse, has power over who these people are and how they are able to function. Events that occurred in previous generations can still have dramatic influence over how decisions are made today. No matter how problematic, congregations arrive at a homeostasis that is constituted by the grand sum of all the interactions that have influenced it over its history. This is the destiny with which the transforming leader must reckon.[5]

As one wrestles with the behavior experienced in a particular context, the transforming leader may detect distinct patterns that are consistent with the insights of pioneer group theorist Wilfred Bion.[6] Bion argued that groups operate always according to a particular belief system that is reflected in how they go about their business.

This theory has implications not only for congregations as systems, but also for each of the groups that function within a congregation—not only the church council, for example, but also the women's group, the youth group, and the choir.

In his research into group dynamics, Bion noticed that only about 20 percent of the time do groups actually behave according to their stated purpose, which he called a "working group." A working group follows its stated reason for existence, makes a plan, sets goals, and acts accordingly. A working group operates with reason and logic. The other 80 percent of the time, groups function instead according to one of three other postures. While this is not an exhaustive list of the patterns congregations follow, the following patterns do account for much of what we observe in the church.

1. Dependency. The first "non-working" posture of a congregation is called "dependency." Such a congregation lacks inner strength and a well-established identity. Therefore it depends on its leader to protect it and keep it safe. Members of such a group often behave dependently, powerless to act on their own. They may become jealous, demanding, or resentful when they feel that their leader is not functioning in the proper way. Therefore, a dependency group may turn hostile to a leader that fails to fulfill its expectations. People may confuse dependency upon God with dependency upon the leader. While a leader may like this for a while, the result is clear: we are not and cannot be God, and parishioners should not assume we are.

We see this pattern very often in the church, especially where there has been an excessive emphasis on the role of the clergyperson as the primary figure who provides ministry. In previous generations, many congregations looked to the *Herr Pastor* model of ministry. Only what the pastor did was really ministry. This led to the abdication of ministry on the part of the people. The people only engaged in ministry when they assisted in clerical functions, such as preaching. The church is now plagued in many contexts for having established a dependency system in which the laity are highly dependent on a pastor in order to be church.

2. Fight/Flight. The second non-working pattern is the "fight/flight" group. Such a congregation engages in diversion from its established identity and purpose either by blaming someone/something for its problems or by some other avoidance behavior. According to the "fight" pattern, a congregation identifies some scapegoat to blame for its problems. This is a very common, human way of dealing with fear and anxiety.[7] Instead of taking responsibility for our situation, we transfer our anxiety to an easily identified scapegoat who we are convinced deserves our wrath. By focusing our attention on the one held blameworthy, we can avoid self-examination and change. In contrast, according to the "flight" pattern, a congregation engages in some other activity that keeps it busy but misses the point of its real purpose.

In the last decades we have witnessed a strong trend toward congregations engaging in fight/flight behavior, rather than claiming their missional purpose. The objects of a congregation's wrath have been many. Some identified scapegoats have been external enemies: the synod, the denomination, or an "issue" that has served as a lightening rod for discontent. Other times the enemy has been internal to the congregation: "those" people, the inactive members, or often, tragically, the pastor. So much energy has been directed at organizing the church for battle that it has neglected its core identity as God's beloved people and its core mission of sharing and witnessing to the gospel of Jesus Christ. We have observed congregations either being consumed by hatred for those they deem dangerous or embroiled in self-destructive internal conflicts. Too often this has also absorbed congregational leaders in concentrating on matters that divert them from a core commitment to transformation. Fighting is the most destructive form of flight, although congregations can concoct a host of other preoccupations that keep them so busy that there is no energy left for participation in God's mission.

3. Pairing. The third non-working pattern is "pairing," which Bion describes as the desire on the part of the group to look for an external solution, beyond the resources already available. A congregation active in pairing is constantly on the lookout for some new savior to deliver it from its doldrums. Such a group is optimistic that all it needs is the right formula to bring it into the Promised Land. Thus it engages in an ongoing search for the new idea, program, or perfect leader to bring deliverance. Yet, somehow, each innovation leaves it disappointed. In its disappointment, a pairing group easily shifts into the blaming behaviors of a fight/flight group.

Congregations engage in pairing behavior when they search for the new program, new worship style, new curriculum, or new leader that can either return them to past glory or make them successful like churches that are growing numerically by leaps and bounds. In a culture so profoundly influenced by marketing success, congregations are sorely tempted to believe that they lack the secret ingredient that can transform them. Only if they can procure what they lack, will they attain the goals they desire. Instead of investing in the relationships with God and one another that can create the transformation for which they long, they keep looking outside themselves for a messiah. Pairing is the antithesis of an assets-based approach to ministry that assumes that all the gifts necessary for a vital ministry are already at hand (see chapter 13).

Congregations also fall into other destructive patterns, particularly when they have suffered under a previous leader who has engaged in sexual misconduct or who functioned according to the unhealthy patterns of narcissism, depression, compulsion, or borderline personality disorder. Conrad Weiser has described these four patterns of unhealthy leaders, noting warning signs and consequences for the church.[8] Weiser estimates that 25 percent to 33 percent of ordained ministers are functioning at any given time according to one of these unhealthy patterns. Whatever the actual numbers, whenever a pastor suffers from such deeply troubling patterns, there is an urgent need for intervention. When such a pastor leaves a given call, there is also a need for the involvement of trained, intentional interim ministers, because the healing process requires both strategic leadership and extensive periods of time. If it takes three to five years to establish a climate of trust in a "normal" congregation, it may take five to seven years (or longer) to establish the climate for transforming leadership in a congregation that is living in the aftermath of a particularly unhealthy leader.

Strategies for Transformation

In the process of intentional listening, the transforming leader is able to read the climate of the faith community in which one is serving. Is the climate punitive, where blame is being placed and outsiders are especially targeted for scapegoating? Is the climate characterized by emotional blackmail? Is there a climate of restlessness, where the real solution is always just around the corner? Or, is there a healthy climate in which there is self-affirmation (without the need for criticizing scapegoats or ranking members in a hierarchy of worth)? The transforming leader wisely recognizes that congregational climates change only over a long period of time through consistent leadership that refuses to be taken in by the "games" congregations tend to assume. The stance of a self-differentiated, non-anxious, transforming leader is to maintain caring relationships with the people, even while expressing a non-reactive point of view regarding the issues facing the congregation.

When transforming leaders find themselves confronted by the unhealthy patterns congregations display, helpful strategies can be employed to disrupt these patterns When congregations act out in *dependency*, especially with dependency upon the pastor, it is first of all important for the leader to recognize that this is a pattern likely developed over a very long period of time. The force of homeostasis for remaining in a dependency system will be very great. In such a system, the transforming leader needs to operate in the mode of empowerment. But this does not mean trying to overturn the dependency system too rapidly; otherwise the pattern could easily become unstable and shift into blaming behaviors.

In transforming a *dependency* system, the leader needs to name God as the giver of gifts to all people, encourage the people to identify their own spiritual gifts, and claim those gifts in their daily lives. The antidote for a climate of dependency is to create a *climate of thanksgiving*. The consistent message is one of thanking God for the gifts that have been given and naming those gifts explicitly. The strategy is that of equipping the saints for the work of ministry by acknowledging the ministry that is already being done by others and inviting people to share their gifts with the whole community. Gradually, the leader hands over responsibility for ministry to the people who have the particular gifts to carry it out, even as the leader remains a partner in encouraging and thanking them. This is not to say that merely saying "thank-you" will change deeply rooted problems. But it is amazing how much modeling saying thank-you genuinely can transform an atmosphere of complaining to one of mutual affirmation.

In a *fight/flight* climate, a different approach is needed. Here the overarching goal is to focus on Christ as the source of reconciliation and peace. Christ died on the cross to be the source of our reconciliation with one another, and the cross offers peace to all those who seek to draw from its power. The theological center for changing from a fight/flight pattern is God's gift of forgiveness and love embodied in Christ's death and resurrection. The antidote for a fight/flight climate is the focus on Christ as the one who came to create a *climate of reconciliation*, reconnecting us to God and to one another. The consistent message is one of God's grace bestowed upon us for Christ's sake.

The central strategy is to put the cross at the center of the community's life and to allow the Crucified One to mediate all relationships. Even while a congregation is yet embroiled in bitter acrimony or estrangement, by the power of the cross Christ has already reconciled them. Believing this may be the most difficult challenge of all. Yet, by believing it, we can live into a new perspective and way of being with one another. Prayer informs this transforming approach as the climate shifts from one of blaming and avoidance toward seeing Christ in the neighbor, especially among the suffering ones of this world. Where there has been alienation from the bishop, synod, or denomination, eventually one will seek to build new relationships with each estranged party. But this is done always in a spirit of prayer that puts Christ at the center.

In seeking to address a *pairing* climate, the leader focuses on the gifts that God in Christ has already given for us to enjoy. In the spirit of an assets-based approach to ministry, one leads with the assumption that God has already given us all the gifts we need to have a vital ministry in this place. Rather than looking at the deficiencies of what we lack, which only an outside party can deliver, we direct attention toward the assets that have been manifested in the life of the congregation in the past and name the assets that continue to bless the present. In transforming such a climate, achieving success is important, so that new patterns of trust and behavior can be established. In order to succeed, the goals need to be realistic and attainable. Step by step, confidence begins to be re-established. The antidote to a climate of pairing (which is in essence a climate of scarcity) is affirming the *climate of abundance* that our generous God has showered upon us. The consistent message is about the power of the Holy Spirit to accompany and activate our efforts. The central strategy is carefully organizing activities on a reasonable scale that are guaranteed success and then celebrating what God has done among us. Thereby we learn to trust our own resources and capacity.

Consistency of leadership over time is crucial in beginning to transform congregational systems. The leader can be leaven, but cannot be the whole loaf. Sometimes our best strategies for changing congregational climate may seem to fail. Leaders can become frustrated at the rate of change or the level of resistance. When one begins to complain about how difficult it is to serve "those" people, often this is the result of lacking the perspective to see the difference that one's ministry has already made. Here again is the reason why a community of support beyond the congregation is so vital for transforming leadership. We need a community to help put our efforts in a larger frame of reference, so that we can trust the difference our involvement has made. Often it is only in retrospect—sometimes decades later—that we can begin to discern the impact of our leadership. In the mean time, we are left to trust in God's providence in the midst of things we cannot understand.

○ ○

Personal Reflection

1. How has your family of origin influenced who you are as a leader?
2. When have you found yourself energized by the group dynamics in your congregation? How do you understand the reasons for that?
3. When have you been frustrated by dynamics in the congregation? What were the major factors contributing to this?

Group Conversation

1. What makes for a constructive decision-making process? What are the key elements? How does your church deal with those who are on the losing side of a contested congregational decision or vote?
2. When has your group engaged in one of the three patterns discussed in the chapter—1) dependency, 2) fight/flight, 3) pairing? Share that experience and discuss it.
3. How have you seen a leader change the climate and dynamics of a congregation positively?

Spiritual Practice

Pray by name for each of those in major leadership roles in your congregation. Pray also for those they love. Consider including this each week in your regular devotions.

Transforming Action

Take initiative with someone in your congregation from whom you are estranged and seek to reconnect. Consider starting with an e-mail or phone call.

Transforming Opportunities: People on the Edge

At any time, in any congregation, there are people on the edge—people on the edge of entering and people on the edge of leaving . . . and people edgy about all sorts of things. Much has been written about how to invite people to church for the sake of mission. Less has been discussed about people who are leaving, or about to leave. This also is a mission concern. We are often sad or embarrassed or ashamed or angry about people leaving. Even those tucked seemingly secure within the bosom of the church may secretly—or not so secretly—be just on the edge, struggling with the desire to leave, or the fear of leaving. The Holy Spirit calls, gathers, enlightens, and brings us into this gift of God, this body of Christ called the church. We may not be that different from each other. We rejoice with one another and we leave each other. Both being on the edge of entering and being on the edge of leaving have the potential for being times of transformation.

Above All, Love the People

We welcome transformative opportunities and, to use the phrase another way, we have the potential to transform the opportunities already before us. The church is always changing, always on the move, sometimes growing, sometimes waning.[1] It is Christ who grows the church. As we minister in Christ's name, we are called to one work above all others, and that is to love the people!

Jesus met people on the road. Sometimes they ran to meet him. Sometimes they approached from behind, feeling they dared only to touch the hem of his garment. Sometimes he confronted them. Sometimes they followed from a distance. He asked them what they wanted him to do for them. He asked who they thought he was. He invited them to trust God and to be part of God's community of unconditional love, disciples together in mission working for justice. Christ transforms lives. Christ transforms us. Christ transforms the church.

So how do we love, especially those who are so far from the church, or those who, though nearby, insist they do not want to come in? How do we love those who are turning their backs on the congregation? How do we love new people when our hearts have been broken because those whom we did love, for such a long time, have died? This call to love others is not easy. We cannot attain or sustain such love all by ourselves. However, God's love remains, no matter what, and in that love, and that love alone, we love the people, both those by our side and those on the edge.

How can we describe these "people on the edge," and how might this inform our leadership? The remainder of the chapter suggests ten such descriptions. Reflect on these and think of additional ways to describe the edges of your ministry and the people you see on these edges.

1. On the Edge of Entering

At a synod assembly workshop on evangelism, a thirty-something man named Eric confessed that he had stepped outside the church for quite a few years. He said that he had considered coming back any number of times. But, he said, "The steps up to the front church door were just too steep." We knew he was speaking metaphorically, because he was young and fit. He went on, "But I smelled the coffee around back, and went in the fellowship hall door." And here he was now, representing his congregation at a judicatory annual meeting.

What aromas and images and sounds come from your church, and how might they beckon people in? Would it be signs out front (and inside in the hallways) that say, "You are welcome" in various languages? Would it be the voices of young children? Children can be very good evangelists, especially if given some role models. Would it be the sight of members living out their faith all week long on their jobs, at school, with friends?

Judy and her husband were reluctant to enter because they had no children. The fact that Hamden Plains Methodist was not *just* a "family" church encouraged them to make the step. Joyce had been away from another congregation for years and was embarrassed to come back. But an open, non-judgmental conversation with Karen at the grocery store encouraged her. Across the country, Jacob was convinced people would not come to church just because he invited them, but then a new man in town, who worked right beside Jacob, almost invited himself to Jacob's church. Jacob now has the courage to speak to others. Kendra, having moved many times, has grown accustomed to her living outside the edges of the church. No church-going acquaintance even bothers trying to get her into the church. But, is Kendra really that rooted in her opposition?

Shelley, on the other hand, would really appreciate being invited to church, but her life as a single mom of three in an urban area, her full-time job and night classes leave her little time or energy to seek out a congregation. Little does she know that in a faith community she might find the support she needs. Likewise, the congregation knows little of Shelley, even though she lives just a couple of blocks from the church building.

Transforming Opportunity: Re-envision those people you label as "non-church-goers." Talk with them; listen even harder. What is their reluctance? What are their deep needs? Their questions? How can you meet them where they are and provide an entry, or re-entry, into the faith community?

2. On the Edge of Leaving

People give many reasons for leaving a congregation. Sometimes the reasons they give are not the real reasons. In addition, people who do not leave are sometimes on the verge of leaving. They may have left emotionally, and their hearts are no longer invested in a particular community of faith. Yes, there are those who threaten to leave every season. But there are also the responsibility-assuming folk who may speak positively while bearing hurt and disappointment without saying a word and who have become bruised and hollow inside. At any one time, many Christians, perhaps ourselves included, are on the edge of leaving. This is hard.[2] We need to tend each other spiritually, noting changes so that we can reach out before the pain is too great. In so doing we might mend broken relationships that cause people unnecessarily to leave.

When leaving is inevitable, how much better it is to understand the reasons and to embrace one another in Christ. Rather than have people sneak away to avoid dealing with the sadness, we can use rituals of sending, including prayers for their journey.[3] We can view the church more broadly than the local congregation. People who leave because they move to a new location take with them not only precious memories but also skills for ministry. That, of course, assumes they will seek out a new congregation. Thousands of people each year do not. Church bodies can provide referral suggestions on how to both send people to and receive people from congregations across the state or across the country.

Still, seeing people leave is difficult. Ann, a long-time member in a growingly transient community, was asked how she had the courage to withstand so many good-byes. She said, "I do feel sad. We worship and grow together and then in two or three years, they leave. We can only say to them, 'Peace be with you,' and turn to welcome the next stranger coming through the door." And that's exactly what she did each Sunday morning, stand in the narthex, at the open door of the church, and greet people who entered.

Transforming Opportunity: Create safe opportunities for people to share their frustrations and fears about leaving and being left. When people must leave, make it an open, communal, experience of blessing.

3. On the Edge of Knowing

One reason adult Christians do not easily and eagerly share their faith is that they do not know what they believe. Oh, they know they trust in God. They may pray. But their faith education has not grown since they were teenagers. On average, only about one-third of most congregations worships weekly; the percentage who regularly attend some educational ministry opportunity is much smaller.

Of course, people are busy; they have many other commitments. But people will find time for that which nourishes them, for that which they enjoy and find meaningful. Each Christian, at each stage of the life cycle, needs opportunity for in-depth conversation around the Word. We face new questions each day. The issues of the world are complex. The opportunity to wrestle with these issues in relation to our beliefs can provide us with strength, comfort, and direction.

Recently, while meeting with a community group dealing with difficult issues of housing, drugs, and jobs, some Lutheran Christians surprised even themselves when discussion of the Lutheran theological perspectives on law and gospel, justification and justice, grace and unconditional love *did* provide a remarkably open and creative, realistic and yet hopeful perspective on the issues. They were able to avoid labeling some people as "good" and others "bad," and look at the issues behind the issues; seek out various views, including the voices of those not usually heard; explore biblical and theological foundations; and then look at the full range of ministries that were needed. Being merely on the edge of knowing is not enough today.

A "blended service" usually refers to music styles in worship. One could pick up on that term, but in a different way, and offer a "blended" Sunday morning experience of worship and education that is for everyone. Challenge people of all ages both to worship *and* to learn. That may mean forums, Bible study, experiential learning through service. It could be a Sunday combination of sanctuary and classroom, or a Tuesday evening Bible study and Compline or a Saturday prayer brunch and interfaith forum. Think creatively about ways to engage people in discussion, faith exploration, and action. Make it harder and harder for people to live only on the edge of knowing by providing exciting opportunities to dig deeper.

Transforming Opportunity. Ask people in the congregation how they like to learn and how they like to teach. Have a variety of different entry points: Bible, issues in daily life, or personal needs. Have some groups leader-led and others participant-led. Some could meet in the fellowship hall, some in homes, others at a local coffee shop. Challenge everyone to pick at least one! Learning leads to mission and mission leads to the need for more learning.

4. On the Edge of Speaking

Many people do not know what to say, because they do not know what they believe. However, even those who faithfully attend some form of education and who hear the Word preached from the pulpit every Sunday may not be verbalizing their faith in the language of their every day lives, either within their family, with their friends, or with others beyond their faith circle. They may want to. They may be on the edge of speaking, but it seems hard or strange.

Laurie said, "I know what I feel like when one of *those* people comes to my door." She is a devoted and well-read Lutheran Christian who wants to speak about her faith. In fact, she has much to say. She understands the complex issues of society, the pain and need. She was clear when she said with deep commitment, "The gospel at core is about God's unconditional love and Jesus Christ." Yet she worries about sounding rude, or simplistic, or irrelevant. In fact, because so many people are looking elsewhere, she wondered if her church *is* irrelevant. Yet as we met with Laurie and other congregational leaders on a Saturday morning to explore what the congregation was doing, even they were amazed to see all of the evangelical outreach they were engaged in: sharing food for the hungry, making quilts, hosting ice cream socials, sharing resources and caring for others, opening up the community room for all kinds of meetings. In the midst of ministry, they were on the edge of sharing in words the hope in Jesus Christ that prompted such care. Mission includes caring ministry and speaking the faith so that the people we serve know about the Christ in whose name we do acts of love and justice.

In this same congregation, Lucy is one of the people who serves refreshments on election days when the congregation's community room serves as a polling place. When neighborhood people come to vote, congregation members take one-hour time slots to offer coffee and conversation in the room to the side. Lucy said, "Well I don't actually say much; I just listen." People sometimes stayed for an hour to talk, and Lucy listened. She ministered powerfully. *And*, she wanted to know how to respond to what she heard.

Mike had an idea about another possibility. "The women of our congregation make wonderful quilts and give them to worthy organizations. We have many single parent families in the neighborhood. If we got to know them, gave them a quilt, and listened to their needs, we could talk about Christ in a more direct, personal way."

Each of these caring Christians is on the edge of speaking. When they leave worship they receive the blessing: "Go in peace, serve the Lord" or, in some liturgical settings, "Go in peace, feed the hungry." What if congregation members asked each other the next Sunday—in an education group—"How did you do?" "What did you say?"

Transforming Opportunity: Provide people such as Laurie and Lucy and Mike with opportunities to practice faith language with one another through discussion or even through role plays of conversations they had or might have had in the preceding week. Have them discuss how they can they make a specific difference, daring to put into words their educated faith, to listen well, to care for the neighbor, and to specifically speak about Christ's care and concern for the world.

5. Shopping from the Edge

"Why *can't* we church shop?" people ask. "It's the American way." Yet it seems so commercial, so, 'meet-my-needs' choosy. Congregations, well aware of this common practice today, are tempted to engage competitively, offering the "best program for youth," "convenient parking," or "kiosk coffee."

Literally, while writing this paragraph, six teenagers rang the doorbell, with an invitation to vacation Bible school in a nearby park. They gave the impression that it was an official neighborhood event. When asked if they were from a church, they said, "Yes, it is New Life Church." While suspect of their stealth invitation, one needed to admire their zeal. They were shopping for people.

"Where has denominational loyalty gone?" people bemoan. It used to be common that if you grew up a Methodist or a Lutheran or a Roman Catholic, that's the church you went to all your life, and you likely looked for when you moved to another city.

Sometimes we speak judgmentally because we fear our congregation will not measure up; the visitors who came last week will find some church they like better, or our members are going to be wooed away by that fast-growing congregation down the street. We are afraid to engage in mission because we fear we will be disappointed.

To believe in Christ Jesus, not *in* the church (see chapter 3) sets a different frame.[4] We are called to build the church, yes, but really we are called to participate in *God's* mission. By grace and the power of the Spirit, as we engage in God's mission, God builds the church.[5] To believe this is hard. In a consumer-oriented culture, it is difficult for people to comprehend discipleship, mission, commitment, and servanthood.

The Spirit has sought us out. We are joined in the body of Christ by God's grace. The congregation that is part of the church, historic and universal, may be small or large, on a prominent street, or set back behind a used car lot.[6] When we shop for something "better," we will be disappointed. Each congregation is beset with difficulties and blessed by opportunities right where it is! The challenge for transformational leaders is to invite people to participate in the unique opportunities for mission and ministry in the congregation and community. This may mean selecting mentors from the congregation to help newcomers recognize their unique gifts and see how they may be called to serve.

Transforming Opportunity: Marilyn said, "People here on the West side (in the neighborhood people say is *not* the right side of town to live in) need Christ just as much as people on the East side, where all those fast-growing churches are." How might Marilyn, and all of us, transform the image of our neighborhood, our church, and even our concept of how one chooses a church? How does your congregation reach out to those who may not even yet know what they are seeking?

6. The Revolving Door: Edging In and Edging Out

People come and go for a number of reasons. It may be the negative fall-out of church shopping. It may be failure to welcome people in a genuine way. The doors of our churches revolve for many reasons.

Jan and Jim wanted to affiliate with the church of their denominational background down the street from their new home, but they found that the people were not as open to their range of beliefs as they had experienced in the town from which they came in another part of the country. Mark was seeking a place where he could worship meaningfully and where his gifts might be used, but the absence of other young men soon left him as lonely in the church as he had been outside. He would have been receptive of a mentoring relationship with an older man, perhaps more open than he or the older men would ever know because it didn't happen.

As writers, we have yet to encounter a congregation that thinks of itself as unfriendly. But, when pressed to describe what this friendship means in the context of their own congregation people give examples of their *own* close church friends. The newcomer may only observe this sense of deep caring and warmth and not really feel it. Oh, the congregation may have ushers at the door who formally act "friendly," but the greeting is surface-deep and short-lived. Congregation members are surprised when new people who came in the front door just as quickly leave by the back.

We live not only in a mobile society, but we live in one where people's lives are almost constantly in transition. Some describe their relationships as seeming like a revolving door. One congregation, recognizing that fact some years ago, stood ready to seek out people who moved into their area, even if they might be there only for a few years, or a few months. Ruth, a new young nurse in town, said about Zion congregation: "I was greeted with genuine warmth. They welcomed me for myself, not as a potential alto in the choir. They did not fall all over me with a 'have-to-be-nice' attitude. Now, six months later I have yet to find the hypocrisy that so many young people say permeates the church today." She was invited to dinner and became part of an education team. By the way, she now does sing alto in the choir. Zion learned how to incorporate transient people into the fiber of the congregation.

Transforming Opportunity: A congregation may need to transform its image of itself and its mission. Ask why people who come do not stay. What views do congregation members hold about newcomers and short-term people? How might those views be intentionally transformed? What skills are needed for welcoming and incorporating new people?

7. Hide and Seek: An Edgy Game

People within the congregation may have a revolving door game of their own. One could call it hide-and-seek. Whether it's a habit they learned from childhood (see chapter 14) or a new pattern, they soon discover the power of such maneuvers. Or, perhaps we should say "we" because all of us do this from time to time.

We need to be a part of community, and yet we need solitude and independence. We want to be noticed and yet we do not want too much attention. Some people intentionally seek out a large congregation so that they can "hide" when they want to. Others do not consider it church unless one knows and is known by everyone. Dietrich Bonhoeffer wrote elegantly and poignantly about this: "Let [the one] who cannot be alone beware of community. . . . Let [the one] who is not in community beware of being alone."[7]

So where do people want to be anyway? On the edge of things? In the middle? A little to the side, but still included? Totally outside? Personality, history, leadership style, relationships, and even ethnicity all contribute to these desires, and they need to be respected.

However, playing hide and seek is another matter. A person may not like a change in the congregation and, instead of speaking directly to the appropriate person or committee in charge of the change, simply goes missing. Their "hiding" is intended to speak for them. Hide and seek is also a way to triangulate, drawing another person in to the middle to speak for them. Furthermore, disgruntled, still-present, people may make use of the absent ones, usually exaggerating their number by saying, "Some people' don't like the changes you made, pastor." A wise pastor clearly makes it known from the start that anonymous complaints or complaints "on behalf" of others are not accepted.

Likewise, people who have used absence as a way to speak, may appear "out of the woodwork," the phrase goes, when an important vote is to come up. Such 'now-you-see-me, now-you-don't' power plays confuse, hurt, and harm congregational life.

If it is a game, a transformation is needed, probably a transformation of the entire system. Congregational leaders need to continue to find ways to build trust and give people direct voice (see Chapter 1). Leaders need to make clear that they will not play this game. Ongoing visitation to everyone, not just in response to hide-and-seek, helps build healthy community. Mission includes ongoing building up of a healthy body of Christ.

Transforming Opportunity. Develop an environment in which people are continually encouraged, empowered, equipped, and held accountable for straightforward communication. Where individuality is honored and community valued, the environment will be more healthy and trusting.

8. Edgy Because of Conflict

Each year multitudes leave congregations because of conflict. People leave because they are angry with the pastor. People leave because they are angry with each other. Unresolved conflict can fester for years. Habitual conflict drains the community of strength for mission.

Conflict, of course, can be constructive as well as destructive. Conflict is part of the human situation; we need to learn to live and work together amidst conflict. To one person conflict may be energizing and adventurous, while another may perceive conflict to be abusive, messy, or even all-out war.

Conflict may be interpersonal or intrapersonal. Conflict may be over issues (beliefs), facts (truth), values (worth), goals (mission), or means (ministry). Discerning the type of conflict and our various roles in the conflict is crucial to being able to move beyond just being "edgy." Conflict, of course, is not static. It can escalate and widen. Sometimes it needs to be broadened in order for the appropriate people to deal with it. Other times it needs to be contained and narrowed. Conflict can even seem to be contagious. A conflict between two people is "caught" by others and either spreads slowly or as quick as lightning through the congregation. How frustrating when the two initial parties "recover," but some people who were audience to the fight now edge themselves out of the congregation.

Leaders with prayerful discernment can learn when to avoid and when to confront, when (on occasion) to compete, and when to take control. Together they can learn ways to accommodate, compromise, and collaborate.

Transforming Opportunity: Together (ideally at a time when the congregation is not in the midst of a huge conflict), have people share their image of conflict. Look at the congregation's history of healthy and unhealthy ways of dealing with conflict. Work together on gaining skill in the various responses to conflict, so that people have options to choose rather than only the option of leaving.[8]

9. On the Edge: Fatigue

Struggling through conflict or through any energy-draining episode is fatiguing for everyone. Leaders worry about budgets, about other people not fulfilling their responsibilities, or about people leaving. How frustrating, then, to find that the leaders themselves, those faithful ones upon whom everyone depends, are now so tired that they are on the edge of leaving. They have heard too many complaints, had too many late-night meetings, or endured too much bickering. They are completely worn out. "Mission" seems like only a word, but no longer a possibility.

Pastors worry about finding new leaders to fill offices in the congregation, but strangely enough a particularly vulnerable time is when a leader is leaving office. The church council president and committee chairs have given much time and energy, perhaps to exhaustion. Now they are being replaced. There is relief, but perhaps also some anxiety about the direction things will go now, or about the relationship with the new set of leaders. It is very human to feel not needed anymore. How might a congregation provide needed rest, maybe a sabbatical? *And* how might this be an occasion for giving people thanks and for re-discernment of gifts and interests, so that retiring leaders might assume a new role to live into at a more healthy pace?

People may leave leadership positions, or leave the congregation altogether because they are too tired. They feel they really need to leave. It may be an opportunity to go to a new challenge. But to leave only because one is dead tired, or feels that as the primary reason, need not be. How can the congregation itself develop a healthy pattern of holy work and Sabbath rest? It is counter-cultural today to live a holy, healthy, well-paced life together (see chapter 12). But living together in a transforming community can provide a counter-cultural experience. Many hands *do* make light work. God created us for interdependence, which releases us from needing to bear too much responsibility, and opens the way to restoring us to new life and mission.

Transforming Opportunity: If only we could take turns being tired. Well, maybe we can. Or at least we can learn when and how to support one another as leaders when one is completely down. In turn, we need to ask for help when we have taken on too much of the burden for the other. Reciprocal responsibility and collaborative leadership make for more life-giving mutual accountability.

10. On the Edge of Belonging

There may be more Lutherans (Presbyterians, Methodists, etc.) around than anyone knows. There are those who were raised in the Lutheran Church who have not attended in years and who hold no membership in a congregation, but who, when asked, say, "I'm a Lutheran." They may hold the tenets of the faith and confess Jesus Christ as their Lord, but they do not belong to a specific faith community

The term *membership* itself is suspect, not only by some people not on the official rolls, but also by the role keepers. Although discipleship is a wonderful New Testament concept, we need not too quickly do away with "membership." The New Testament does, after all, talk about being "members" of the body of Christ (1 Corinthians 12, Romans 12, Ephesians 4). Of course, "membership" can convey exclusivity, and some people stay away because they do not want to be "dues-paying" members. Can you belong without belonging?

Congregations do need to be realistic about who really is still there, and, perhaps even more important, about where people are who have not been present or participating for a long time. A term that has strange connotations is "cleaning" the records. Were they dirty? Certainly clarity of role keeping is essential. But who decides when to drop people? One day in a seminary class on leadership, when we were discussing this very topic, a senior said he had received a letter from his home congregation that week which read that since he had not been in attendance for more than three years (he had been at seminary preparing for pastoral ministry), he was being removed from the rolls. Now one could say that it was the responsibility of this man, and every person, to keep a congregation regularly informed. The reality is that we forget people who are on the edge. We lose track of the sheep and more than one is lost.

What would it mean for us to re-member those whom we would forget, to really believe we are members together in the body of Christ?[9] We do belong to Christ, and in Christ we belong to each other.

Transforming Opportunity: Be creative in thinking about "membership" and belonging. What can "associate membership" include? How does the congregation send young adults forth into the world and continue to provide a congregation for them to belong to? How might those on the edge be incorporated?

Above all, love the people!

○ ○

Personal Reflection

1. Recall a time when you were on the edge, in any sense of that word. What did it feel like? What did you do? Or not do? Or not feel like doing?
2. Did someone reach out to you? Who? How? If so, or if not, where did you go from there?

Group Conversation

1. Ask the group to select one or more of the list of ten "edges" above. Discuss the "Transforming Opportunity" provided. If the group is large, divide into smaller groups and later share your conversations with the whole group.
2. Extend the list beyond ten. In what other ways are people on the edge? How does that relate to our common calling of evangelizing?

Spiritual Practice

1. Read 1 Corinthians 12. Reflect particularly on "If the foot would say, 'Because I am not a hand, I do not belong to the body,' that would not make it any less a part of the body" (v. 15). Do we feel the pain of being devalued or dismissed? Do we feel the pain of others whom we may devalue or dismiss?
2. Prayerfully consider "The eye cannot say to the hand, 'I have no need of you,' nor again the head to the feet, 'I have no need of you'" (v. 21). The hand and the feet are the extremities, on the "edge" of the body of Christ, perhaps working in mission beyond what we realize.

Transformative Action

The terms, "Actives" and "Inactives," when used to describe congregational members, can create misconceptions that prevent healthy conversation. A role play may help people discover how they understand these terms. At an evangelism committee or church council or adult forum, try this (Have a little fun with it; exaggeration can reveal some things about ourselves.):

1. Invite four people to take part. All others will be observers. Two people will represent a stereotypical active and inactive member running into each other at the grocery story. The other two, standing behind, will be the voices in their heads representing what they may be thinking as the first two carry on a polite conversation. (Let the four pick their parts.) As the "active" and "inactive" person meet and engage in conversation, leave a few seconds between each exchange for the "inside-their-heads" people to say out loud that which, in real life, would probably never be said. As a leader, see where the role-play goes and determine when to stop, after a minute or two, or perhaps even 3 to 5 minutes. It does not have to be a long role-play in order for the whole group to have a lot on which to reflect.

2. After the role-play is stopped, ask, "What were you feeling?" to the inactive, and then the active roll players. Listen. Then ask the "inside-their-heads" people the same question. Then invite the group for their observations. Together discuss what this might mean for your congregation.

Transformed for Daily Life: Ministry of the Baptized

chapter
sixteen ●

SHELLY, A WOMAN IN HER late thirties, is the only woman on a team of about twenty people that staffs two firehouses, a calling that requires concentration, dedication, skill, and cooperation. She is daily challenged to deal with the physical and emotional demands of her job in addition to being a wife and mother of three. One of her greatest challenges, however, was helping people see that this slight-of-frame woman could handle the job. In so doing, she has earned the respect of her male co-workers.

Saying table grace is a part of her pattern of life. Shelly says that her ability to address the challenges and become an accepted, vital team member are due in great part to her faith in God, as well as her understanding of God's mission and how she is called to be part of that mission. That faith also gives her strength in the face of searing fires, icy winter roads, multiple car accidents, and the aftermath of drive-by shootings. In the midst of an emergency she calls upon God for the safety of the crew and offers prayers for the safety of the victims. She also offers up prayers during services at her church on behalf of those she has treated.

Shelly displayed her paramedic skills and genuine care for God's people on a recent medical mission trip to Haiti. After supper at the clinic one evening, Shelly walked to the home of a pregnant woman with a high fever who had been at the clinic that day. Before Shelly went, she filled plates full of food for the woman and her family. Shelly had provided what this woman needed: genuine concern for her welfare, medical treatment for her body, and prayers for health and healing.

Shelly has said on a number of occasions that as difficult as it may be to juggle her family life with the demands of her profession, she knows that God has called her to this vocation, because she has the gifts and skills that can make a difference in the lives of those she treats, as well as those with whom she works and lives."[1]

Transformation Taken to the "Extremes"

When people think of "transforming leadership," they may have thought first of the necessity of leaders themselves being transformed, "changed" into better leaders. In this book we have considered ways for leaders to not only *be* transformed but to lead in transformational ways. We have considered the church itself being a transformational body. In this chapter we carry the concept of transformation to the extremities of the body of Christ: all members of the church by the power of the Spirit are being transformed daily for their various ministries in the arenas in which they live and work all week long.

The people of God are set apart in order to be sent back into the world.[2] What do the gathered people of God need to become in order to be the transformed, equipped, and empowered people of God serving in the world through their ministries in daily life? How are their skills for ministry and leadership in the congregation being strengthened? And as we move beyond the church doors, do we recognize the ways in which we are each being called to various ministries in daily life? How will we walk with one another in those varied arenas, any and all of which are places for potential ministry and for working toward a more just and peaceable world? And what about the many people outside the congregation whose lives the congregation members touch? What does daily transformation of the body of Christ mean in the lives of those people? How can we really make a difference in the world?

Leaders who are charged to equip people for their ministries in daily life may say, "I already have too much to do now." However, to believe in the communion of saints is to believe that God is the Creator of the whole world, that Christ is and continues to be incarnate in that world, and to claim the Spirit's power. As leaders walk with the laity, listening to and engaging the theological questions people raise *from* being involved in the world, ministerial leadership becomes more interesting, more vital, more theologically challenging and alive. And ministry is multiplied.

Those who have been called to faith in Jesus Christ have been faithfully ministering in the world in each generation. Full *recognition* of this ministry and these ministers by the church is the issue. In that regard we have a transformation—an unfinished reformation—waiting to happen.

Concepts: A Variety of Images

A number of terms describe this radical reformation concept, each of which contains its own wisdom.

1. *The Priesthood of all believers.* By God's grace through faith in Jesus Christ, the Spirit creates the priesthood we all share. Christ became the faithful high priest, not only to make a sacrifice for the people but to become the sacrifice (Hebrews 2:17-18; 7:26-27; 9:14). Patriarchal hierarchies historically have reserved the bestowing and assurance of salvation to priests. But Scripture proclaims that all Christians are called to be a royal priesthood to "proclaim the mighty acts" of the one who called us out of darkness into light (1 Pet. 2: 5-9). The word *priesthood* is plural: Within the priesthood of all believers some are called and ordained to Word and Sacrament ministry and others to Word and Service ministry.

Through faith Christians are transformed by the Spirit and called to pursue peace, to show hospitality to strangers, and to remember those in prison (Heb. 12 and 13). Because Jesus, our high priest, died not on an altar, but "outside the city" (Heb. 13:12), the priesthood of all believers is called to go with him "outside the camp" (Heb. 13:13) and be willing to praise God, to do good, and to share what we have (Heb. 13:15-16). We need distinct offices and roles within the church, but together as the priesthood of all believers we are transformed to be the church in the world, proclaiming the grace of God and living out ministry "outside the camp."

2. *Ministry of the baptized.* We do not baptize ourselves. By the power of the Holy Spirit in water and Word, we are liberated from sin and death through being joined together in the death and resurrection of Jesus Christ. In the baptismal rite of the ELCA, the entire congregation hears, "By water and the Word God delivers us from sin and death and raises us to new life in Jesus Christ."[3] Christians often feel unclean. All people, including Christians, are sinful and in need of God's gracious forgiveness. In Baptism, the promise of God's forgiveness is proclaimed, and the baptized becomes a child of God, part of the Body of Christ. Even so, we need the washing clean of forgiveness and the refreshment of the daily remembrance of baptism, so that the sins and struggles of the day do not overwhelm us.

How is our baptism linked to Christ's baptism, and what does that have to do with ministry? For that matter, why was Christ, who was not sinful, baptized? Mark's Gospel dramatically begins with Jesus being baptized by John in the River Jordan. In Mark 10:38, Jesus asked his disciples, "Are you able to drink the cup that I drink, or be baptized with the baptism that I am baptized with?" Jesus was baptized into his ministry of servanthood, death, and resurrection; Christian disciples are baptized into Christ. Jesus said, "whoever wishes to become great among you must be your servant, and whoever wishes to be first among you must be slave of all. For the Son of Man came not to be served but to serve, and to give his life a ransom for many" (Mark 10:43-45). The congregation says to the newly baptized:

> We welcome you into the body of Christ and into the mission we share:
>> join us in giving thanks and praise to God
>> and bearing God's creative and redeeming word to all the world.[4]

3. All people in ministry. All of us are part of the *laos*, the "people" of God. Because God is Creator, all peoples are God's people. We need to take care that "people of God" language does not sound exclusionary in a pluralistic world. Although we need to be clear on roles to which we have been called, it is not helpful to separate *people* in artificial or ultimate ways. We use the original Greek word *laos* because "lay" in the English carries the connotations of "not clergy" or in general, of someone who is not very knowledgeable in a certain field.[5] Such hierarchical distinctions can lead some pastors to simply delegate to laity work they themselves do not like to do. Just as worship is the "work of the people" so, too, ministry is the work of the *laos*.

In Hosea, a child is named "Not my people" to signal the unfaithfulness of the people of God: "You are not my people and I am not your God" (Hos. 1:9). And, yet, in the very next verse we hear God's covenant faithfulness, "...in the place where it was said to them. 'You are not my people,' it shall be said to them, 'Children of the living God'" (Hos. 1:10). That Hosea passage is recalled in 1 Peter:

> You are a chosen race, a royal priesthood, a holy nation, God's own people, in order that you may proclaim the mighty acts of him who called you out of darkness into his marvelous light.
>> Once you were not a people,
>> But now you are God's people:
>> Once you had not received mercy,
>> But now you have received mercy. (1 Pet. 2:9-10)

Through God's mercy, a redeemed *people* is called to live ministries of mercy.

4. *Ministry of the Whole People of God.* The ministry of the church in the world belongs to the whole people. Wholeness, however, is not a matter of health or perfection. Individual Christians are not totally capable, experienced, or well. Congregations may be broken in conflict. In the midst of this reality, Christ imputes wholeness and salvation. It is a matter of believing that the church is whole, even while it is broken.

The Body of Christ is not whole unless all people are using their gifts to serve in the world.[6] In Ephesians 4, Paul urges the Ephesians saying, "I . . . beg you [plural] to lead a life worthy of the calling to which you have been called" (v. 1). This calls for humility, gentleness, patience, and bearing with each other. That's hard. Paul writes that there is one body, one spirit, one Lord, one faith, one baptism, one God, and one "hope of your calling" (vs. 4-6). Then Paul describes the variety of gifts (vs. 11-13), just as he does in Romans 12 and 1 Corinthians 12. But note that the lists of gifts are not closed and the roles are not ranked. The purpose of the gifts is "to equip the saints for the work of ministry" (v. 12). When the "whole" people of God is in pain, when the body of Christ is actually torn apart, Christ heals and grows the body: "Speaking the truth in love, we must grow up in every way into him who is the head, into Christ, from whom the whole body, joined and knit together by every ligament with which it is equipped, as each part is working properly, promotes the body's growth in building itself up in love"(vs. 15-16).

5. *Ministry in Daily Life.* Each of us is called. Each of us has a daily life. Although our lives may be long or short, each person has a 24-hour day. Not everything we do is automatically ministry, but everything we do carries the potential for ministry. Einar Billing wrote, "Call" is an "everyday word, with a splendor of holy day about it, but its holy day splendor would disappear the moment it ceased to be a rather prosaic everyday word." [7] "Calling" also means Christians being called by grace to faith. "When it began to dawn on Luther that just as certainly as the call to God's kingdom seeks to lift us infinitely above everything that our everyday duties by themselves could give us, just as certainly the call does not take us away from those duties, but more deeply into them, then work became calling. . . ."[8]

To Luther "call is primarily gift, and only in second or third place a duty."[9] Our roles and relationships in daily life are transformed in Christ. Even though they seem mundane or problematic, in Christ's cross we can now receive our work and each other not as burden but as gift.[10] Calling for Luther was rooted in forgiveness of sins, the ultimate transformation. "In the degree that our life becomes a life of forgiveness of sins, to that degree we receive a calling."[11] "Life organized around the forgiveness of sins, that is Luther's idea of the call."[12]

These reformation breakthroughs provided radical new possibilities for all people to serve in the church and to make significant contributions to society. There was a break from reliance on authority for what to think and what to do in the world. People were able to read the Scriptures for themselves. But what more needs to happen? Freedom *from* is freedom *for*. It's the "freedom for" that is left not fully realized. The power of the priesthood of all believers, even these many years later, has not fully been unleashed. Why?

Vocatio: Rooted in the Forgiveness of Sins

If our calling (our *vocatio*) is rooted in the forgiveness of sins, what does that mean for the real ways people live? What does forgiveness mean for living out this calling? How are we freed *for* ministry? These are core questions for living out our transformation in the Spirit. Each of the baptized, who together make up of the priesthood of all believers, needs to hear the gospel, God's grace, in terms of their own specific situation. Theologian Letty Russell wrote that Jesus did not say to the blind person, "You can walk," nor to the person who could not walk, "You can see."[13] Christ met people on the road in the midst of their lives and asked, "What do you want me to do for you?" Jesus cared about people and also about the societal problems related to human need in the world in which they lived.

We who have been transformed by the power of the Spirit each meet Jesus in our own need, and in the midst of society's need. If the human problem is brokenness, the good news is that Jesus makes us whole. If the human problem is alienation, the good news is God reconciles and restores relationships. If the human problem is guilt, the good news is that God through Jesus Christ forgives. If the human problem is being lost, the good news is that the Good Shepherd looks for and finds the lost. If the human problem is death, the good news is that Jesus Christ has brought new life. If the human problem is judgment, the good news is that in Jesus Christ there is unconditional acceptance. If the human problem is bondage, the good news is that Jesus brings freedom.[14]

Not everything we do is ministry, but everything we do in each arena of our daily lives has the potential for becoming ministry. Luther's concept of ministry is linked with his definition of the church as the communion of saints. The naked and the hungry are our neighbors.[15] Every Christian is a priest in the sense of being a servant. All of the baptized, including children, are called to minister to the neighbor. Martin Luther did not begin his reform of the church on the basis of pious leaders, but through a transformed concept of the church itself. Therefore, not just priests but the one who bakes bread or serves in civic government or cleans a house is part of the priesthood and called to ministry in that very place.

Our neighbors are everywhere. Luther wrote about our "stations" and "vocations." We today might think about "stations" as the whole range of roles and relationships of our daily lives and our "vocations" as our calling to minister to the neighbor. We sit beside a "neighbor" at our work "station" or school desk. This neighbor is the person right next to us and also the person on the other side of the world. We may just sit there and do nothing to serve the neighbor, thereby missing our calling. But if we regard the other as one also made in the image of God, as one for whom Christ died, then, by the power of the Spirit, whatever the service we do, it is our ministry.

When we deeply believe that all of our ministries are rooted in the forgiveness of sins, then we will submit our roles and relationships to Christ in confession, knowing that through the cross and resurrection we are freed for powerful servanthood. Such ministries make a difference in people's real lives. In order to do this daily we will need spiritual guidance and faithful conversation with trusted brothers or sisters in the faith.

For example, I may be a financial consultant, but it is not by my fine consulting that I gain God's favor. In fact, it may be that not only my "worst," but my very "best," work needs forgiveness. Then I am freed from worrying only about my own performance and able to really serve the needs of my clients. Or, I might be struggling with how to serve—or how even to like—members of my family. That, too, can be placed before the cross. Then I am freed from my need to control another, to save another, or to "fix" another's life, so that I might minister with love, even tough love, as God calls me to do.

It is helpful to take some time to quietly make a list of our roles and relationships (stations), asking of each, who is my neighbor there? Some roles and relationships may be ongoing, such as relationship of parent and child, but even those constantly change throughout the life cycle. There may be new roles—a different job, a new colleague, an invitation to a volunteer position in the community, a global challenge. What is the potential for ministry there? We will need the caring guidance of a friend in Christ to help us discern our calling. What are the challenges and barriers? What are our own dilemmas in that relationship?

Is there alienation in the family? Alienation need not be permanent. When our vocation is rooted in the forgiveness of sins, we know we live already reconciled in Christ with the potential for restored relationships. We are then freed to engage in the work of reconciliation, within ourselves and within our family. Is there guilt about the thousands who die of hunger each day? Mere guilt does not help poor people. When our vocation is rooted in the forgiveness of sins, we are freed to minister by actually helping a poor person and by working for change in systems that keep people in bondage to poverty. We are freed in Christ for powerful serving ministry. How might we reflect on our other roles and relationships? Who might help us hear God's Word of law and gospel? If a congregation wants to be transformed in order to equip and empower people for their vocations in daily life, what challenges will they face, and what key questions do they need to explore?

1. What Do People Need for Ministry in Daily Life?

One evening, while speaking at a conference meeting of congregational church council members, we asked the gathered group of faithful—and tired—leaders to imagine erasing all of their collective responsibilities. Note that we did not call for them to disband councils, committees, and meetings. We simply invited them to imagine what their congregations might look if they began not *inside* the church walls, but in the arenas of people's lives all week long. What would the baptized—the *laos*, this priesthood of all believers, this whole people of God—need when they gathered together in order for them to be equipped and sustained for their ministries in daily life?

The group of leaders had no trouble saying what was really needed. People spoke from their hearts. They appreciated the work of their congregation, but they had not been asked before what they really needed to survive all week long and to be transformed for ministry in their daily lives. As each spoke we put their words on the board. Then, together, we drew a transformed image of what they thought should be the components of their life together as the gathered people of God.

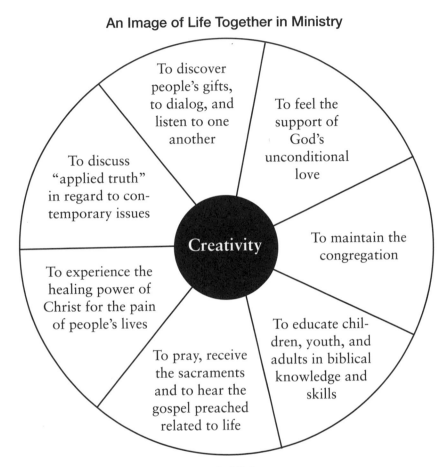

An Image of Life Together in Ministry

To discover people's gifts, to dialog, and listen to one another

To feel the support of God's unconditional love

To discuss "applied truth" in regard to contemporary issues

Creativity

To maintain the congregation

To experience the healing power of Christ for the pain of people's lives

To educate children, youth, and adults in biblical knowledge and skills

To pray, receive the sacraments and to hear the gospel preached related to life

Figure 5. An Image of Life Together in Ministry

Ask leaders in your congregation to draw their own circle. What components of a blank circle would they put in to equip the congregation for transformational ministry as they go forth in mission?

2. Why Is "Volition" Missing from "Volunteer"?

As noted in chapter 13, ask leaders the question, "What's the problem with the Time and Talent Sheet?" and they answer in chorus, "They are put in a drawer and forgotten." When people are invited to identify their gifts, but those gifts are not used, or the lists are referred to only in a desperate attempt to get someone to fill an office or volunteer for a job within the congregation, rather than in creative ways to extend the congregation's mission to all of daily life, the outcome is often not transformative at all. Why is that? Are leaders too busy to follow up? Is the congregation unsure if they really want vision and change? Is it unsure it wants all those gifts multiplied in ministry? Those are real questions and deserve thoughtful consideration. In the Ephesians 4 cited above, we clearly see that varied gifts are for equipping the saints for the work of ministry. The body that does not honor and develop all of its members will wither. In using all gifts in the church's mission in the world, the "whole" body is built.[16]

Leaders need a transformed view of volunteerism. It is not a matter of sitting in one's office and pondering, "Who can I find to take care of this church job?" Perhaps I will cajole someone to do some work *I* think they should do under the guise of "good delegation." Transformational leadership is not about making "little helpers" for "me" in the congregation. Such leadership remains at a hierarchical level.[17] The ministry of the baptized is about all being joined in the death and resurrection of Jesus Christ for the sake of becoming a servant community in the world. To *this* end the church is blessed with capable, faithful, committed, and collaborative volunteers.

At the root of the word *volunteer* is the concept of "volition," the act of choosing, using one's own will. Nothing can squelch ideas for transformational congregational ministry faster than people "volunteering" one another. I know people who are reluctant to mention an idea they have—maybe even a very good idea—for fear someone will say, "Okay, you do it!" (Or, on the other hand, some are reluctant to miss a meeting for fear that someone will "volunteer" them for work when they are not there.) One *cannot* actually volunteer another. It cannot be done. To try is merely to goad with guilt.

To volunteer is to think one's own ideas, exercise one's own will, or offer one's own gifts. People use their gifts to serve within the congregation so that the congregation is strengthened for ministry in daily life. The *laos* includes pastors. Might pastors also volunteer in the community, maybe in one of the arenas where a congregation member serves all week long? We need to create an atmosphere where people's ideas flourish and where we develop a truly shared vision for ministry. In such an atmosphere free of guilt, manipulation, and coercion, people can genuinely offer themselves, their gifts, and their time, as well as ultimately their vision.[18]

What would such an atmosphere look and feel like? How can we move from "volunteering" each other to the exercise of real volition?

3. How Does God Transform People through Invitation, Empowerment, and Mutual Accountability?

Christian people are engaged in ministry in the arenas of their daily lives in all sorts of ways. When we view people only as we see them on Sunday morning at the usher's post or in the choir, we may not recognize the full range of their many gifts. Surely their specific gifts of hospitality and song, and their other gifts such as teaching and cooking and organizing, are needed within the congregation as Christ builds up the body of Christ. But where is Kevin engaged in ministry on Tuesday afternoon, or Kristin on Thursday morning? How is Ruth caring for her husband with Alzheimer's? How is Bryant ministering as a member of his high school chorus? Do we understand the ministries to which they are called? How can we invite each other more deeply into the callings we already have? Do we thank people, and give thanks to God, for these many and varied ministries? How can we help people discover emerging gifts for new possibilities of service?

In the midst of ministry we need to ask, "How is it going?" and to really listen to the response. At such deep levels of care, people can share their difficulties. Whether speaking about our ministry within the congregation or beyond, we may say to each other, "I need your support." But one person's concept of support may be another's idea of rescue. We need to complement with integrity. Positive support invigorates, while disingenuous compliments may leave people second-guessing whether their work really was good enough. Perhaps people should not need affirmation to validate their work, but each of us does thrive when our work is thoughtfully recognized and appreciated. Professionals need to learn to self-assess, but we can also develop skills to give and receive productive feedback. Sustainable collaborative ministry includes open, honest, support for ongoing growth in skills, provision of resources, and genuine affirmation.

The ministry of the whole people of God is relational, lifting up invitation, empowerment, support, and yes, accountability. Mutual accountability! Although that term is used frequently in school and business, it is less often used in the church. "Accountability" should not mean "checking in with the pastor," as though he or she is the boss. Nor is it passing a test or being "good" in the eyes of a diaconal minister. No, we are not justified by human judgment nor saved by stellar performance.

Accountability is living faithfully in the promises of God. Mutual accountability means trusting the promises of God so that we can keep the promises we make to one another about faithfully carrying out our callings. Having low, or no, expectations of each other as disciples is neither nice nor "forgiving." It is rather a sign of unfaithfulness to what God can do through us—together. Lack of accountability muffles our prophetic voices and undermines bold ministry.

There are practical ways we can exercise mutual accountability. For example, at the end of a meeting we might review the decisions made and make clear who is going to do what and when, and to whom they are accountable. When we install people into new offices, we can provide position descriptions and expect regular attendance not only at meetings but also at worship and in Bible class. When we go apart from each other for our ministries in daily life, we should know that brothers and sisters in Christ will expect us to live out our baptismal callings in courageous ways. Such expectation is not judgment, but belief in the power of a loving, healing God who has invited us all into mission.[19]

Discuss with one another: "What do you find helpful in support for your ministries? How do you wish to be held accountable for this work?"

4. What If Your Ministry Is Different from Mine?

Picture all of the gathered people of God going forth from the worship service, walking or driving home in different directions. Yes, we are to ask, empower, support, and hold each other accountable for discipleship. The Spirit transforms entire communities for ministries in daily life. But what if those ministries take us in opposite directions culturally, economically, or politically? What if one person is in advertising and another is a consumer advocate? What if one is working to keep local property taxes low and another is working on a bond issue to build a new elementary school? What if some are Republicans and others Democrats? We often assume that such subjects are not to be talked about in church. After all, we have enough trouble getting along with each other in our debates over church council issues. Our callings will take us in many different directions, perhaps further than we know. No matter.

Differences reside in the congregation anyway. Why not know about them and embrace them? And embrace one another in those differences. Surely we will need to create and work to maintain a trustworthy place for us to be different together (as we stated in chapter 1). That trustworthy place will need to be broad enough to encompass all the individual differences among us with our extended ministries all week long. Can our circle be that large? Yes, if we continue to return to the center—to Christ.[20] Radical transformation is at the cross. As the people of God gathers at the communion table, they are restored, strengthened, and empowered to go forth to serve in the world as one body of Christ with many members, even as they go in differing directions. As we return again and again from our various directions, we are able to move out further and further each time. One person's actions don't cancel another's out. Strengthened by the Spirit, we need to act, and we also need to search the Scriptures more deeply. In a safe and open learning environment we need to hear about each other's ministries, and yes, learn from each other, even while yet holding opposing views. This is not easy. But the harmful alternatives are doing nothing or hiding what we are doing from each other.

A pastor had just moved to a small city divided decades ago over a strike in a meat packing plant that tore apart the town and the churches. The legacy of that painful time lives on, even as a newer issue of immigration has been rising. The pastor told of leading a worship service in a nursing home. When asked for whom to pray, one resident who had become well acquainted with an immigrant family, requested prayer for them. Another resident, in the same service, requested prayers because the town faced "danger from all these immigrants." What to do? The pastor included both people and their prayers. She noted that afterwards the two women began to speak to each other about their concerns—and perhaps begin to learn from one another about God's amazing broad mission.

In the midst of our diverse ministries, there also will be ministries we do together. A congregational care group or choir starts out visiting a nursing home. In listening to the residents and staff they begin to care about the economic conditions. This may move the congregational group to action in the community, perhaps even advocacy work for nursing home care at a state or national level. As individual members of the body of Christ and as a community, when we become more deeply involved, we are called to issues of justice and mercy.

What are some of the different callings of members of your congregation? How might you as a faith community deal with the challenge of that diversity?

A Method for Discerning Transformative Ministry

Individually and as a faith community we are called to discern our ministries in daily life. Realistically, we face challenges in those callings. Here is a method[21] to use in the process of dealing with difficult issues. Take one specific issue and work through the method carefully, step by step:

Step 1: Pay attention, listen, observe

- What is going on? What is the surface, or apparent issue?
- What is the context?
- What are the issues behind the issue?
- What are the obstacles to our understanding?

Step 2: Explore, seek perspective

- What is going on from the perspective of different people?
- Who is not present? Who is voiceless? What might they say?
- What cultural influences are at work here?
- What systemic evils, or "isms," might be at work?

Step 3: Reflect, search

- What beliefs are represented here?
- What are some worldviews on the issue?
- What theological issues do we see?
- What images of God, and of God at work, do we see?
- What biblical themes do we see?
- How do Scripture, creeds, and confessional understandings inform our deliberation?

Step 4: Ministry Options and Opportunities

- How do we become part of the solution rather than part of the problem?
- What is the call for God's righteousness and justice here?
- What is the need for the gospel, for grace, in this situation?
- Who needs ministry here?
- What obstacles might we encounter?
- How do we decide what roles are needed and who is called for what role?
- How do we call each other to faithful accountability in Christ?

○ ○

Personal Reflection

1. Reflect on just one day in your life (maybe yesterday). Walk though the day in your mind hour by hour. What were you doing? What happened? Who was there? What, do you imagine, was God doing there?
2. How does the death and resurrection of Christ free you for servanthood in those daily places?

Group Conversation

1. Have each member of the group make a list of his or her "stations" (roles and relationships in the various arenas of one's life). Divide into pairs and talk about the list. Note how some may be in flux or transition.
2. Have each person take a few quiet moments to discern what might be a calling (*vocatio*) in one of those roles or relationships. Return to conversations among partners: listen well, speak thoughtfully, and discern ministry together carefully and prayerfully.

Spiritual Practice

Invite a layperson to talk about faith in the language of their workplace, e.g. medicine, engineering, coffee shop worker, parenting. Together write prayers or a faith statement that might be used daily in that setting and in congregational worship.

Transforming Action

Walk with a layperson in one of the arenas of their daily life. Listen deeply to their hopes, their struggles, and their challenges. Converse about how they see God's creating, redeeming, and transforming activity in that place. Continue that conversation regularly.

 # Conclusion

It ALL BEGINS AND ENDS with the gospel. Our Transforming God is ultimately the source for all transforming leadership and transformed congregations. This God seeks to establish us in life-giving relationships in Christ with one another in the Church. This means the gospel is at the heart of all that we are and do. The gospel grounds transforming leaders in prayer, sustains them in times of conflict, and strengthens them for life-giving relationships. While the contexts in which we serve are different and need to be taken with utmost seriousness, the gospel sends us forth into the world, promoting transforming leadership in every context as we claim assets and work together collaboratively.

We dwell in the gospel not only for ourselves and for the sake of the Christian community. Our Transforming God sends us into the world individually and collectively to be agents of God's saving purposes for the world. The members of the body of Christ are never alone in this endeavor. Because we have been joined together as one, as we serve in our ministries in daily life our brothers and sisters accompany us and provide the encouragement we need, lest we give up in the face of the enormity of the task. At the same time, the church is called collectively to be an agent of change, courageously engaging the principalities and powers. God is seeking through the church to make a transforming effect on the world. God's purpose goes by many names: salvation, shalom, or justice.

Justification and justice belong together at the heart of transforming leadership. Justification is God's liberating act that sets God's people free to become who they were first created to be—beloved, precious, dear. Justification centers us as human beings in gracious relationship with the Living God. At the same time, sin is always close at hand to endanger our trust in this reality. Sin always also distorts how we view and relate to others. We need to repent and hear God's promise of reconciliation and forgiveness anew every day. Transformation has been completed by Christ's death and resurrection, while the full transformation of the world is not yet so. We are summoned to make a difference in the world, to live out of this power as our calling in life while we await the eschatological fulfillment of this reality.

God's Spirit spurs us on in our efforts to engage God's people through transforming leadership. The challenges are immense: peace does not rule, justice is fragmentary, people are hungry, violence tears us apart, creation groans. Yet through the work of the Spirit, this Transforming God continues to call, equip, and empower us to live boldly in transforming ways. Daring to care each new day, we are encouraged to risk for the sake of all the people in the world and creation itself. Sent into the world for the life of the world, we are transformed by God's transforming power.

 **Notes**

Chapter 1. Living in Trust: Setting the Environment

1. See Susan K. Hedahl, *Listening Ministry* (Minneapolis: Fortress Press, 2001).

2. See James F. Hopewell, *Congregation: Stories and Structures* (Philadelphia: Fortress Press, 1987).

3. See Gaylord Noyce, *Why Can't I Believe?* (St. Louis: Chalice Press, 1999). This is a book of conversations with all kinds of people struggling with faith and doubt.

4. James Glasse, *Putting It Together in the Parish* (Nashville: Abingdon, 1971), 56.

5. Glasse, 53–61. Glasse wrote that the pastor must pay the rent in order to earn the right to be creative and prophetic, including marching for peace, becoming involved in youth problems in the community, pursuing advanced education, or working for the denomination. But for Glasse, paying the rent "consists of more than the congregation demands of its pastor. The pastor has a responsibility to maintain [his] whole ministry. That includes [himself] (physical, mental, spiritual) and [his] professional practice (skill and situational specialties), as well as parish maintenance (which includes the involvement of the parish in the larger mission of the church)," (p. 55).

6. See Richard Bliese, and Craig Van Gelder, eds., *The Evangelizing Church: A Lutheran Contribution* (Minneapolis: Augsburg Fortress, 2005).

7. Augustine, *The Confessions of St. Augustine*, trans. John K. Ryan (New York: Image, 1960), 43 (1.1).

8. This is a term used in the denomination we serve to describe a committee focused on support, evaluation, personnel issues, and parish relations. See *Pastor and People: Making Mutual Ministry Work* (Minneapolis: Augsburg Fortress, 2003).

9. Although there have been periodic proposals in U.S. churches about salary equalization (with implementation in the Adventist Church), and while many churches have adopted salary guidelines, this remains an issue that has great bearing on the fundamental capacity for the emergence of transforming leadership. More serious deliberation on this issue needs to be undertaken.

10. James D. Whitehead, and Evelyn E. Whitehead, *The Promise of Partnership* (San Francisco: Harper, 1991), 27–36. See also chapter 3, "Healing the Wounds of Authority."

11. Musimbi Kanyoro, "Cultural Hermeneutics: An African Contribution" in *Women's Visions: Theological Reflection, Celebration, Action*, ed. Ofelia

Ortega (Geneva: World Council of Churches, 1995), 19. When trying to create a safe environment for cultural dialog, Kanyoro emphasizes that "cultural critique is possible only where the vulnerability of all the participants is transparent." Even oppressor and oppressed can be in a transformative community if inequalities are acknowledged and addressed.

12. Jamie L. Manson, ed., "The Future of the Prophetic Voice," in *Yale Divinity School Reflections* 93 (Winter 2006): 76. This special tribute edition to William Sloane Coffin, Jr., Yale '56 BD (June 1, 1924–April 12, 2006) is filled with articles that are not only about Coffin but that deal with the biblical legacy, history, and contemporary imperative for the prophet to speak truth to power.

13. See Christine D. Pohl, *Making Room: Recovering Hospitality as a Christian Tradition* (Grand Rapids: Eerdmans, 1999). Pohl explores the biblical and historic traditions of hospitality as well as topics such as "Hospitality from the Margins," "The Fragility of Hospitality," and "The Spiritual Rhythms of Hospitality."

14. See Letty Russell, *Household of Freedom* (Philadelphia: Westminster, 1987).

15. For more on setting and maintaining a trustworthy environment, see chapter 2 of Norma Cook Everist, *The Church as Learning Community* (Nashville: Abingdon, 2002).

16. See Juan Luis Segundo, *The Community Called Church* (New York: Maryknoll, 1973). Segundo says that Christianity is something to give away and that the church was not instituted simply to save those within, but to be of service to all humanity, p. 55.

17. Whitehead and Whitehead, *The Promise of Partnership*, 28.

18. See Hans Kung, *The Church* (Garden City, NY: Image Books, 1976).

19. Tilden Edwards, *Sabbath Time* (New York: Seabury, 1982), 71. See chapter 9, "Community."

20. Dietrich Bonhoeffer, *The Communion of Saints,* trans. James Schaef (New York: Harper and Row, 1960), 106–120.

21. Letty Russell, *Growth in Partnership* (Philadelphia: Westminster, 1981), 12. Russell writes in regard to partnership, "I find that one educates for partnership by a method of participation in that partnership with God, with the world, with self, and with others. We educate for partnership by being a partner."

Chapter 2. Honoring the People: Congregational Realities

1. For rationale and methodology in studying congregations, see James F. Hopewell, *Congregation: Stories and Structures* (Philadelphia: Fortress Press, 1987).

2. A useful introduction to ethnography is James P. Spradley, and David W. McCurdy, *The Cultural Experience: Ethnography in Complex Society,* 2nd edition (Prospect Heights, IL: Waveland Press, 2004).

3. For the following categories I draw upon the work of James R. Nieman from the team-taught course at Wartburg Theological Seminary, "Theology in Context."

4. Nancy Tatom Ammerman, Jackson W. Carroll, Carl S. Dudley, and William McKinney, eds., *Studying Congregations: A New Handbook* (Nashville:

Abingdon, 1998). See also in the Congregational Leader Series, Mark D. Johns, *Our Context: Exploring Our Congregation and Community* (Minneapolis: Augsburg Fortress, 2002).

5. Laurie J. Hanson, and Ivy M. Palmer, eds., *Pastor and People: Making Mutual Ministry Work* (Minneapolis: Augsburg Fortress, 2003).

6. Martin Luther, "The Small Catechism," in Robert Kolb and Timothy J. Wengert, eds., *The Book of Concord: The Confessions of the Evangelical Lutheran Church* (Minneapolis: Fortress Press, 2000), 353 (16).

7. On emotional systems, see Michael E. Kerr and Murray Bowen, *Family Evaluation: An Approach Based on Bowen Theory* (New York: Norton, 1988), 27–58.

8. Dietrich Bonhoeffer, *Life Together*, trans. and intro. John Doberstein (New York: Harper and Row, 1954), 27.

9. Edwin H. Friedman, *Generation to Generation: Family Process in Church and Synagogue* (New York: Guilford Press, 1985), 24–25.

10. For an excellent meditation on the central work of the pastor in worship, see Gordon W. Lathrop, *The Pastor: A Spirituality* (Minneapolis: Fortress Press, 2006).

11. David K. Switzer, *The Minister as Crisis Counselor* (Nashville: Abingdon, 1974), 26–27.

12. See Henri Nouwen, *The Wounded Healer* (New York: Doubleday Image, 1979).

13. On anxiety and reactivity in systems, see Ronald W. Richardson, *Creating a Healthier Church* (Minneapolis: Fortress Press, 1996), 91–100.

14. Rene Girard, *The Girard Reader*, ed. James G. Williams (New York: Crossroad, 1996).

15. William H. Willimon, *Clergy and Laity Burnout* (Nashville: Abingdon, 1989).

16. John Calvin, *Institutes of the Christian Religion*, trans. Ford Lewis Battles (Philadelphia: Westminster, 1960), 1:108 (1.11.8).

17. Susan K. Hedahl, *Listening Ministry: Rethinking Pastoral Leadership* (Minneapolis: Fortress Press, 2001).

18. Wilhelm Loehe, *Three Books About the Church*, trans. James L. Schaaf (Philadelphia: Fortress Press, 1969), 55.

Chapter 3. Hearing the Wisdom: Twelve Ecclesial Foundations

1. James D. Whitehead, and Evelyn E. Whitehead, *Method in Ministry: Theological Reflection and Christian Ministry* (Kansas City: Sheed and Ward, 1995), 8. The Whiteheads acknowledge both the scandal of disunity and the scandals of mispractice but also appreciate the richness of the diverse voices in the church's pluriform history.

2. H. Richard Niebuhr, *The Purpose of the Church and Its Ministry* (New York: Harper and Row, 1956), 24.

3. This relates to number 1 and number 10 of chapter 2, Congregational Realities: "the congregation was there before you were" and "the congregation will abide even after you leave."

4. See Norma Cook Everist, *Open the Doors and See All the People: Stories of Congregational Identity and Vocation* (Minneapolis: Augsburg Fortress, 2005).

5. Jürgen Moltmann, *The Church in the Power of the Spirit* (New York: Harper and Row, 1975), 22.

6. Hans Küng, *The Church* (Garden City, NY: Image Books, 1976), 46–59.

7. Norma Cook Everist, ed., *The Difficult but Indispensable Church* (Minneapolis: Fortress, 2002), xxi–xxii, 45–48.

8. Rosemary Radford Reuther, *Women–Church: Theology and Practice* (New York: Harper and Row, 1985), 25. Reuther describes and calls for exodus communities of women, and liberated men, free of the domination of male hierarchies, to nurture the journey of faith beyond patriarchy as the model of not just women-church but the church itself.

9. Ibid., 23.

10. Ibid., 32–33.

11. Letty M. Russell, *Church in the Round: Feminist Interpretation of the Church* (Louisville: Westminster John Knox, 1993), 12.

12. Christian Grumm, "In Search of a Round Table," in Musimbi R. A. Kanhoro, *In Search of a Round Table: Gender, Theology and Church Leadership* (Geneva: World Council of Churches, 1997), 28–39.

13. Martin Luther, *Luther's Works*, vol. 39: *Church and Ministry* (Philadelphia: Fortress Press, 1970), xi.

14. See Suzanne de Dietrich, *The Witnessing Community* (Philadelphia: The Westminster Press, 1958). De Dietrich was considered by some to be the outstanding lay theologian of Europe during the twentieth century. She worked in connection with the Ecumenical Institute at Bossey, Switzerland, and had a devotion to biblical and evangelical faith.

15. Ibid., 13–15.

16. Ibid., 16

17. Ibid., 16–17.

18. Juan Luis Segundo, *The Community Called Church* (New York: Maryknoll, 1973), 55.

19. Jürgen Moltmann, *The Church in the Power of the Spirit* (New York: Harper Collins, 1991; first printed in 1977 in English translation by SCM Press), 64.

20. Wilhelm Loehe, *Three Books About the Church* (Philadelphia: Fortress Press, 1969), 54-57.

21. Carol Lakey Hess, *Caretakers of Our Common House: Women's Development in Communities of Faith* (Nashville: Abingdon Press, 1997), 45.

22. Ibid., 38.

23. Parker Palmer, *The Company of Strangers* (New York: Crossroad, 1981), 40-46.

24. Harold Wilke, *Creating the Caring Congregation* (Nashville: Abingdon, 1980), 17.

25. Dorothy Soelle, *The Strength of the Weak,* trans. Robert and Rita Kimber (Philadelphia: Westminster, 1984), 30.

26. Karen L. Bloomquist, ed., *Communion, Responsibility, Accountability* (Geneva: The Lutheran World Federation, 2004), 16.

27. Ibid., 115.

28. Ibid., 94.

29. Dietrich Bonhoeffer, *The Communion of Saints,* trans. James Schaef (New York: Harper and Row, 1960), 106–120. This is Bonhoeffer's first work, a dissertation presented in 1927 at the age of 21. It is a sociological theology of the church.

30. Dietrich Bonhoeffer, *Life Together,* trans. John Doberstein (New York: Harper and Brothers, 1954), 26–28. *Life Together* is based on Bonhoeffer's earlier work, *The Communion of Saints*. In this quote male language has been changed to the more inclusive plural.

Chapter 4. Leading for Mission: Problems and Practices

1. Sharon Daloz Parks, *Leadership Can Be Taught: A Bold Approach for a Complex World* (Boston: Harvard University Press, 2005), 26.

2. See Craig L. Nessan, *Beyond Maintenance to Mission: A Theology of the Congregation* (Minneapolis: Fortress Press, 1999), 6–9.

3. See Kenneth Stokes, *Faith is a Verb* (Mystic, CN: Twenty-Third Publications, 1989). Stokes goes beyond faith as content to be believed or trusted to the action of faith and to the important work of lifelong faith development.

4. Robert Greenleaf, *The Servant as Leader* (Westfield, IN: The Robert K. Greenleaf Center, 1991), 11.

5. See David P. Mayer, *Our Gifts: Identifying and Developing Leaders* (Minneapolis: Augsburg Fortress, 2002); Bob Sitze, *The Great Permission: An Asset-Based Field Guide for Congregations* (Chicago: Evangelical Lutheran Church in America, 2002); and Luther K. Snow, *The Power of Asset-Mapping: How Your Congregation Can Act on Its Gifts* (Bethesda: Alban Institute, 2004).

6. Parks, *Leadership Can Be Taught: A Bold Approach for a Complex World,* 52f.

7. Craig L. Nessan, "Missionary God; Missionary Congregations," *Dialog* 40 (Summer 2001): 112–117.

8. Ronald J. Sider, Philip N. Olson, and Heidi Rolland Unruh, *Churches That Make a Difference: Reaching Your Community with Good News and Good Works* (Grand Rapids: Baker, 2002).

9. See Richard H. Bliese, and Craig Van Gelder, eds., *The Evangelizing Church: A Lutheran Contribution* (Minneapolis: Augsburg Fortress, 2005), 128–132.

10. Dietrich Bonhoeffer, *The Cost of Discipleship,* trans. R.H. Fuller (New York: Macmillan, 1959).

11. For a masterful description of the theological significance of the stewardship metaphor, see Douglas John Hall, *The Steward: A Biblical Symbol Come of Age,* rev. ed. (Grand Rapids: Eerdmans, 1990).

Chapter 5. Leading with Authority

1. Jackson W. Carroll, *As One with Authority: Reflective Leadership in Ministry* (Louisville: Westminster John Knox, 1991), 14.

2. Celia Allison Hahn, *Growing in Authority, Relinquishing Control: A New Approach to Faithful Leadership* (Bethesda: Alban Institute, 1994), 7.

3. James D. Whitehead, and Evelyn Eaton Whitehead, *The Promise of Partnership* (San Francisco: Harper, 1991), 29.

4. It may be valuable to take a spiritual gifts inventory as a way of claiming one's own unique gifts. For example, see Gary L. Harbaugh, *God's Gifted People: Discovering and Using Your Spiritual and Personal Gifts* (Minneapolis: Augsburg, 1988).

5. On the threefold offices of ministry, see *Baptism, Eucharist and Ministry* (Geneva: World Council of Churches, 1982), 24–27.

6. Marc Kolden, "Ministry and Vocation for Clergy and Laity," in *Called and Ordained: Lutheran Perspectives on the Office of the Ministry,* ed. Todd Nichol and Marc Kolden (Minneapolis: Fortress Press, 1990), 195–207.

7. "Consecration of Diaconal Ministers and Deaconesses," adopted by the Church Council of the Evangelical Lutheran Church in America, August 1997, Rubric 5.

8. "Ordination," in *Occasional Services: A Companion to Lutheran Book of Worship* (Minneapolis: Augsburg/Philadelphia: Board of Publication, 1982), 193–194.

9. See information on Bridgebuilders and Healthy Congregations at http://www.hcongregations.net.

10. One resource is Norma Cook Everist, *Church Conflict: From Contention to Collaboration* (Nashville: Abingdon, 2004).

11. Carroll, *As One with Authority*, 57ff., makes the distinction between "official authority" and "personal authority."

12. For the following, see Hahn, "Authority in Different Voices," *Growing in Authority, Relinquishing Control*, 72–109.

13. Carroll, *As One with Authority*, 124–133.

14. For strategies to strengthen excellence in pastoral ministry, see Jackson W. Carroll, *God's Potters: Pastoral Leadership and the Shaping of Congregations* (Grand Rapids: Eerdmans, 2006), 219–238.

Chapter 6. Transforming Servant Leadership

1. Some of the material in this chapter was first published in Norma Cook Everist, "Servant Leaders," *Lutheran Partners* 9 (July/August 1993), 11–14.

2. Robert K. Greenleaf wrote the essay "The Servant As Leader" in 1969, and since that time the term *servant leader* and *Greenleaf* are frequently said in the same breath. Published in 1970, this essay brought forth the wisdom of listening, foresight, and the necessity of leaders to serve. However, Greenleaf, noting the problems with coercive leadership, uses as his examples only white men such as Woolman, Jefferson, and Grundtvig. Greenleaf does not even mention Martin Luther King Jr., the outstanding model of powerful servant leadership of that era

of nonviolent social change. The essay later became the first chapter in *Servant Leadership* (New York: Paulist Press, 1977), 7–38.

3. Jackson Carroll, *As One with Authority* (Louisville: Westminster John Knox, 1990), 34–60.

4. John Gardner, *On Leadership* (New York: The Free Press, 1990), 1–10.

5. Robert K. Greenleaf, "The Servant as Leader." This essay, written in the middle of the civil rights and feminist movements, urged leaders with power of office to be first servants. The author may have presumed a white, male audience. However, those presumed to already be in the servant class by virtue of race, gender, staff position, etc., usually do not need to hear, "First be a servant." From that perspective, one needs to hear that one is freed from subservience for powerful servanthood.

6. See Celia Allison Hahn, *Growing in Authority, Relinquishing Control: A New Approach to Faithful Leadership* (Bethesda, MD: Alban, 1994).

7. Martin Luther, "The Freedom of a Christian" in *Luther's Works*, vol. 31: *Career of the Reformer I*, ed. J. J. Pelikan, H. C. Oswald, and H. T. Lehmann, 344.

8. For Martin Luther "idolatry" is the core in all sin. He begins his explanation to each commandment with, "We should fear and love God so that." R. Kolb, T. J. Wengert, and C. P. Arand, *The Book of Concord: The Confessions of the Evangelical Lutheran Church* (Minneapolis: Fortress Press, 2000), 351–354.

9. "The Deaconess Litany" of The Lutheran Deaconess Community (Lutheran Deaconess Association, Valparaiso, Indiana, 1959; revised, 1997).

10. Carol Lakey Hess, *Caretakers of Our Common House* (Nashville: Abingdon, 1997), 38.

11. Elizabeth Howell Verdesi, *In but Still Out: Women in the Church* (Philadelphia: The Westminster Press, 1975), 176–177. Verdesi shows that church people who protest they are "not interested in power" have power, whether used irresponsibly or responsibly. Those with inordinate power go to great lengths to ignore, trivialize, or do away with those they fear will gain access to power.

12. See Mary Beth Rogers, *Barbara Jordan: American Hero* (New York: Bantam Books, 1998).

13. See Marie Augusta Neal, *A Socio-Theology of Letting Go* (New York: Paulist Press, 1977).

14. Gardner, *On Leadership*, 5.

15. See Richard Osmer, *A Teachable Spirit* (Louisville: Westminster John Knox, 1990), 139–147. Osmer calls for a recovery of teaching authority among church leaders.

16. Mary Belenky, et al., *Women's Ways of Knowing* (New York: Basic Books, 1986), 35–51.

17. Sandra Moen Kennedy, "Ordinary Listening," in *Ordinary Ministry: Extraordinary Challenge,* ed. Norma Cook Everist (Nashville: Abingdon, 2000), 29–34. Kennedy describes the many untold stories within a congregation. Listening to these stories can free people, not only from locked-in secrets but to become caring communicators and good listeners themselves.

Chapter 7. Leading Theologically

1. Wesley Carr, *The Pastor as Theologian: The Integration of Pastoral Ministry, Theology, and Discipleship* (London: SPCK, 1989).

2. Jacob Neusner, *The Mishnah: An Introduction* (New York: Jason Aronson, 1994).

3. Martin Buber, *Israel and the World: Essays in a Time of Crisis* (New York: Schocken, 1963), 139.

4. Joseph Sittler, "The Maceration of the Minister," *The Ecology of Faith: The New Situation in Preaching* (Philadelphia: Muhlenberg Press, 1961), 76–88.

5. Ibid., 78.

6. The meaning of the term is expounded in Herber H. Farmer, *The Servant of the Word* (Philadelphia: Fortress Press, 1964).

7. For a historical and systematic treatment of ministry of and to the Word, see Bernard J. Cooke, *Ministry to Word and Sacraments: History and Theology* (Philadelphia: Fortress, 1980).

8. On the ministry of the Word, see Mary E. Hinkle, *Signs of Belonging: Luther's Marks of the Church and the Christian Life* (Minneapolis: Augsburg Fortress, 2003), 19–30.

9. Regarding the importance of ministers modeling the speaking of the faith, see Richard H. Bliese, and Craig Van Gelder, eds., *The Evangelizing Church: A Lutheran Contribution* (Minneapolis: Augsburg Fortress, 2005), 130.

10. Mark A. Olson, *Moving Beyond Church Growth: An Alternative Vision for Congregations* (Minneapolis: Fortress, 2002), 56–62.

11. Thomas H. Groome, *Sharing Faith: A Comprehensive Approach to Religious Education and Pastoral Ministry* (San Francisco: HarperSanFrancisco, 1991).

12. For fascinating documentation about clergy reading habits, see Jackson W. Carroll, *God's Potters: Pastoral Leadership and the Shaping of Congregations* (Grand Rapids: Eerdmans, 2006), 108–110.

13. Barbara E. Bowe, *Biblical Foundations of Spirituality: Touching a Finger to the Flame* (Lanham: Sheed and Ward, 2003).

Chapter 8. Transforming Power for Partnership

1. Parts of this chapter first appeared in Norma Cook Everist, "Gender, Power and Leadership" in *Journal of Religious Leadership,* vol. 1, no. 2 (Fall 2002): 45–67.

2. See Pam McAllister, ed., *Reweaving the Web of Life* (Philadelphia: New Society Press, 1982), for a classic work on the connection between misogynist and militaristic styles and tactics. See also Aruna Gnanadason, Musimbi Kanyoro, and Lucia Ann McSpadden, *Women, Violence and Non-Violent Change* (Geneva: World Council of Churches, 1996).

3. Based on the doctoral research of Elizabeth Howell Verdesi, *In but Still Out: Women in the Church* (Philadelphia: The Westminster Press, 1973 and 1976).

4. See Letty Russell, *Church in the Round* (Philadelphia: Westminster John Knox, 1993); and Christine Grumm, "In Search of A Round Table," in *In Search*

of a Round Table: Gender, Theology and Church Leadership, ed. Musimbi R. A. Kanyoro (Geneva: World Council of Churches, 1997), 28–39.

5. See Marie Augusta Neal, *A Socio-Theology of Letting Go* (New York: Paulist, 1977) for a "theology of relinquishment." See also Celia Hahn, *Growing in Authority, Relinquishing Control* (Bethesda: Alban, 1994).

6. See Linda Babcock, and Sara Laschever, *Women Don't Ask: Negotiation and the Gender Divide* (Princeton: Princeton University Press, 2003). Now that women have risen in corporate ranks, they are not less but more likely to be subject to gender stereotypes. Ambitious, successful leaders are sent to programs to teach them to be "nicer" because they are said to "scare men." (85–111).

7. Schools are beginning to address bullying behavior that is no longer being seen as just adolescent pranks but as attitudes and actions to gain and retain power fed by a violent cultural environment.

8. Letty Russell, *Growth in Partnership* (Philadelphia: Westminister, 1981), 12.

9. Babcock and Laschever, *Women Don't Ask*. Men are more comfortable with negotiation than women. Most women leaders today try to align their requests with shared goal and are more concerned about relationships when making suggestions or requests (1–16).

10. Russell, *Church in the Round*. "Like the eucharist and like the church that gathers at Christ's table, the round table is a sign of the coming unity of humanity. It achieves its power as a metaphor only as the *already* of welcome, sharing, talk, and partnership opposes the *not yet* of our divided and dominated world" (17).

11. The body of work of Verdesi's *In but Still Out* (see note 3 above) describes two places where women had power in numbers in the Presbyterian Church, the women's home mission movement and Christian education. In each case when their numbers and budgets and effectiveness became powerful, they allowed themselves and that power to be co-opted.

12. These questions were developed as part of a proposed curriculum for a global consultation on "Engendering Theological Education for Transformation" by The Lutheran World Federation, Geneva, Switzerland, 2001–2002.

Chapter 9. Stewardship of Life:
Spiritual Practices for Sustainable Ministry

1. For very useful examples of this genre, see Roy M. Oswald, *Clergy Self-Care: Finding a Balance for Effective Ministry* (Bethesda: Alban Institute, 1991); and Gwen Wagstrom Halaas, *The Right Road: Life Choices for Clergy* (Minneapolis: Fortress Press, 2004).

2. For a fascinating snapshot of the changing face of the clergy family, see Jackson W. Carroll, *God's Potters: Pastoral Leadership and the Shaping of Congregations* (Grand Rapids: Eerdmans, 2006), 69–71.

3. Augustine, *The Confessions of St. Augustine,* trans. John K. Ryan (New York: Image, 1960), 43 (1.1).

4. An excellent resource on spiritual disciplines is Richard Foster, *The Celebration of Discipline: The Path to Spiritual Growth* (San Francisco: HarperSan Franciso, 1998).

5. A guide for the contemporary reappropriation of classic spiritual practices is Marjorie J. Thompson, *Soul Feast: An Invitation to the Christian Spiritual Life* (Louisville: Westminster John Knox, 1995).

6. Such books include Joan Chittister, *Called to Question* (Lanham, MD: Sheed and Ward, 2004); and Gordon W. Lathrop, *The Pastor, A Spirituality* (Minneapolis: Fortress Press, 2006). Several titles relating to spiritual disciplines or spirituality and leadership exist.

7. For a disturbing account of the need for mental health among clergy, see Conrad W. Weiser, *Healers Harmed and Harmful* (Minneapolis: Fortress, 1994).

8. See Gary L. Harbaugh, *Caring for the Caregiver: Growth Models for Professional Leaders and Congregations* (Bethesda: Alban Institute, 1992).

9. For an account of a particular case that reveals the dynamics of clergy sexual abuse, see Marie M. Fortune, *Is Nothing Sacred? The Story of a Pastor, the Women He Sexually Abused, and the Congregation He Nearly Destroyed* (San Francisco: HarperSanFrancisco, 1989). See also G. Lloyd Rediger, *Beyond the Scandals: A Guide to Healthy Sexuality for Clergy* (Minneapolis: Fortress Press, 2003).

10. See Marie M. Fortune, *Love Does No Harm: Sexual Ethics for the Rest of Us* (New York: Continuum, 1995).

11. For an insightful analysis, see Martha Ellen Stortz, *Pastor Power* (Nashville: Abingdon, 1993), especially 49–68.

12. An excellent resource regarding sexual boundaries is Nils C. Friberg, and Mark R. Laaser, *Before the Fall: Preventing Pastoral Sexual Abuse* (Collegeville, MN: Liturgical Press, 1998).

13. Another valuable resource on the themes discussed in this chapter is Norman Shawchuck and Roger Heuser, *Leading the Congregation: Caring for Yourself While Serving the People* (Nashville: Abingdon, 1993).

Chapter 10. Relational Ethics: Admiration, Affection, and Respect

1. Evelyne Jobe Villines, speaker at the Fourteenth Annual Dr. Martin Luther King, Jr., Breakfast in Dubuque, Iowa, on January 16, 2006.

2. See books by Marie Fortune. Dr. Fortune founded the FaithTrust Institute (formerly the Center for Prevention of Sexual and Domestic Violence), which offers many resources for congregations and leaders in ministry. The Institute's website is http://www.faithtrustinstitute.org.

3. Bell Hooks, *All About Love* (New York: HarperCollins, 2000; Perennial, 2001), 87. Hooks writes, "A love ethic presupposes that everyone has the right to be free, to live fully and well," 87.

4. Ibid. Hooks, drawing on definitions from M. Scott Peck and Erich Fromm, uses the definition of *love* as "the will to extend one's self for the purpose of nurturing one's own or another's spiritual growth," 4.

5. See the discussion of Dietrich Bonhoeffer's *The Communion of Saints* in chapter 3.

6. Hooks, *All About Love*. Hooks encourages us to choose work with "individuals we admire and respect," 87. She does, however, say that embracing a love ethic means utilizing care, commitments, trust, responsibility, respect, and knowledge in our everyday lives, 94.

7. C. S. Lewis, *Four Loves* (New York: Harcourt Brace Jovanovich, 1960). Lewis explores Affection, Friendship, Eros, and Charity. For him "Charity" is the "Gift-love" that comes by grace, within which God bestows two other gifts, need-love of God and of one another, 178.

8. Ibid. Lewis says, "Affection is not simply one of the natural loves but is Love Himself working in our human hearts and fulfilling the law," 61.

9. Ibid., 59–60.

10. Martin Luther, *A Treatise on Christian Liberty*, trans. W. A. Lambert, ed. Harold J. Grimm (Philadelphia: Fortress Press, 1957), 7. Luther says, "A Christian is a perfectly free lord of all, subject to none. A Christian is a perfectly dutiful servant of all, subject to all," 7.

11. Deborah Tannen, *The Argument Culture: Moving from Debate to Dialogue* (New York: Random House, 1998), 4. Tannen makes the point that in day-to-day life, "nearly everything is framed as a battle or game in which winning or losing is the main concern," 4.

12. Lewis, *The Four Loves*. "Friendship arises out of mere companionship when two or more of the companions discover that they have in common some insight or interest or even taste which the others do not share and which, till that moment, each believed to be his own unique treasure or burden," 96.

13. Evangelical Lutheran Church in America, *Vision and Expectations: Ordained Ministers in the Evangelical Lutheran Church in America* (Chicago, ELCA, 1990). "The Evangelical Lutheran Church in America has high expectations for those who serve within the ordained ministry of this church. It does so because it recognizes that when offense is given by an ordained minister, the witness of the gospel may be impaired and the ability to carry out public ministries is threatened," 11. Other church bodies have similar documents outlining the expectations of ministers.

14. Parker Palmer, *A Company of Strangers* (New York: Crossroad, 1981). Chapter three of this book cautions readers about too quickly turning stranger into friend. Affection represents the other as other, not someone I can shape to meet my own needs.

Chapter 11. Ethical Leadership: Confidentiality, Collegiality, and Finances

1. The English word *integrity* derives from the Latin word *integritas*, meaning "whole, entire, a quality or state of being complete (wholeness), in perfect condition (soundness), the quality or state of being sound."

2. For example, *Visions and Expectations: Ordained Ministers in the Evangelical Lutheran Church in America* (Chicago: ELCA, 1990).

3. W. D. Ross, *The Right and the Good* (Oxford: Clarendon Press, 1930), chapter 2.

4. Karen Lebacqz, *Professional Ethics: Power and Paradox* (Nashville: Abingdon, 1985), 25.

5. Richard M. Gula, *Ethics in Pastoral Ministry* (New York/Mahwah: Paulist, 1996), 142–152.

6. Craig L. Nessan, *Ethics in Lutheran Perspective*. Study Guide (Columbus: Select, 2005).

7. Adapted from H. Newton Malony, "Confidentiality in the Pastoral Role," in H. Newton Malony, Thomas L. Needham, and Samuel Southard, eds., *Clergy Malpractice* (Philadelphia: Westminster, 1986), 119–120.

8. John C. Bush, and William Harold Tiemann, *The Right to Silence: Privileged Clergy Communication and the Law* (Nashville: Abingdon, 1989), 39–46.

9. Robert Regan, as quoted by Thomas W. Klink in "Pastoral Confidences: A Modern Dilemma," *Pastoral Psychology* 17:162 (1966): 6.

10. Maloney, *Clergy Malpractice,* 111.

11. Ronald K. Bullis, "When Confessional Walls Have Ears: The Changing Clergy Privileged Communications Law," *Pastoral Psychology* 39:2 (1990): 76.

12. The following schema was first published in Craig L. Nessan, "Confidentiality: Sacred Trust and Ethical Quagmire," *The Journal of Pastoral Care* 52:4 (1998): 356.

13. Arthur B. Becker, "Professional Ethics in Ministry," *Trinity Seminary Review* 9:2 (1987): 72.

14. For a constructive resource on building staff ministry, including the importance of establishing a covenant, see Anne Marie Nuechterlein, *Improving Your Multiple Staff Ministry: How to Work Together More Effectively* (Minneapolis: Augsburg, 1989).

15. For example, William E. Hulme, "A Prophetic Merger?" *Lutheran Partners*, no. 1 (Jan/Feb 1987): 17–18, 27.

16. For an excellent resource on stewardship, including the role of the minister, see Eugene Grimm, *Generous People: How to Encourage Vital Stewardship* (Nashville: Abingdon, 1992).

17. For a descriptive portrait of the ethical life of pastors, see Joseph E. Bush Jr., *Gentle Shepherding: Pastoral Ethics and Leadership* (St. Louis: Chalice Press, 2006).

Chapter 12. Leaders Under Stress: The Transformation of Time

1. Some of this material first appeared in Norma Cook Everist, "The Tyranny of Time," *The Lutheran* 14 (July 2001): 12–16.

2. See Arlie Russell Hochschild, *Time Bind* (New York: Henry Holt, 1997).

3. Tilden Edwards, *Sabbath Time* (New York: Seabury, 1982). Edwards notes differences also due to different states of life, cultures, life stages, and rhythms (75).

4. "The Small Catechism of Martin Luther" as printed in *Evangelical Lutheran Worship* (Minneapolis: Augsburg Fortress, 2007), 1160–1161.

5. Harvey Cox, *Turning East* (New York: Simon and Schuster, 1977). In chapter 5, "Meditation and Sabbath," Cox discusses how the Hebrew word for God's resting as used in the Sabbath commandment literally means "to catch one's breath."

6. Robert Kolb, and Timothy J. Wengert, eds., "Martin Luther's Large Catechism" in *The Book of Concord: The Confessions of the Evangelical Lutheran Church* (Minneapolis: Augsburg Fortress, 2000), 396.

7. Ibid., 397.

8. Ibid.

9. Ibid., 398.

10. Ibid.

11. Ibid.

12. Ibid., 399.

13. Edwards, *Sabbath Time,* 74–75 and 124.

14. "Martin Luther's Large Catechism," 399.

15. Kolb and Wengert, "Martin Luther's Small Catechism," 352.

16. Ibid., "Martin Luther's Large Catechism," 400.

17. Joyce Sequichie Hifler, *A Cherokee Feast of Days,* vol. 2 (Tulsa: Council Oak Books, 1996), 111.

18. Ralph F. Smith, "Hold Him Close; Hold Him Lightly," in Norma Cook Everist, ed., *Gentle Strength: Homilies and Hymns of Ralph F. Smith* (Dubuque: Wartburg Theological Seminary, 1995), 124–125. This sermon on Luke 10:38-42 was preached October 26, 1994, just one month before he was killed in an automobile accident at the age of 44.

19. Joan Chittister, *Called to Question* (Lanham, MD: Sheed and Ward, 2004), 83–87. Chittister writes about the spirituality of balance.

20. Gay Gaer Luce, *Body Time* (New York: Bantam, 1973). This groundbreaking book and many studies since describe the significance of and differences in internal body time.

21. Edwards, *Sabbath Time.* Edwards wrote words that might be especially helpful to leaders of worship who find it difficult to find a fulfilling Sabbath rest when they are at work: "Corporate worship can be the pinnacle of the Christian Sabbath, but it is not the Sabbath" (p. 105).

Chapter 13. Transforming Gifts: Assets-Based Congregations

1. Gary Goreham, "Appreciative Inquiry," presentation for the Center for Theology and Land, Wartburg Theological Seminary, June 2003.

2. Luther K. Snow, *The Power of Asset Mapping: How Your Congregation Can Act on Its Gifts* (Bethesda: Alban Institute, 2004), 3–12. This book is an excellent primer for those desiring to develop basic competence in leading groups in asset mapping.

3. See Snow, *The Power of Asset Mapping,* 5, in reference to the work of John McKnight and Jody Kretzmann.

4. An excellent practical resource with a variety of materials for congregational use is David P. Mayer, *Our Gifts: Identifying and Developing Leaders* (Minneapolis: Augsburg Fortress, 2002).

5. Snow, *The Power of Asset Mapping,* 117–120.

6. For the following, see Snow, *The Power of Asset Mapping,* 93–95.

7. Another useful resource with many practical ideas is Bob Sitze, *The Great Permission: An Asset-Based Field Guide for Congregations* (Chicago: Evangelical Lutheran Church in America, 2002).

8. For a critique of clericalism, see Richard H. Bliese, and Craig Van Gelder, eds., *The Evangelizing Church: A Lutheran Contribution* (Minneapolis: Augsburg Fortress, 2005), 115–116.

9. For example, Neal F. McBride, *How to Build Small Groups Ministry* (Colorado Springs: NavPress, 1994).

10. Jeffrey Arnold, *Starting Small Groups: Building Communities That Matter* (Nashville: Abingdon, 1997).

11. Eugene Grimm, *Generous People: How to Encourage Vital Stewardship* (Nashville: Abingdon, 1992), 19. This book provides a wealth of information about various types of stewardship programs and the appendices contain practical tools for use by stewardship committees.

12. Craig L. Nessan, *Beyond Maintenance to Mission: A Theology of the Congregation* (Minneapolis: Fortress Press, 1999), 68–77.

13. Douglas John Hall, *The Steward: A Biblical Symbol Come of Age* (Grand Rapids: Eerdmans, 1990), 178.

14. According to Kim Wilson, in Norma Cook Everist, *Open the Doors and See All the People* (Minneapolis: Augsburg Fortress, 2005), 88–93.

Chapter 14. Transforming Congregational Systems

1. The established primer in family systems theory is Edwin Friedman, *Generation to Generation: Family Process in Church and Synagogue* (New York: Guilford, 1985). Particularly useful for applying the constructs of family systems theory to congregational life are the works of Ronald W. Richardson, *Creating a Healthier Church: Family Systems Theory, Leadership, and Congregational Life* (Minneapolis: Fortress, 1996); and Peter Steinke, *Healthy Congregations: A Systems Approach* (Bethesda: Alban Institute, 1996).

2. See Craig L. Nessan, "Surviving Congregational Leadership: A Theology of Family Systems," *Word and World* 20 (2000): 390–399.

3. See Kenneth C. Haugk, *Antagonists in the Church: How to Identify and Deal with Destructive Conflict* (Minneapolis: Augsburg, 1988); and G. Lloyd Rediger, *Clergy Killers: Guidance for Pastors and Congregations Under Attack* (Louisville: Westminster John Knox, 1997). While these books have many valuable insights about dealing with conflict, the premise of labeling one's enemies with such epithets is fundamentally unhelpful.

4. A very useful manual for preparing a family genogram is Monika McGoldrick and Randy Gerson, *Genograms in Family Assessment* (New York: Norton, 1985).

5. For the meaning of *destiny*, see Langdon Gilkey, *Message and Existence: An Introduction to Christian Theology* (New York: Seabury Press, 1981), 36–37.

6. See the summary of Bion's work in Conrad W. Weiser, *Healers Harmed and Harmful* (Minneapolis: Fortress Press, 1994), 121–128.

7. For a concise summary of scapegoat theory, see Craig L. Nessan, "Violence and Atonement," *Dialog* 35 (Winter 1996): 26–34.

8. Weiser, *Healers Harmed and Harmful*, 67–111.

Chapter 15. Transforming Opportunities: People on the Edge

1. Wilhelm Loehe, *Three Books About the Church*. (Philadelphia: Fortress Press, 1969), 54–55.

2. C. S. Lewis, *The Great Divorce* (New York: HarperCollins, 2001). In the "twilight lands," Lewis describes the situation where people keep moving further and further away from each other.

3. See *Evangelical Lutheran Worship* (Minneapolis: Augsburg Fortress, 2006), 75.

4. Hans Küng, *The Church* (Garden City, NY: Image Books, 1976), 46–59.

5. Ibid.

6. Norma Cook Everist, *Open the Doors and See All the People: Stories of Congregational Identity and Vocation* (Minneapolis: Augsburg Fortress, 2005), 1–3.

7. Dietrich Bonhoeffer, *Life Together,* trans. John W. Doberstein (New York: Harper and Brothers, 1954), 77.

8. For much more on this topic see Norma Cook Everist, *Church Conflict: From Conflict to Collaboration* (Nashville: Abingdon, 2004).

9. See Norma Cook Everist, "Re-membering the Body of Christ" in Norma Cook Everist, ed., *The Difficult but Indispensable Church* (Minneapolis: Fortress Press, 2002), 45–56.

Chapter 16. Transformed for Daily Life: The Ministry of the Baptized

1. Excerpts from an interview with the Reverend Kathy Johnson, Milwaukee, Wisconsin, printed with permission.

2. Suzanne De Dietrich, *The Witnessing Community* (Philadelphia: Westminister Press, 1958). "The church has to rediscover again and again its vocation, its corporate vocation as the witnessing community taken out of the world, set apart for God, but set apart in order to be again sent to the world" (16).

3. *Evangelical Lutheran Worship* (Minneapolis: Augsburg Fortress, 2006), 227.

4. Ibid., 231.

5. Frederick C. Marsh, ed., *The Merriam-Webster Dictionary* (Springfield, MA: Merriam-Webster, 2004). According to Merriam-Webster, the fourth definition of *lay* is "of or relating to the laity" and "lacking extensive knowledge of a particular subject" (p. 409).

6. Note the reference in chapter 3 to Harold Wilke, *Creating the Caring Congregation* (Nashville: Abingdon, 1080), 17.

7. Einar Billing, *Our Calling,* trans. Conrad Bergendoff (Rock Island: Augustana Press, 1958), 5.

8. Ibid., 6.

9. Ibid., 8.

10. Note the reference in chapter 3 to Dietrich Bonhoeffer that when through the cross we are placed in community, we no longer see one another as claim but

as gift. Dietrich Bonhoeffer, *The Communion of Saints,* trans. John Doberstein (New York: Harper and Brothers, 1960), l06–120.

11. Billing, *Our Calling,* 19.

12. Ibid., 11.

13. Letty M. Russell, *Human Liberation in a Feminist Perspective: A Theology* (Philadelphia: Westminster, 1974) 53.

14. Norma Cook Everist, and Craig L. Nessan, eds., *Forming an Evangelizing People* (Dubuque: Wartburg Theological Seminary, 2005), 20.

15. Martin Luther, *Luther's Works,* Volume 39: *Church and Ministry.* (Philadelphia: Fortress Press, 1970), xi.

16. Norma Cook Everist, "Let God Build the Body! The Body of Christ Proverb" in Paul Hill, ed., *Up the Creek with a Paddle: Building Effective Youth and Family Ministry* (Minneapolis: Augsburg Fortress, 1998), 45–51.

17. Mark 10:43: Jesus said "It is not so among you" in description of the servant community in contrast to leaders who "lord it over" or disciples who want a special place in the kingdom.

18. Jürgen Moltman, *The Church in the Power of the Spirit* (New York: HarperCollins, 1977), 64. Note the reference in chapter 3 to Jürgen Moltmann. Moltman wrote that it is not the church that has a mission of salvation to give to the world but rather it is the mission of God that includes the church, creating church as it goes. It is not that the church ceases to exist but that, while participating in God's acts of love and justice in the world, God transforms, strengthens, and shapes the church for yet more service.

19. Norma Cook Everist, and Nelvin Vos, *Where in the World Are You?* (Bethesda: The Alban Institute, 1996), 87–93.

20. Dietrich Bonhoeffer, *Christ the Center,* trans. Edwin H. Robertson (New York: Harper and Row, 1978), 60. "It is the nature of the person of Jesus Christ to be in the centre, both spatially and temporally. The one who is present in Word, Sacrament and the Church is in the centre of human existence, of history and of nature," 60.

21. Adapted from *Called to Deal with Difficult Issues: A Method for Theological Reflection and Decision Making in Ministry in Daily Life* (Chicago: Women of the ELCA, 2002) 9–10. This booklet was based on material presented by Norma Cook Everist during three-day conference events around the United States entitled "Feasting at Katie's Table."

Indexes

Names and Subjects

abdication, 66, 69, 73, 99, 177

abundance, 35, 122, 161, 163, 181

accountability/accountable, 12, 33, 35, 37, 40, 50, 54-55, 113, 155, 193, 209

anxiety/anxious (non-anxious), 8, 24, 104, 139, 149, 151, 173–175, 178, 180, 194

appreciative inquiry, xii, 44, 160–163, 169

assets/assets mapping, 44, 108, 144, 160–163, 165, 169–170, 173, 179, 181, 213

Augustine 4, 109

authority/authoritarianism, x, 6–7, 9, 11, 23, 32, 42, 53-56, 59–68, 71, 73, 97, 109, 142, 165, 203

Bion, William 176–178

blame/blaming, 24, 42, 82, 126, 143, 151, 177–181

Bloomquist, Karen 36

Bonhoeffer, Dietrich 20, 37, 38, 50, 192

boundaries, xi, 3, 103–105, 11, 114–118, 120, 129, 134, 138, 141–143, 157

Buber, Martin 77

call/calling, vii–x, xii, xiii, 1–5, 8, 10–12, 16, 22, 24, 26–27, 29, 31, 33, 35, 37, 40–42, 47, 50, 54, 56-59, 63, 65–66, 68, 71, 73, 75–84, 87, 89, 97, 104–105, 108, 110–111, 113, 117, 120, 122, 124–125, 127, 130–132, 134, 139, 141–142, 153, 157, 165–170, 173–174, 179, 184–185, 190, 198–205, 208–211, 213–214

Calvin, John 25

Carroll, Jackson W. 55

change, vii, ix, 9, 20–21, 26, 32, 44–45, 67, 70, 80, 86–88, 90–91, 93, 95–96, 106–109, 122, 125, 143, 147, 153, 156, 172, 174, 178–181, 186, 192, 199, 205, 207, 213

Christ, vii–x, xii, 1, 3, 7, 9–11, 14, 21–22, 24–25, 29–30, 32–38, 40–41, 46–47, 49–50, 54–55, 57–58, 65–68, 70–72, 74, 79, 81, 83, 86–87, 94, 97, 100, 107, 120, 122–125, 132, 151–152, 155, 160, 169, 174–176, 178, 180–181, 184, 186, 188–190, 193, 195, 199–211, 213

collaboration/collaborative, viii, x, xiv, 1, 8, 12, 53, 66, 71, 93, 100, 124, 129, 155, 195, 207–208, 213

collegiality/colleagues, x–xi, xiii–xiv, 17, 23, 45, 84, 111–113, 115, 121, 136, 140–141, 143–144, 145, 147

community, viii–x, xiii–xiv, 1–4, 6–11, 13–14, 17, 19, 29–39, 45, 60, 63, 66, 71–73, 77–78, 80, 90, 92, 94, 105–106, 108, 111–114, 116–117, 120–121, 123–127, 129, 131, 136–137, 152, 157, 159, 163–164, 166–167, 170, 179, 180–182, 184, 186–187, 189, 190, 192–195, 205, 207, 210–211, 213

Communion of Saints, 32, 199, 204

competition/competitive, 87, 127, 145, 190

confidentiality, xi, 103, 113, 117–118, 134–140, 147

conflict, ix–x, xii, xiv, 4–5, 7, 17, 24, 35, 37, 41–42, 44, 46, 60–61, 67, 72, 79–80, 96, 118, 131, 145, 155, 164, 173–175, 178, 193–194, 202, 213

Jordan, Barbara 69
justice/injustice, vii–ix, xii, 3, 7, 24, 31, 34–37, 47–49, 70, 81–82, 87, 115, 135, 156, 184, 187, 189, 210–211, 213–214

Kleingartner, Connie 78
Kung, Hans 12, 30

Large Catechism, 152
law, 42, 47, 76, 92, 115, 129, 132, 135, 137–139, 187, 205
leadership development, xii, 164, 166
leaving, xii, 92, 155, 159, 184, 186–187, 194
Lebacqz, Karen 135
Lewis, C. S. 123
liberation/liberator, xiv, 36, 69
listening, x, 2, 8, 19–20, 25–26, 33, 43, 59–60, 73, 78, 80, 128–130, 172, 179, 199, 210
Loehe, Wilhelm 27, 34
love, viii–ix, xiv, 2, 4, 7, 10, 13–14, 18, 25, 29–30, 32, 34, 37–38, 40, 43, 46–48, 50, 58, 70, 73, 82, 87, 97, 120, 123–124, 128–129, 132, 134–135, 151–154, 156–157, 169, 175, 178, 180, 184–185, 187–189, 196, 202, 204, 206, 213
Luther, Martin 32, 46, 66, 129, 132, 151–153, 165, 202–204

members/membership, viii, xii, 2–3, 7, 9–10, 12–14, 17, 19–25, 29–30, 33, 37–38, 44–45, 57, 65, 96, 105, 107–108, 111, 115–116, 121, 125, 135–137, 140–142, 144–147, 160, 163–165, 167–168, 173–174, 176–179, 185, 189–192, 195–196, 199, 204–205, 207, 210, 213
mission, vii–x, xii, xiv, 1, 3, 5, 10–12, 16, 18, 25–26, 30–36, 40–50, 58, 65, 70–71, 75–76, 78–79, 84, 87, 91–92, 116, 118, 124, 137, 140–141, 143–144, 149, 153, 155–156, 161, 164–167, 169–170, 174, 176,

178, 184, 188–190, 192–194, 196, 198, 201, 206–207, 209, 210
Moltmann, Jurgen 30, 34
money, xii, 48, 50, 96, 126, 150, 160–161, 163, 167–170
multi-tasking, xi, 103

Neal, Marie Augusta 69
Niebuhr, H. Richard 29

office/public office, x, xii, 3, 10–12, 42, 54–55, 57–61, 63, 66, 71, 77–80, 83, 105, 115, 124, 126, 143–144, 150, 194, 200, 207, 209
Olson, Mark 81
ordination, x, 57–58

Palmer, Parker 35
partnership, ix, xi, 5, 18, 23, 26, 45–46, 53, 61–62, 67–68, 86–96, 98–100, 136, 143-146, 155, 166–167, 169
patriarchy (patriarchal systems), 31, 61, 86, 89, 93, 95–97, 99, 100, 200
patterns (congregational), xii, 2, 8, 19, 26, 32, 105, 111, 130, 155–156, 162, 176–177, 179–181
power, vii–viii, x–xii, 7, 10–12, 14, 19, 21, 29, 31–37, 40–44, 46–47, 53–55, 61, 65–70, 72–73, 84, 86–100, 109, 114, 120, 122–126, 130, 132, 134–135, 139, 141–142, 146, 150, 153, 155–157, 159, 161, 163–166, 172, 176–177, 180–181, 189, 192–193, 199, 200, 203–206, 208–210, 213–214
power cycle, xi, 87–94, 96, 98–99
practices/spiritual practices, x–xi, 5, 40–42, 47, 50, 110, 118, 141
prayer, xiii, 5, 7, 13, 21, 25, 42, 45, 58, 77, 79, 80, 83, 110, 141, 152, 154, 156, 163–164, 167–168, 174, 181, 186, 188, 193, 198, 210, 213
predecessors, 19, 141–142
Priesthood of All Believers, 10, 32–33, 77, 165, 200, 203, 205

Bible Verse Index